WAFWW9-AFW-367

# PRACTICING THE ART OF LEADERSHIP

*A Problem-based Approach to Implementing the ISLLC Standards*

# REGINALD LEON GREEN

*The University of Memphis*

Merrill
Prentice Hall

Upper Saddle River, New Jersey
Columbus, Ohio

**Library of Congress Cataloging-in-Publication Data**

Green, Reginald Leon.
  Practicing the art of leadership : a problem-based approach to
implementing the ISLLC standards / Reginald Leon Green.
    p. cm.
  Includes bibliographical references and index.
  ISBN 0-13-020364-5
  1. Interstate School Leaders Licensure Consortium. 2. Educational
leadership–United States. 3. School management and organization–
United States. 4. Problem-based learning—United States. I. Title.

LB2805.G687 2001
371.2'00973–dc21                                          00-036174

**Vice President and Publisher:** Jeffery W. Johnston
**Editor:** Debra A. Stollenwerk
**Editorial Assistant:** Penny S. Burleson
**Production Editor:** Linda Hillis Bayma
**Copy Editor:** Karen Slaght
**Design Coordinator:** Diane C. Lorenzo
**Cover Designer:** Thomas Borah
**Cover art:** © Don Bishop/Artville
**Production Manager:** Pamela D. Bennett
**Director of Marketing:** Kevin Flanagan
**Marketing Manager:** Amy June
**Marketing Services Manager:** Krista Groshong

This book was set in Bembo by Carlisle Communications, Ltd. It was printed and
bound by R.R. Donnelley & Sons Company. The cover was printed by Phoenix
Color Corp.

10 9 8 7 6 5 4 3 2
ISBN: 0-13-020364-5

*To Jean, my best friend*

# ABOUT THE AUTHOR

**Reginald Leon Green** is Associate Professor of Educational Leadership at The University of Memphis. He received the Ed.D. in Educational Administration and Supervision from the University of Missouri–Columbia. He has served at the teacher, principal, deputy superintendent, and superintendent levels of K–12 education, and has been in higher education for seven years. In 1977, Reginald was one of five educators chosen nationally to participate in the Rockefeller Foundation's Superintendency Preparation Program, and, in 1996, he was selected as an associate to the Institute for Educational Renewal, under the leadership of Dr. John Goodlad.

Reginald has published a book on inner-city education and articles on educational restructuring, primary grade restructuring, gang violence, and other contemporary educational issues. Most recently, he completed national inquiries into nurturing characteristics that exist in schools and standards and assessment measures being established as a part of school reform. Dr. Green teaches courses in educational leadership, organizational behavior, and participatory governance and change. His research interests include school leadership, superintendent/board relations, school district restructuring, and the effects of nurturing characteristics on the academic achievement of students.

# PREFACE

The challenges in today's schools are increasing in frequency, complexity, and intensity, requiring school leaders to enter the schoolhouse with practical experience that prepares them to take immediate and definitive action regarding multifaceted issues. The need for the beginning administrator to have practical experience is so great that many universities are changing their leadership preparation programs to reflect a more practice-oriented approach. One organization advocating this change is the Interstate School Leaders Licensure Consortium (ISLLC). The change advocated by this organization is very influential and offers a "new leadership paradigm," one that incorporates what ISLLC believes is required behavior for school leaders.

Through a series of six standards, ISLLC presents a common core of knowledge, disposition, and performances that link leadership to productive schools and enhance educational outcomes. The standards represent an effort to refine the skills of school leaders and to couple leadership with effective educational outcomes (ISLLC, 1996). These standards, the recommended changes in educational leadership preparation programs, and the development of other related performance assessment instruments have influenced a renewal of the approaches used to prepare school leaders. This change is occurring in terms of classroom instruction, assessment of leadership skills and attributes for licensure, and practical application of theoretical concepts.

This text is designed to support the new thrust by providing a series of scenarios that incorporate the behaviors informed by the ISLLC Standards. Also, theory is connected to practice in a manner that allows the prospective school leader an opportunity to reflect on problems and issues that exist in today's schools. A second, yet crucial, objective is to connect the standards and the literature on school leadership to scenarios, questions, and suggested solutions. In this regard, the indicators of the ISLLC Standards are embedded in the scenarios in both a positive and negative manner, allowing the reader to view their practical implications for school leaders.

*Practicing the Art of Leadership: A Problem-based Approach to Implementing the ISLLC Standards* is a compilation of scenarios and related exercises that represent the kinds of challenges and issues that surface in today's schools. It is significantly different from the traditional case study format, which probes in an in-depth manner issues that build on one another and need to be resolved. Instead, this work recognizes that definitive action is extremely critical to the success of school leaders as they function on a day-to-day basis in a setting inherently filled with complex challenges.

This text is designed for use in a culminating course of a leadership preparation program. Therefore, the content is written based on the assumption that individuals who utilize it have already developed a basic knowledge of administrative theories and concepts that inform leadership behavior. However, if the text is used in an earlier course, it will need to be supplemented by a text that treats the theoretical concepts of leadership in a more comprehensive manner. The caution to be remembered in the use of this material (as with most behavioral material) is that there is no substitute for reflective reasoning. The reader must take care to select a solution based on the interrelationships between the people, the situation, the skills needed, and the environmental forces. An appropriate mix of theory, reflective thinking, and prescription must be identified.

I hope the prospective school leaders and the practitioners who read this text and work through the scenarios enjoy it and find it beneficial.

## Acknowledgments

I hereby gratefully acknowledge all the help, encouragement, support, and sacrifice given me by my wife, Jean; my son, Reginald, who developed the charts; and my daughters, Cynthia, Stephanie, and especially Reginique, who motivated me to write this book.

Obviously, the contents of a work of this nature come from a number of sources. First and foremost, I express appreciation to all my leadership students at Wright State University and The University of Memphis for their reflections, assistance, and support during the many class sessions in which these scenarios were refined. Expressions of appreciation are also given to Georgia Edwards and Shirley Johnson, District 89, Maywood, Illinois; Dr. Lirah Sabir and Dr. William Sweet (retired), Memphis (Tennessee) City Schools; James Trent, Wright State University; Katheline Ware, Cincinnati (Ohio) Public Schools; and Dr. Thedore Myers and Dr. John Petry, The University of Memphis, for reviewing the scenarios and providing me with invaluable feedback. I am deeply indebted to Dr. Glynda Cryer, Memphis (Tennessee) City Schools, who read and proofed each and every draft.

In addition, the comments of the following reviewers were invaluable: Renee A. Alley, Youngstown State University; Philip Arbaugh, Western Maryland College; Dale Brubaker, University of North Carolina at Greensboro; Carol Carter-Lowery, Central Connecticut State University; Virginia Doolittle, Rowan University; Larry W. Hughes, University of Houston; Jacqueline E. Jacobs, University of South Carolina; Judith A. Kerrins, California State University, Chico; Charles E. Kline, Purdue University; Frances Kochan; Auburn University; Price M. Michael, State University of West Georgia; and Robert Millward, Indiana University of Pennsylvania.

Reginald Leon Green

# CONTENTS

# A FRAMEWORK FOR USING THE TEXT: A SUGGESTED GUIDE FOR PROFESSORS

The text is designed to provide support for the professor and has multiple uses. It is structured in a manner that allows the professor to utilize it in the context of his/her curriculum. One purpose of the scenarios is to provide support for presentations made by the professor and to serve as a framework for group discussions, reflective questioning, individual problem analyses, and class interaction. Students are provided an opportunity to examine their values and beliefs and to formulate or refine their leadership styles. The material can be used in a variety of ways. The following process describes just one way that has proven to be effective:

Chapter Introduction
Professor's Presentation
Reading the Scenario
Small Group Interaction
Reflective Thinking and Scenario Analysis
Multiple-Choice Questions
General Class Discussion

## Chapter Introduction

Each chapter begins with an introductory section that provides an explanation (in summary format) of theoretical concepts. When coupled with prior course work, the content of the section is sufficient to establish a frame of reference for responding to questions about the scenarios. The section places the scenarios of the chapter into a leadership process area and assists the reader in developing an appreciation for the practical application of embedded concepts. It must be understood that it

is not the intention of the author for this section to be comprehensive or to introduce new concepts. Rather, the introductory section suggests a framework for
consideration of the scenarios and motivates the recall of concepts given in-depth
treatment in class lectures, previous readings, and/or courses.

## Professor's Presentation

Prior to presenting a scenario to the class, the professor may choose to present
information or lead a discussion on the subject of the content material
addressed in the scenario. Such a presentation will assist students in revisiting
the theoretical concepts necessary to respond to the challenges posed in the
scenario. Also, it helps build a foundation for translating principles into practice. It is unlikely that students will be able to adequately respond to the challenges posed in the scenarios without prior exposure to the key concepts in a
previous class, lecture, or prior readings.

## Reading the Scenario

Each student should read a scenario two to three times individually. The
first reading should be a general reading to familiarize the student with the
scenario content and characters. The second reading should be to identify
the key issues and formulate a position on how the issues relate to theoretical principles and the ISLLC Standards. Because of the comprehen-
siveness of the standards, multiple standards may be cross-referenced in a
single chapter and/or scenario. The student will want to make notes as
ideas occur.

The third reading should allow the student to formulate a position on the
issues and develop tentative action plans to identify appropriate solutions to the
scenario challenges. In so doing, the student should take care to respond to
such questions as:

1. What should the principal do next?
2. What factors should the principal consider before responding?
3. What additional information, if any, will the principal need to develop
   an effective response?
4. What are the sources of additional information?

## Small-Group Interaction

After the presentation by the professor (if the professor elects to) and the reading of the scenario by each student, the class might be divided into small
groups. By participating in small groups, students have an opportunity to analyze the scenario using theoretical principles and making behavioral compar-

isons of the characters in the scenario with those advocated by the standards. It will also allow for reflective responses, the exchange of ideas, and the formulation of positions on the issues. Students should:

▶ Think about the scenario from multiple points of view.
▶ Identify the critical issues in the scenario.
▶ Determine the knowledge base necessary to address the issues (models).
▶ Project a course of action to be taken.
▶ Identify the probable consequences of the course of action selected.
▶ Identify the theoretical principles that apply to suggested alternative actions.
▶ Review the suggested response to each issue.
▶ Suggest alternative actions from those given in the text.
▶ Pose reflective questions to members of the group.

## Reflective Thinking and Scenario Analysis

The reflective thinking and scenario analysis section is heavily based on the ISLLC Standards and designed to provoke thoughtful discussion among class members. Quite clearly, it provides an opportunity for each student to analyze issues, make comparisons, and apply theory to practice. It allows for the consideration of both obvious and subtle issues and motivates students to search for evidence to build their responses. In addition, the process of addressing the reflective questions is designed to strengthen the student's ability to analyze interpersonal implications, influence the consideration of equity principles, encourage the development of action plans, and assess mastery of the ISLLC Standards. When more than one group is involved, the reflective questions can provide a means to make comparative analyses between the groups. Discussions resulting from the comparative analyses often provoke questions that stimulate action research.

A professor might also choose to make in-class and/or out-of-class assignments using these questions. In the in-class mode, the class could be divided into groups for interaction and discussion of the questions, identification of various implications, and development of possible solutions. After an allotted time period, each group might make a presentation to the entire class, generating further discussion and analysis. Out-of-class mode assignments could include:

▶ Developing a written analysis of select questions.
▶ Relating select questions to an experience the student may have had in the past several years.
▶ Relating select questions to elements of school reform.
▶ Creating a newspaper article that focuses on some aspect of the issues.
▶ Developing a scenario of a similar nature.

The reflective questions involve analysis, synthesis, evaluation, and recall. They assist in the development of higher-order thinking skills that allow the professor to assess students in the areas of trust, oral and written communication skills, sensitivity, judgment, attention to details, and willingness to develop others.

## Multiple-Choice Questions and Class Discussion

A student-guided discussion using multiple-choice questions can be a part of the in-class presentation. Responding to the multiple-choice questions is most effective, beginning as an out-of-class written assignment and concluding in a general in-class discussion. Used in this manner, the questions become an excellent review tool, bringing a focus to the critical factors in a scenario and motivating students to research their responses. This activity also provides practice in responding to the type of questions that appear on some local and national examinations. Once the responses have been addressed in writing as an out-of-class assignment, students might review and compare their responses in a subsequent class meeting. Such a presentation creates another opportunity for the professor to assess students on the attributes previously cited.

The multiple-choice questions are organized into three parts: (1) addressing the issues, (2) discussion of the solution, and (3) summary and conclusion.

1. *Addressing the issues.* In this section, students are asked to respond to a series of questions about a scenario. Responding to these questions facilitates a student's personal interaction with the key issues in the scenario and challenges the student to establish a position on those issues. In some instances, the student might disagree with the suggested response. In such instances, additional research by the student will become necessary; if an alternative response is suggested, it should be justified and the source cited. The generation of multiple points of view fosters a deeper understanding of the key issues and enhances the leadership skills of students.

2. *Discussion of the solution.* After responding to each of the questions, the students are provided an opportunity to compare their responses with the author's suggested responses, which are supported by an extensive list of researchers and writers who have studied leadership in schools. In addition, the suggested response to each question has been sanctioned by a number of practicing administrators. In this activity, the student is challenged to recall and use factual information in identifying solutions to real-life issues. With the development of a response to these questions, the student is connecting theory to practice.

3. *Summary and conclusion.* The summary and conclusion section is an attempt to bring purpose, process, and outcomes together. It is based on current literature and is comprehensive in nature. The section provides

an explanation of previous content, helps the student relate theory to practice, and provides definitions of key terms. Many underlying concerns are addressed, and pitfalls for prospective administrators are identified. The student is presented with issues involving values, cooperation, cultural diversity, and collaboration for reflection and consideration.

## Purpose of the Text

It is not the author's intent to offer new research or to treat the concepts in an in-depth manner; rather, the findings of previous researchers are used to establish a conceptual framework for classroom instruction through case scenario analysis. In that regard, an extensive review of the literature has been conducted to identify theories that advocate best practices in the field of educational administration. The works of Bennis, Senge, Covey, Barth, Sergiovanni, Greenleaf, Gardner, Bolman and Deal, Hersey and Blanchard, Blake and Mouton, Lunenburg and Ornstein, Hoy and Miskel, Ubben and Hughes, and many others have been examined to identify theories, models, designs, concepts, and practices to comprise the main section of each chapter. These works, along with others, were also used to support suggested responses to the challenges posed in the case scenarios. If the text is selected for use in a course that precedes the culminating experience, it will be necessary to identify a companion text that addresses the concepts in a more comprehensive fashion.

# USING THE SCENARIO FORMAT:
# A SUGGESTED GUIDE FOR STUDENTS

In reviewing many educational leadership case-based instruction books, you are likely to observe that writers offer no "right answers" to the challenges posed in the cases. In fact, in many instances, writers stress the point that there are no "right answers" to the challenges posed in the cases. Yet, case-based instruction is not hopelessly mired in relativism; there are certain points of view and approaches to issues in administrative practices that are more effective than others (Merseth, 1997, p. 5). What seems clear is the need to formulate a case scenario instructional approach that sensitizes the prospective leader to the problems of practice, rather than one that is simply a device to stimulate discussions (Hoy & Tarter, 1995). Classroom discussions that simply allow participants to foster opinions appear to be inconsistent with the new direction of school leader preparation.

*Practicing the Art of Leadership: A Problem-based Approach to Implementing the ISLLC Standards* addresses the new thrust. Though not an easy task, in this text an attempt has been made to develop a case scenario approach with suggested responses grounded in theory and best practices. It provides the prospective leader an opportunity to explore a somewhat unique approach to moving beyond mere reflective discussions. The text offers suggested responses to the challenges posed in the scenarios, a practice common in case study textbooks used in other disciplines. By using such an approach, the prospective school leader has an opportunity to examine, compare, and make judgments about well-documented responses. Such an approach appears to be warranted, given the standards-based instruction advocated by the Interstate Leaders Licensure Consortium (ISLLC). The following section describes the composition of the text.

# The Composition of the Text

Specifically, the text is designed for use in a course that offers the student or practitioner a culminating experience, one in which he/she reflects on information previously acquired and uses that information to solve complex school challenges. The text does not attempt to address all of the functions of a school leader; rather, it addresses five processes and/or procedures that contemporary literature (Barth, 1990; Conley, 1997; Fullan, 1999; Sarason, 1996; Sergiovanni & Starratt, 1998; Yukl, 1994) suggests a leader must effectively use in fulfilling his/her roles and responsibilities. The five areas addressed are decision making, communication, change, conflict management, and the establishment of an effective teaching and learning climate.

Using a circular design, the format of the text is as depicted in the illustration. Leadership appears in the center of the inner circle and is surrounded by three triangles that encompass decision making, change, and conflict management. Adjacent to each triangle are the category indicators of the ISLLC Standards, denoting the standard of excellence that must be achieved in each of the identified areas. Leadership is presented in the center in an attempt to characterize leadership as the focal point of the school. Each of the three triangles surrounding leadership identifies processes and procedures in which the effective leader must be proficient. Communication appears in an outer circle to indicate that it is the linchpin, comprising all areas and providing the lifeblood that generates substance, allowing them to function. The internal field represents the internal environment of the school and the influences of internal forces. Then there is the outer circle, reflecting the external environment that influences the school's transformation process.

The chapters follow this format. The main section of each chapter is designed to serve as a framework for consideration and to inspire critical thinking and responses to questions posed. Thus, the theoretical concepts in that section are presented in summary format and are not all-inclusive.

The scenarios selected to comprise the text cover the processes and procedures a leader must effectively use in fulfilling his/her responsibilities on a daily basis. Whereas all functions a leader might perform in a school situation are not covered, the processes a leader is likely to use in addressing those situations are presented. The scenarios are about real-life situations that have occurred in school districts, schools, and classrooms. They are constructed to provoke thought, motivate reflections, and establish a setting in which prospective school leaders can explore multiple options and perhaps enhance their leadership skills before entering an actual school situation.

In addition, the performances specified by the ISLLC Standards appear in scenarios in both a negative and positive manner, allowing the reader to consider behaviors that are appropriate and inappropriate. To further accentuate the standards, those addressed within the context of the chapter are listed at the beginning of the chapter. The indicators of the standards precede each scenario to serve as a guide for reader inquiry with the intent of adding to the growing body of knowledge that links the reality of school leadership to university classroom instruction.

## General Class Discussion

A general in-class discussion of the scenarios will afford you an opportunity to exchange ideas on the key issues. The reflective questions reveal many philosophical aspects of belief systems and suggest areas that warrant additional attention. The different points of view on the multiple-choice suggested responses can be presented, and a rationale can be provided for alternative responses. Extensive discussion is often generated, yielding valuable information of a theoretical nature. This general discussion will also allow the professor an additional opportunity to clarify any misconceptions and to provide summary remarks and comments. The following principles of conversation tend to establish and maintain collegiality as issues are discussed:

- *Engage in conversation.* "Conversation" means "sharing ideas" and exchanging "informed opinions." The key to an effective conversation is to share only informed opinions (a position taken as a result of past reading, writing, and discussion of an issue).
- *Exchange informed opinions.* State your ideas and beliefs and try to maintain an unbiased view. Be honest and foster open dialogue.
- *Don't argue.* Try to make the people around you feel comfortable.
- *Be a good listener.* Stay focused on the issues, and listen carefully to each member of the group.

# INTRODUCTION

## Using Scenarios to Enhance Standards for School Leaders

For a number of years, in the fields of law, business, and medicine, case studies have proven to be a very effective instructional tool. Today, there is increased enthusiasm for the use of this pedagogical approach in the field of educational administration. In fact, the case format is becoming a part of a national movement to reform the field of educational administration, forging a new vision of educational leadership for tomorrow's schools (CCSSO, 1996).

In 1987, the National Commission on Excellence in Educational Administration recommended that "administrative preparation programs should be like those in professional schools which emphasize theoretical and clinical knowledge, applied research, and supervised practice" (p. 20). Giving consideration to this recommendation and others, many institutions of higher education are revising their leadership preparation programs and, in their revisions, some are changing their pedagogical approach to include scenario-type strategies (Murphy, 1993).

The Interstate School Leaders Licensure Consortium (ISLLC), a nationwide organization composed of public officials who head departments of elementary and secondary education in the 50 states, the District of Columbia, the Department of Defense Education Activity, and five extra state jurisdictions, is one of the organizations influencing this movement. According to ISLLC (1997), the new vision should include a common core of standards that can be used to inform program instructional content, as well as assessment tools for awarding new principal licensure, and advanced certification. To this end, ISLLC has developed six standards that focus on the knowledge, performance, and disposition of school leaders. Each of these standards has indicators of effectiveness in each of the identified areas. Figure I.1 contains a listing of the ISSLC Standards; specific indicators of these standards appear later in each chapter.

**FIGURE I.1   ISSLC Standards**

**Standard 1:** A school administrator is an educational leader who promotes the success of all students by facilitating the development, articulation, implementation, and stewardship of a vision of learning that is shared and supported by the school community.

**Standard 2:** A school administrator is an educational leader who promotes the success of all students by advocating, nurturing, and sustaining a school culture and instructional program conducive to student learning and staff professional growth.

**Standard 3:** A school administrator is an educational leader who promotes the success of all students by ensuring management of the organization, operations, and resources for a safe, efficient, and effective learning environment.

**Standard 4:** A school administrator is an educational leader who promotes the success of all students by collaborating with families and community members, responding to diverse community interests and needs, and mobilizing community resources.

**Standard 5:** A school administrator is an educational leader who promotes the success of all students by acting with integrity, fairness, and in an ethical manner.

**Standard 6:** A school administrator is an educational leader who promotes the success of all students by understanding, responding to, and influencing the larger political, social, economic, legal, and cultural context.

SOURCE: Interstate School Leaders Licensure Consortium of the Council of Chief State School Officers, 1997, *Candidate Information Bulletin for School Leaders Assessment* (p. 5). Princeton, NJ: Educational Testing Service.

Also, at the time this book is being written, four of the ISLLC states and the District of Columbia have joined together to fund the Educational Testing Service's (ETS) development of a performance assessment instrument that will be used in some states to license principals. A portion of the content of the instrument will be designed using a scenario or vignette type of format. The District of Columbia, Illinois, Kentucky, Mississippi, and North Carolina took this action (ISLLC, 1997). With the increased use of scenarios and vignettes in leadership preparation programs, it is becoming evident that this is a powerful tool that offers a unique approach to the successful blending of theory and practice in a variety of settings. Therefore, the scenario and vignette approach has been selected for use in this text.

## The Value of Using Scenarios

The value of scenarios and vignettes, as used in this text, is that they provide a way for the reader to relate theory to practice and to identify the relationship that exists between the literature and the ISLLC Standards. Understanding this relationship should endow the "new practitioner" with a greater appreciation for the complementary connection, thus enhancing the skills necessary for practice.

Scenarios also offer another approach to testing whether the readers can apply the theory acquired in the classroom to practical situations in schools and whether they display the behaviors suggested by the ISLLC Standards. They can also be used to assist prospective leaders to gain skills of critical analysis and problem solving. The acquisition of these skills will foster their capacity to analyze situations, make decisions, and communicate with constituents. They will also equip them to develop, implement, and evaluate action plans and to secure the assistance of others in the process (Ashbaugh & Kasten, 1995; Christensen & Hansen, 1987; Conley, 1997; Fullan, 1999; Merseth, 1997).

Further, the scenario approach allows prospective leaders to examine the conceptions or misconceptions they bring to the learning process, which, if not addressed, can block new learning (Merseth, 1997). When the prospective leader is given the opportunity to analyze concepts and principles through the perspective of scientific management (Taylorism), the result is rational decision making guided by rational policy. Scientific management leaves no questions as to the values that govern policy development (Ashbaugh & Kasten, 1995). Therefore, the use of scenarios provides the prospective leaders with evidence that will influence them to explore and perhaps revise their personal conceptions and motivate a search for new knowledge.

The scenario (cases) approach was expanded to the field of educational administration a number of years ago. However, in spite of considerable effort to establish the case method in the field of educational administration, the concept has not received the credibility that it has been afforded in other disciplines. Notwithstanding, the actions of ISLLC, coupled with pedagogical changes in higher education leadership preparation programs, signal a return of this approach to educational administration with greater acceptance and expanded use as an instructional tool in preparing educational leaders. Considering the fast adoptions of the standards developed by ISLLC, a book of scenarios that reflects the leader behaviors informed by those standards, if coupled with effective instruction, is likely to be a valuable addition to the field of school administration. This work is presented for that purpose.

## SUGGESTED READINGS

In addition to the instruction the prospective leaders receive in the classroom, reading the references listed below will provide additional background information in administrative theories, research, and practice sufficient to understand the content issues and address the challenges posed in each scenario.

Barth, R. (1990). *Improving schools from within*. San Francisco: Jossey-Bass.

Bennis, W., & Nanus, B. (1985). *Leaders: The strategies for taking charge*. New York: Harper & Row.

Council of Chief State School Officers. (1996). *Interstate school leaders consortium standards for school leaders*. Washington, DC: Author.

Fullan, M. (1999). *Change forces: The sequel*. New York: Farmer Press.

Gardner, J. W. (1990). *On leadership*. New York: The Free Press.

Goodlad, J. I., & McMannon, T. J. (1997). *The public purpose of education and schooling*. San Francisco: Jossey-Bass.

Greenberg, J. (1996). *Managing behavior in organizations*. Upper Saddle River, NJ: Prentice Hall.

Interstate School Leaders Licensure Consortium of the Council of Chief State School Officers. (1997). *Candidate information bulletin for school leaders assessment*. Princeton, NJ: Educational Testing Service.

Ryan, K. D., & Oestreich, D. K. (1991). *Driving fear out of the workplace: How to overcome the invisible barriers to quality, productivity, and innovation*. San Francisco: Jossey-Bass.

Sarason, S. (1996). *Revisiting the culture of the school and the problem of change*. New York: Teachers College Press.

Senge, P. (1990). *The fifth discipline: The art and practice of the learning organization*. New York: Doubleday.

Sergiovanni, T. J. (1994). *Building community in schools*. San Francisco: Jossey-Bass.

Short, P., & Greer, J. (1997). *Leadership in empowered schools: Themes from innovative efforts*. Upper Saddle River, NJ: Merrill/Prentice Hall.

Smith, D. M. (1997). *Motivating people* (2nd ed.). Hauppauge, NY: Barron's Educational Series.

Ubben, G. C., & Hughes, L. W. (1997). *The principal: Creative leadership for effective schools* (3rd ed.). Needham Heights, MA: Allyn and Bacon.

# 1

# LEADERSHIP IN TODAY'S SCHOOLS

## Leadership Theories Informing Practice

The literature on education is filled with descriptions of the challenging nature of schools. Of all the challenges posed, the one that appears to be most pronounced is providing the type of leadership necessary to assist schools in expanding their traditional boundaries. As society becomes more complex, schools become equally complex, placing a greater demand on the individuals who lead them. But what is leadership? Do leaders have special personality and physical traits? Is a leader an individual who closely monitors the performance of others? Are leaders individuals who articulate a vision and inspire other members in the organization to believe in that vision? Do leaders tell people what to do, tell them when to do it, and punish them if things are not done as prescribed? Do leaders have a specific set of behaviors that they perform in the course of their interaction with others? Or, perhaps leaders are individuals who can cultivate a special type of relationship with people, making each individual feel unique.

In pursuit of an answer to these questions and to establish a clear definition of leadership, theorists, researchers, and practitioners have spent over a century researching and analyzing various theories on the subject of leadership. The first studies of leadership were conducted by traditionalists who attempted to differentiate between leaders and nonleaders by identifying characteristics or traits necessary to complete tasks in the organization. A second group of theorists attempted to identify leaders by observable behaviors. Then there were the theorists who took a situational or "contingency" approach to the study of leadership. Although these studies have not provided a clear and definitive answer to the questions previously raised, they have provided insight into the subject and established a foundation on which contemporary leadership theories are built. From these early leadership studies, there tends to be common agreement in three areas. First, leadership involves the ability of an individual to influence others to pursue defined goals and objectives. Second, leadership involves establishing relationships with individuals affiliated with the organization sufficient to gain their commitment, and third, leadership involves acquiring a knowledge of individuals and situations (Conger, 1991).

More recent work offers a similar response, but in quite a different manner. Contemporary researchers and writers (Barth, 1990; Bennis & Nanus, 1985; Depree, 1992; Fullan, 1999; Gardner, 1990; Senge, 1990; Sergiovanni, 1992; Smith, 1997) suggest that leaders should be servants, coaching, influencing, and empowering subordinates to participate in building learning communities. They view leadership as a process with elements that are interactive and influential (Gardner, 1990). In this process, leaders manage meaning, self, trust, and attention (Bennis, 1995). They provide a clear vision, identify strategies, and establish policies that will enable followers to share and achieve the vision. Diversity is seen as an asset, and equity includes equity of treatment, opportunity, communication, recognition, and reward (Depree, 1992). The leader recognizes each person as an individual who has his/her own set of expectations and beliefs and understands that these inner forces are the prime motivators for achievement (Smith, 1997). Somewhat interesting is the premise that although writers and researchers continue to explore definitions of leadership, we find the principles of new discoveries to be derivatives of those that emerged from early studies. As will be explained in this chapter, both the traditional principles and the new ones inform leadership practices in today's schools.

The underlying purpose of this chapter is to review theoretical frameworks that informed early leadership practices, as well as contemporary ones. In addition, the relationship between the theories emerging from early studies and contemporary practices that suggest strategies for effective leadership in today's schools is identified. The chapter begins with a presentation of leadership theories, proceeds to a discussion of contemporary ideas relative to leadership practices in today's schools, and concludes with four scenarios that afford the reader an opportunity to consider the practical aspects of leadership. Through these scenarios, the reader will be exposed to various leadership styles that are utilized in an attempt to promote the success of students. To assist the reader in relating the ISLLC Standards to the behaviors exhibited in the scenarios, the knowledge, disposition, and performance indicators of the standards precede each scenario.

## Studies of Leadership Traits

One of the first series of theories concerning leadership emerged from the study of leadership traits. These early studies attempted to identify traits that could be used to differentiate between leaders and nonleaders. The organization was designed in a hierarchical fashion, and individuals in leadership roles functioned at or near the top of the hierarchy. The work of the organization was clearly defined, and tasks were broken down into key components. Such traits or characteristics were classified under the headings of capacity, friendliness, achievement, responsibility, participation, and status.

Leaders were believed to be a select group of individuals who focused their attention on completing the identified tasks. Their primary functions were to tell people what to do, monitor the progress of individuals in the workplace, see that organizational rules and regulations were followed, reward excellent performance, and penalize poor performance. The major focus of individuals functioning in leadership roles was task completion, and effectiveness was judged by the productivity of the organization. The more productive the organization was in achieving its goals, the more effective the leader.

In summarizing over 100 of these early studies, Stogdill (1948) pointed out that even though leaders exhibited some general managerial advantages over nonleaders relative to some characteristics and traits, there were no characteristics or traits exhibited by leaders that were clearly superior to nonleaders. Thus, these early studies were unsuccessful in distinguishing leaders from nonleaders. In fact, this top-down perspective was criticized because it implied that leaders were in a select group. This type of thinking minimized the contributions of other employees and perhaps reduced their level of motivation toward organizational goal attainment. Further, it was determined that leaders with one set of traits might be successful in one situation but not in others. Also, leaders with the same traits might be successful in different situations (Stogdill, 1948).

In reviewing the study of traits, one might come to understand that the top-down perspective is not a popular one. However, equally important, our attention can be drawn to traits of leaders who have achieved established goals. One in particular is Sam Walton. According to Walton and Huey (1992), Sam had passion and vision, was an effective communicator, empowered subordinates, and motivated them to share his vision. Through his vision, he was able to influence and motivate others by empowering them and creating a feeling of ownership and responsibility. He communicated his passion and vision to his subordinates through words and action.

## Studies of Leader Behaviors

In the early 1930s, researchers began to explore the behavior of leaders. With the collapse of the trait approach in the early 1940s, research on the behavior of leaders took center stage. Of the many behavior studies conducted, three that have provided insight into the behavior of school leaders were those conducted at the University of Iowa, The Ohio State University, and the University of Michigan. A brief summary of each of these studies follows.

### The Iowa Studies

At the University of Iowa, under the direction of Kurt Lewin, researchers who were in search of a style or pattern of leadership behavior conducted studies on the productivity of subordinates using three basic styles: autocratic, democratic, and laissez-faire (Lewin, Lippitt, & White, 1939).

Using the autocratic style, leaders were very direct, and decision making and power were centralized in the role of the leader. Leaders with this style allowed little or no participation in the decision-making process and tended to take full responsibility from the initiation of a task to its completion. When a leader used a democratic style, emphasis was placed on shared decision making and viewing the follower as an equal. Group discussion and decisions were encouraged. The leaders with a laissez-faire style gave complete freedom to the group and displayed little concern for completing a job. Subordinates were left to make decisions on their own.

In various instances, different styles had different effects on subordinates. However, the results of the studies showed the democratic style was considered to be most effective and most preferred by subordinates. The laissez-faire style was next, with the authoritarian style being the least preferred by subordinates (Lewin, Lippitt, & White, 1939).

In a general sense, these studies assist in understanding the behavior exhibited by individuals in practical school situations today. When an individual tends to be direct and highly task oriented, allowing members of the faculty and staff little or no participation in the decision-making process, the individual is considered to be autocratic. The individual who is relationship oriented, showing concern for the faculty and staff and inviting their participation in the administration of the school, is considered to be using a democratic style. Finally, the individual who offers little or no direction and allows followers complete freedom is characterized as laissez-faire. It is strongly advocated that to be effective in today's schools, the leader must be democratic, driving fear out of the workplace and fostering a community of learners who collaborate on all major issues. Such a relationship can have a huge impact on the teaching and learning process (Ryan & Oestreich, 1991).

## The Ohio State Studies

At The Ohio State University, a more contemporary view of leadership emerged. Whereas the concern had previously been with the identification of traits of effective leaders, the question became: What type of behaviors do effective leaders display? Researchers (Stogdill & Coons, 1957) addressing the latter question defined leadership as the behavior an individual displays when directing a group toward goal attainment. Having compiled a list of behavioral functions that they believed to be good examples of effective leader behavior, a questionnaire was designed and administered to a variety of individuals. The questionnaire asked individuals to delineate the behavior of their supervisor. An analysis of the responses to the questionnaire placed the behavior of supervisors into two categories: Initiating Structure and Consideration.

The *initiating structure* dimension (task-oriented leader behaviors) consisted of behaviors that related to the degree to which the leader defined his/her own behavior and the behavior of subordinates for the completion of tasks within an organization. The focus was on the manner the leader used in establishing well-defined patterns of organization, channels of communication, methods, and procedures. Such behaviors as maintaining performance standards, enforcing work deadlines, and scheduling were included.

The second dimension, *consideration* (people-oriented leader behaviors), consisted of behaviors that related to the degree to which the leader expressed a concern for the welfare of other individuals in the organization. Such behaviors as being approachable, exhibiting warmth, trust, respect, and a willingness to consult with subordinates before making decisions were included.

The researchers used the Leader Behavior Description Questionnaire (LBDQ) to assess the behavior of individuals relative to the two dimensions. These studies indicated that the two factors seemed to be separate and distinct. Thus, four quadrants of leadership could be formed: Quadrant 1: High Consideration/Low Structure; Quadrant 2: High Structure/High Consideration; Quadrant 3: Low Structure/Low Consideration; and Quadrant 4: High Structure/Low Consideration. Hoy and Miskel (1991) reported Halpin's analysis of the original data, which concluded that the combination of high initiating structure/high consideration leads to higher satisfaction and performance among school leaders than do any of the other three combinations. From these studies, it was clearly demonstrated that leader behavior in organizations can be observed through these two dimensions. Whereas the results of the studies are not conclusive, it seems reasonable to believe that some combination of these dimensions influences leadership effectiveness.

There are times in school situations when various combinations of the dimensions are appropriate. The challenge for the school leader is matching the appropriate combination in a manner that will produce a win–win situation. By developing a rapport with subordinates and acquiring an understanding of the situation, the leader is likely to select such an approach (Zuker, 1991).

## The Michigan Studies

At the University of Michigan, researchers conducted additional studies on the behavior of leaders. The Michigan research focused on the identification of relationships among leader behavior, group processes, and measures of group performance using Likert's (1961, 1967) theory of organization. The initial and subsequent studies revealed that three types of leader behaviors differentiate effective and ineffective managers: task-oriented behavior, relationship-oriented behavior, and participative leadership behavior. These behaviors were described in the following manner:

1. Task-oriented behavior: Effective leaders focused on subordinates, set work standards that were high but obtainable, carefully organized tasks, identified the methods to be used in carrying them out, and closely supervised the work of subordinates. The task-oriented behaviors found to be important in these studies were quite similar to the initiating structure behaviors found to be important in the Ohio State studies.

2. Relationship-oriented behavior: Effective leaders who displayed relationship-oriented behavior emphasized the development of interpersonal relations, while focusing on the personal needs of subordinates and the development of the kind of relationships that would motivate subordinates to set and achieve high performance goals. The relationship-oriented behaviors found to be important were similar to the consideration behaviors found to be important in the Ohio State studies.

3. Participative leadership: The third factor, participative leadership, involved extensive use of group supervision, rather than the separate supervision of each subordinate. In their experiments, the Michigan researchers placed considerable emphasis on the use of groups. Likert proposed that the role of leaders in group meetings should be to enhance follower participation in decision making, communication, cooperation, and resolving conflict. During group meetings, the leader took on the role of being directive, constructive, and supportive, allowing some degree of autonomy regarding group work. Researchers concluded that when subordinates participate in making decisions, they tend to reach a higher level of satisfaction and performance (Likert, 1967).

An analysis of the behaviors of leaders in the Michigan studies revealed that effective leaders were generally task oriented, set high performance goals, and focused on such administrative functions as planning, coordinating, and facilitating work. It was also found that effective leaders gave consideration to good interpersonal relations, allowing subordinates some degree of autonomy in deciding how to conduct their work and at what pace. Leaders who were relationship oriented, rather than task oriented, tended to have the most productive work group. It was also determined that high morale, in some instances, did not result in high productivity. However, as leaders used the kind of practices that resulted in high productivity, it was found that they often also resulted in high morale (Likert, 1967).

From the University of Michigan studies and others that followed, the possibility of shared leadership became a major focus. Leadership that involved allowing followers to participate in procedures (i.e., site-based management) that influenced leaders' decisions became a major thrust. The participative movement is alive in today's schools in the form of power sharing, decentralization, democratic management, and shared decision making.

Contemporary works support this line of reasoning, and in addition to being concerned with task completion, effective leaders are demonstrating a concern for people as they have come to realize that you cannot mandate what matters (Fullan, 1993). Covey (1989) writes that effectiveness lies in a balance between the desired results and the leader's ability to produce the desired results. To that end, teams are being established in schools through strong interpersonal relationships, and individuals are bonding to solve problems at the lowest organizational level. Principals are providing avenues for teachers, students, parents, and other stakeholders to feel a sense of personal dignity and purpose regarding their involvement with the school. As a result of this involvement, individuals can experience confidence and fulfillment and remain committed to the organizational process. A review of Blake and Mouton's (1985) Managerial Grid offers additional insight into this position and suggests various leader behaviors that might be used to influence the behavior of subordinates.

## Blake and Mouton

Blake and Mouton's (1985) Managerial Grid identifies two dimensions of leader orientation: *concern for production (task)* and *concern for people (relationship)*. These dimensions contribute to an understanding of the style a leader might use in influencing the behavior of subordinates. Using these two concepts, five leadership styles are portrayed on the grid:

1. Country club management: Even if production is less than desired, the leader places major emphasis on developing good relations among colleagues and subordinates.
2. Authority obedience: Power, authority, and control are used to maximize production.

3. Impoverished management: The leader completes the minimum requirements necessary to remain employed.
4. Organization nonmanagement: Leaders maintain the status quo and display an attitude of go-along-to-get-along.
5. Team management: Leaders emphasize a high concern for both task
completion and maintenance of positive interpersonal relationships
(Blake & Mouton, 1985).

Of the five styles portrayed, the team management style (which allegedly is
equally effective and equally applicable in all situations) is identified as the one
that is superior to all other styles (Blake & Mouton, 1985).

In general, studies of leadership behavior offered two basic elements concerning effective leadership, relationship-oriented behaviors and task-oriented
behaviors. In some instances, they revealed that leaders who are both task oriented and relationship oriented have the best production record (Bowers,
1977). In schools, it seems advisable for leaders to be true to this practice.
When the school leader is well organized, has a plan of action that has been
developed with the cooperation of the faculty, and implements that plan using
a fair process, the end results tend to be goal attainment and high faculty
morale (Barth, 1990). However, because another group of theorists added
variables to the equation that influences contemporary leadership styles and
practices in schools, it is necessary for us to review contingency and situational
theories of leadership behavior.

## Contingency and Situational Leadership Theories

In the late 1970s, a group of theorists began to explore a set of variables
believed to influence the relationship between leadership styles and subordinate responses to those styles. This definitive approach attempted to determine
how behavior influences outcomes differently from situation to situation.
These studies resulted in a series of situational theories. According to Yukl
(1989), "a situational theory is more complete if it includes intervening variables to explain why the effect of behavior on outcomes varies across situations" (p. 98). In the following section, a brief description of three widely
discussed situational theories is presented. In presenting these theories, the
author attempts to raise the reader's awareness of the benefits that can be
derived from having a knowledge of subordinates and the situation in question
and allowing that knowledge to influence his/her behavior.

### Vroom and Yetton Normative Model

Vroom and Yetton (1973) analyzed the effects of leader behavior on decision
quality and subordinate acceptance of the decision. They theorized that decision quality and decision acceptance are intervening variables that work collectively to affect group performance. They further theorized that aspects of

**FIGURE 1.1   Aspects on which decision effectiveness depends as outlined in the Vroom-Yetton Model**

The Vroom-Yetton Model offers that decision effectiveness in a given situation can depend on:
1. The amount of relevant information the leader and the follower possess.
2. The amount of disagreement among followers regarding the desired alternative.
3. The extent to which the decision/problem is structured or unstructured and the extent to which creativity is needed.
4. The likelihood followers will cooperate, if allowed to participate.
5. The likelihood followers will be receptive to an autocratic decision.

SOURCE: Yukl, 1989, p. 113.

the situation moderate the relationship between decision procedures and the intervening variables of quality and acceptance. Decision acceptance refers to "the degree of subordinate commitment to implement a decision effectively, whereas decision quality refers to the objective aspect of the decision that affects group performance aside from any effects mediated by decision acceptance. A basic assumption of the model is that participation increases decision acceptance if it is not already high. Also, the more influence subordinates have, the more they will be motivated to implement a decision" (Yukl, 1989, p. 113).

The researchers reasoned that a subordinate who is not consulted regarding a decision might not understand either the decision or the reason for it. As a result, subordinates may believe the decision to be detrimental to their interests. Also, if a decision is made in an autocratic manner, subordinates may resent not being involved and refuse to accept the decision. Therefore, group decision making is likely to result in greater decision acceptance.

A leader should be concerned with decision quality when a variety of alternatives exist and the alternative selected holds important consequences for the performance of the group. When the best alternative is selected, a decision is of high quality. The Vroom-Yetton model offers that subordinate participation will result in higher-quality decisions when subordinates possess relevant information and are willing to participate in the decision-making process. The model outlines five aspects on which decision effectiveness in a given situation can depend. Those aspects are listed in Figure 1.1.

The model also provides a list of seven rules that a leader can apply in conjunction with these assumptions. The rules are listed in Figure 1.2.

## Vroom and Jago Revision Model

A later model developed by Vroom and Jago (1988) offered revisions to the original model. The revised model denotes actions that the leader should not take, but refrains from advising of actions to take. It also contains features that

**FIGURE 1.2    Rules that guide a leader in determining the type of leader behavior to use in decision making**

1. Autocratic decisions are not appropriate when subordinates have important relevant information lacked by the leader. In such an instance, the leader would make decisions with inadequate or incomplete data.
2. Group decisions are not appropriate if decision quality is important and subordinates do not share the leader's concern for task goals. Group involvement gives too much influence to possibly uncooperative or hostile individuals.
3. When the quality of a decision is important, if the leader lacks the information and expertise necessary to address the problem and the problem is unstructured, interaction should occur among people who have the relevant information to make the decision.
4. When decision acceptance is important and subordinates are not likely to accept an autocratic decision, then an autocratic decision should not be made by the leader. Subordinates may not effectively implement such a decision.
5. Autocratic decision procedures and individual consultations are not recommended when decision acceptance is important and there is likely disagreement among subordinates relative to the best alternative. Such action is not likely to resolve the differences that exist among subordinates and between subordinates and the leader.
6. When decision acceptance is critical and unlikely to result from an autocratic decision and if decision quality is not in question, the only appropriate procedure is a group decision. In such instances, acceptance is maximized without risking quality.
7. When decision acceptance is important but is not likely to occur from an autocratic decision and if subordinates share the leader's task objective, subordinates should be given equal partnership in the decision process; then acceptance is maximized without risking quality.

SOURCE: Yukl, 1989.

enable the leader to prioritize the different criteria, thus reducing the feasible set used in the original model to a single procedure. To describe a situation in the revised model, leaders are required to differentiate between five choices (no, probably no, maybe, probably yes, yes). In addition, the Vroom-Jago model takes into account time constraints, geographical dispersion of subordinates, and amount of subordinate information, whereas the Vroom-Yetton model uses only two outcome criteria in reaching the decision rule, decision acceptance, and decision quality.

The Vroom-Yetton model has been tested by a number of studies, and a number of weaknesses have been identified. Nevertheless, of the situational leadership theories, it is probably the best supported. The model places the focus on specific aspects of behavior, addresses meaningful intervening variables, and identifies factors about the situation that allow the relationship between behavior and outcomes to be moderated.

**FIGURE 1.3   House's categories of leader behavior**

▶ Supportive Leadership: A supportive leader is approachable, maintains a pleasant work environment, is considerate, and shows concern for the needs and well-being of subordinates.

▶ Directive Leadership: A directive leader sets performance standards, lets subordinates know what is expected of them, schedules the work, and establishes specific directions.

▶ Participative Leadership: A participative leader consults with subordinates concerning work-related matters and takes their opinion into consideration when making decisions.

▶ Achievement-Oriented Leadership: An achievement-oriented leader stresses excellence in performance, sets goals that are challenging, and shows confidence in the ability of subordinates to achieve challenging performance standards.

SOURCE: House, 1971.

## Path-Goal Theory

R. J. House (1971) theorized that the behavior of leaders has an effect on the performance and satisfaction levels of subordinates. House took the position that the motivational function of the leader is to clarify the routes subordinates must travel to reach work–goal attainment and remove any roadblocks and/or pitfalls that may exist. He offered that this type of leader behavior improves the work performance and increases the opportunity for subordinates to receive personal satisfaction en route to work–goal attainment.

He further theorized that the type of behavior displayed by the leader to motivate and bring satisfaction to subordinates is dependent on the situation, adding another dimension to the equation. Such factors as the ability and personality of subordinates, characteristics of the work environment, and work group preferences contribute to the satisfaction and motivational level of subordinates and must be given consideration. Using the principles of this theory, House (1971) suggested that there are four categories of behavior from which leaders may choose, depending on the situation. The four categories suggested by House appear in Figure 1.3.

This theory holds many implications for the effective administration of a school. Assessing the ability of the faculty and staff, understanding individual personalities, and identifying factors in the environment that influence the transformation process of the school can prove to be of considerable benefit to the school leader in achieving established goals.

## Hersey and Blanchard's Theory of Situational Leadership

Another theory that has application for educational leaders is Paul Hersey and Kenneth Blanchard's (1977, 1982) Situational Leadership Theory. These researchers attempted to provide some understanding of the relationship between effective leadership styles and the maturity level of followers by adding the variable of level of maturity to Fiedler's (1967) contingency factors. They argued that to be effective, the leader must take into account the followers' maturity level. In their research, maturity level was defined as the extent to which a follower demonstrates the ability to perform a task (job maturity) and a follower's willingness to accept responsibility (motivational level) for its completion.

Using a similar design, as was the case in the Ohio State studies, Hersey and Blanchard (1977) developed a leadership effectiveness model consisting of two dimensions of leader behavior—task and relationship. The two variables were defined in the following manner:

> *Task behavior:* the extent to which the leader engages in one-way communication by explaining what is to be done, how it is to be done, and when it is to be completed
>
> *Relationship behavior:* the extent to which the leader engages in two-way communication to provide supportive and facilitative behaviors

Using the possible combinations of the two dimensions, leadership behaviors were aligned in four quadrants:

- Q1—High task and low relationship
- Q2—High task and high relationship
- Q3—High relationship and low task
- Q4—Low relationship and low task

Depending on the condition of the relationships among the leader, the follower, and the situation, the leader may elect to use one of four styles: directing, coaching, supporting, or delegating. The following is the suggested leader behavior for each style:

- When leaders choose to use a directing style, they provide the follower with specific instructions regarding the completion of a task and closely supervise the performance of the subordinate throughout the process (high task, low relationship).
- If the leader chooses to use a coaching style, he/she gives specific directions, closely supervises the task, explains directions, solicits suggestions, and supports the progress toward task completion (high task, high relationship).
- When the supportive style is chosen, the leader facilitates and supports the efforts of subordinates toward task accomplishment and shares responsibility for decision making with them (low task, high relationship).
- The leader may find it acceptable to turn over the responsibility for decision making and problem solving to subordinates. In such instances, the leader behavior is referred to as delegating (low task, low relationship).

In a continuous search for the right approach to influence the desired outcome behavior, many theorists have focused on the situation and characteristics of the situation that would be effective. However, like the theorists who probed traits and leader behavior, the results remain inconclusive; leadership effectiveness may occur for any number of reasons. The major factor to be considered in achieving success with situational leadership theory is selecting the leadership style that is appropriate for the specific situation and the individuals of the group involved (Hanson, 1996). In making that determination, the leader is wise to give consideration to the source and use of power.

## Power and Authority

Power and its source are important factors in leadership effectiveness. The nature and use of power, influence, and authority often determine the effectiveness of the leader. John French (1993) presented four sources from which a leader might acquire power. Quite clearly, one source is the position held (legitimate or position power). A leader has legal power that is vested in his/her position, or role, in the organizational hierarchy. Another source of power is the personality of the leader (referent or personality power). Many leaders are able to influence followers from the strength of their personality. This type of power is also referred to as charismatic power. A third source of leader power is known as reward power. Leaders have the ability to control and administer punishment to subordinates for noncompliance with the leader's directives or to reward selected behavior. In such instances, the leader is using reward power. Finally, there is expert power, which is derived from the special ability and/or knowledge possessed by the leader and needed by followers.

In many instances, the manner in which a leader exerts his/her power and authority determines his/her effectiveness. Followers in the organization grant power to the leader (by shared agreement) as they accept his/her influence and directions. Individuals in a higher position also grant power to the leader as they assign tasks and share responsibility. These two sources build on one another. As one gets stronger, the other is likely to get stronger. However, the reverse is also true; as one gets weaker, so does the other. The power of the leader is likely to be most effective when he/she uses a combination of legitimate and referent power to facilitate inquiry, mastery, and collaboration (Fullan, 1993).

## Bridging the Past and the Present

As noted very early in this chapter, the theories on leadership previously presented are of long standing and have provided and continue to provide tremendous insight into practices that inform effective leadership in today's schools. From a review of Table 1.1, the reader can begin to connect these theories, behaviors, and practices to those that are suggested for leaders of today's schools.

**TABLE 1.1** Leadership Studies and Theories

| THEORIES | AUTHORS OF STUDIES AND/OR MODELS | MAJOR FOCUS | BASIC ASSUMPTION | IMPLICATIONS FOR LEADERSHIP IN SCHOOLS |
|---|---|---|---|---|
| *Early Trait Theories*<br><br>*Recent Studies* | Ralph M. Stogdill (1948)<br>R. D. Mann (1959)<br>Gary Yukl (1981) | Identification of specific characteristics that contribute to an individual's ability to perform in a leadership role | Relative to their effectiveness, leaders have specific characteristics and/or traits that differentiate them from the people they lead. | Traits of leaders do not contribute highly to their performance. An individual does not become a leader because of the possession of some combination of traits.<br><br>Leaders have vigor and use persistence in their pursuit of goals. They have self-confidence, sense of personal identity, and the ability to influence others. |
| *Behavior Theories* | Ohio State Studies<br>Univ. of Michigan Studies<br>Iowa Studies Managerial Grid (Blake and Mouton, 1964) | Leader patterns of activities and categories of behavior: What do leaders do? How do effective leaders behave? | Leader behavior has an influence on the performance of the group. One behavior style of leadership can be developed and applied across all situations. | When the traits of the leader match the situation, the leader is likely to be effective in achieving organizational goals. There must be a good fit between the leader's personality and the favorableness of the situation that produces leader effectiveness. |
| *Contingency Theories* | House's Path-Goal Theory | The importance of situational factors on task accomplishment and psychological state of subordinates and processes | Leader behavior is shaped and constrained by situational factors. | |
| | Vroom and Yetton Normative Model | Decision and procedures | Participation increases decision acceptance. | Followers are likely to be receptive to decision outcomes when they are involved. |
| *Situational Theories* | Hersey and Blanchard (1982) | Relationship between effective leadership styles and the maturity level of followers | Leader effectiveness depends on a match between the leader's behavior and the follower's maturity level. | Leadership behavior that changes with the maturity level of the individual or group should produce leader effectiveness. |
| *Power Theories* | John French and Bertrom Raven (1968)<br>Gary Yukl (1981)<br>Henry Mintzberg (1983) | How effective leaders use power: source, amount, and leader use of power over followers | Leaders influence followers through power acquired from various sources. The behavior of the leader and his/her influence on the follower are determined by the source of power and its use. | A combination of referent and expert power should lead to greater follower satisfaction and performance. |

Findings from these early studies hold many practical implications for today's school leaders. The knowledge acquired about task completion, leader behavior, and the behavior of followers when a particular leadership style is used is very informative. They underpin what current writers and researchers characterize as participatory governance, servant leadership, site-based management, collaborative leadership, teaming, empowerment, learning communities, and shared governance. To complete the connection, the following section draws the reader's attention to some key approaches appearing in the literature that incorporate these concepts into contemporary practice. Because it is assumed that individuals using this text have previously addressed these approaches in an in-depth manner, they will be treated in a brief summary format.

## Contemporary Approaches to School Leadership

Building on the works of early theorists, current literature (Bennis & Nanus, 1985; Covey, 1989; Fullan, 1999; Gardner, 1990; Lundy, 1986; Manz & Sims, 1989; Senge, 1990; Smith, 1997) offers that today's leaders should create a learning environment that fosters the development of a shared vision and the pursuit of that vision through various forms of participatory decision making. After spending a number of years studying leadership, Bennis (1995) suggests that leaders should concern themselves with doing the right thing, whereas managers emphasize doing things right. "Doing things right" includes such activities as planning, organizing, and monitoring, whereas individuals who are concerned with "doing the right thing" manage the four areas of attention, meaning, trust, and self (p. 396).

According to Bennis (1995), the leader manages meaning by being highly committed to a vision that is compelling. He suggests that leaders manage meaning when they use words and symbols to make ideas seem real and tangible to others. Leaders manage trust by demonstrating that they are reliable and congruent so people know that for which they stand. Regarding the fourth area, which is self, the leader knows his/her skills and uses them effectively. He/she learns from mistakes and focuses on success, rather than on failure (p. 397).

### A Shift in the Leadership Paradigm

The leadership paradigm is shifting; in schools today, it is no longer effective to threaten people into compliance. Our society, through its laws and practices, is emphasizing the worth of the individual. To address this shift, rather than directing and assigning, today's leaders are coaching, influencing, and assisting followers in fulfilling individual as well as organizational goals. Responsibility for addressing organizational challenges is shared, and leaders are identifying problems that fall within the realm of subordinates and empowering them to share in the decision-making process. (Blanchard, Oncken, & Burrows, 1989).

Today, leadership involves working with individuals to establish teams and motivating them to focus on the vision of the school to share leadership responsibility (Gardner, 1990). To accomplish this, the leader must use the power of influence that can best be displayed through the use of motivation (Gardner, 1990). The prime motivators for achievement are the inner forces that drive an individual's expectations and beliefs (Smith, 1997). Therefore, the leader must establish a climate in which he/she builds relationships that influence a desire within subordinates to achieve school goals. Priorities are set, and individuals understand the mission of the school, buy into that mission, have a personal vision, feel empowered to participate in the decision-making process, and communicate the benefits that will be derived from mission attainment (Covey, 1989).

Leaders are establishing this type of productive work environment, and it is occurring because they establish the roles of followers, build trust, and participate in humanistic interaction that allows them to know constituents on a personal level. They recognize the value of stakeholder involvement and consider cooperative working relationships essential to organizational effectiveness.

## The Moral Dimension of Leadership

There are a number of writers who argue that the leader must be prepared to address moral dilemmas that will occur in schools (Fullan, 1999; Goodlad, 1994; Sergiovanni, 1992; Strike, Haller, & Soltis, 1988). These writers argue that objective ethical reasoning is possible and should be used by leaders of today's schools. They further argue that the leader should be a moral agent who applies the principles of equal respect and benefit maximization. The principle of equal respect requires that human beings be regarded as having intrinsic worth and should be treated accordingly. "The principle of benefit maximization holds that whenever we are faced with a choice, the best and most just decision is the one that results in the most good or the greatest benefit for the most people" (Strike, Haller, & Soltis, 1988, p. 16). The challenges faced by leaders of today's schools appear to warrant the use of these two principles.

In espousing moral leadership, the leader takes into account the best interest of all children, teachers, parents, and himself or herself. Sergiovanni (1992) writes that leaders have a moral responsibility to make people feel welcome, wanted, and a part of the school with which they are affiliated. Individuals in schools have a common purpose, a shared vision, and seek mutual goals. People are drawn to leaders who first have a vision to serve others and a willingness, when necessary, to experience personal sacrifices in order to promote their ideas (Greenleaf, 1977). They reflect what Sergiovanni (1992) describes as the heart, head, and hand of leadership.

## Summary

In many schools, the principal is the instructional leader, and in order to effect quality instructional programs, he/she must acquire a new picture of leadership.

Fear must be removed from the workplace, and the challenges of the school must be addressed from within (Barth, 1990; Ryan & Oestreich, 1991). Teachers will necessarily have to share the vision of the school, conduct inquiries into the teaching and learning process, take risks, explore new methods of doing things, and expand their role outside of the classroom to include activities and programs that affect the entire school (Conley, 1997). This means redistributing power, establishing effective committee structures and engaging in comprehensive planning.

In addition to the concept of moral leadership and the others previously mentioned, there are a number of other contemporary theories and postulates that offer explanations concerning the qualities and attributes of effective leaders, a list that is much too extensive to include in a text of this nature. *Practicing the Art of Leadership through Scenarios: Meeting the ISLLC Standards* adopts the view that a leader is an individual who has the capacity to influence others to use their skills and expertise to move the organization toward established goals. In this process, the leader must assist individuals in understanding and adjusting to the environment of the organization. Ineffective patterns of behaviors that inhibit progress must be replaced by behaviors that aid in the process of managing change, and the delicate balance between task and relationship must be achieved. Above all, it is the leader's predisposition about schools, teachers, children, parents, and the community that forms the foundation upon which leadership for school improvement is based. Constructs characterizing the disposition of effective leadership appearing most frequently in the literature are listed in Figure 1.4. The reader might review this list to identify those that hold meaning for him/her.

The scenarios that follow will allow the reader an opportunity to explore his/her disposition and apply some of the constructs, as well as the theoretical principles previously discussed. Supporting variables, which appear in Chapter 2, help to further establish a foundation for selected constructs and other organizational influences that effect leadership.

## The Scenarios

In Scenario 1, Principal Williams has the responsibility of selecting and orientating a new teacher to the fourth-grade faculty. Members of her faculty who are not desirous of participating in that process challenge her. The reader will want to review the leadership skills necessary to influence faculty participation in the completion of tasks, while maintaining a climate that is conducive to teaching and learning.

In Scenario 2, Principal Johnson makes a major change in the science program and acquires the cooperation of the entire faculty in the process. The leadership style and strategies she used are reflective of those advocated for leaders of today's schools.

Scenarios 3 and 4 are related. In fact, Scenario 4 is an outgrowth of Scenario 3 and is presented to illustrate what can happen if the leader gets too far ahead of followers. In Scenario 3, the leader makes several adjustments in her

**FIGURE 1.4   Leadership constructs that comprise the disposition of effective leaders**

| | | |
|---|---|---|
| compassion | accuracy | judgment |
| persuasion | influence | logic |
| insight | trust | communication |
| sensitivity | knowledge | tact |
| respect | vision | diplomacy |
| creativity | management | predictability |
| rapport | dignity | courage |
| credibility | consistency | decisiveness |
| organization | fairness | equity |
| morality | diversity | honesty |
| support | planning | openness |
| reasoning | timeliness | adaptability |
| reliability | accountability | |

SOURCE: Compiled from various writings and studies on leadership.

style to fit changes in faculty attitude. Adult motivation, the effects of school culture and climate, and leadership behaviors that are effective in working cooperatively with a faculty entrenched in tradition are exhibited.

As a result of working through these scenarios, the reader will have an opportunity to review the indicators of ISLLC Standards 1, 2, and 3 in practical situations.

## SCENARIO 1
## THE NEW FOURTH-GRADE TEACHER

### STANDARD 2

A school administrator is an educational leader who promotes the success of all students by advocating, nurturing, and sustaining a school culture and instructional program conducive to student learning and staff professional growth.

*In Scenario 1, Principal Williams advocates sustaining a school culture and instructional program conducive to student learning. Because she believes that professional development is an integral part of school improvement and wants to utilize the faculty in a collegial manner, she seeks the cooperation of the fourth-grade faculty in selecting and providing professional development for a new teacher.*

## ISLLC Standards Indicators Exhibited in Scenario 1

### Knowledge Indicators
The administrator has knowledge and understanding of:
▲ Adult learning and professional development models
▲ The change process for systems, organizations, and individuals
▲ School cultures
▲ Human resources management and development

### Disposition Indicators
The administrator believes in, values, and is committed to:
▲ Making management decisions to enhance learning and teaching
▲ Taking risks to improve schools
▲ Accepting responsibility
▲ Involving stakeholders in management processes
▲ Professional development as an integral part of school improvement
▲ The benefit that diversity brings to the school community

### Performance Indicators
The administrator facilitates and engages in activities ensuring that:
▲ All individuals are treated with fairness, dignity, and respect
▲ Professional development promotes a focus on student learning consistent with the school vision and goals
▲ There is a culture of high expectations for self, students, and staff
▲ The school is organized and aligned for success
▲ Organizational systems are regularly monitored and modified as needed
▲ Stakeholders are involved in decisions affecting schools

Mrs. Williams has served as principal of Jacksonville Elementary School for 15 years. She is an experienced principal and realizes the benefits to be derived from involving her faculty and staff in the selection and orientation of new personnel.

It was just three weeks prior to the end of the school year when the registrar provided her with the estimated student enrollment figures for the next school year. According to the numbers received, she will need an additional fourth-grade teacher. Currently, the fourth-grade faculty consists of three teachers who have their own styles, and there is very little cooperative teaching or interaction among them.

Following her practice of involvement, Mrs. Williams informed the teachers that an additional fourth-grade teacher was needed and that she wanted them to participate in the selection process. She also asked one of them to volunteer to serve as mentor to the newly employed teacher.

The current fourth-grade teachers showed little interest in the new position, knowing how it would affect their grade level, or being included in the selection process. Each of the teachers offered reasons for not being interested in accepting the assignment. "I have a computer club to organize and maintain next year, so I won't have the time," said one teacher. Another teacher remarked, "I am doing an inclusion class next year, and I will also have a student teacher." The third teacher stated, "I have been assigned Parent's Night, and the planning of that activity is going to really take a lot of extra time."

Concerned by the situation, Mrs. Williams replied, "All fourth-grade teachers will serve on the selection committee; I will look over everyone's obligations and assign one of you the mentoring responsibility." Fully respecting the wishes of the current faculty members, but being in a situation where she needed a mentor for the incoming teacher, she exercised her authority in order to implement one of her proven leadership concepts. The selection process began and within three weeks, the position was filled. Although each of the fourth-grade teachers had reasons for not volunteering to accept the commitment of mentoring the new teacher, one of the teachers received the assignment. The teacher receiving the assignment was not pleased with the principal's decision; however, he agreed to it.

The new school year began with the assigned fourth-grade mentoring teacher and the newly employed teacher working together. The new teacher was acquainted with policies, schedules, activities, and procedures of the school. Aware of the lack of motivation the senior teacher showed for mentoring the new teacher, Mrs. Williams closely supervised the process and often stopped in to check on how the mentoring was progressing.

## REFLECTIVE THINKING AND SCENARIO ANALYSIS

1. Identify several factors that would serve as a basis for a characterization of the existing state of the fourth-grade faculty.
2. At Jacksonville Elementary, what might be occurring that would influence faculty members to resist serving on a selection committee and mentoring a new colleague?
3. Which adult learning and professional development models would best inform the actions needed in this scenario?
4. Identify the system, organization, and individual change process that Mrs. Williams might have used to influence the participation of her faculty without making a direct assignment.
5. Using the Vroom-Yetton model, give a theoretical rationale for why Mrs. Williams should be concerned with the decision she made. In addition, cite the decision rule that is most applicable.
6. What long-term provisions could Mrs. Williams make to sustain an effective mentoring program?

## ADDRESSING THE ISSUES

Select the one best answer to the following questions:

1. Which of the following best exemplifies the leadership disposition of Mrs. Williams?

   **a.** She is willing to allow teachers to decide whether or not to participate in the personnel selection process.

   **b.** Achieving an outcome that is in the best interest of the total school program is of primary importance.

   **c.** Being responsive to the needs, concerns, and interests of each faculty member is more important than achieving an established goal.

   **d.** Utilizing the expertise of the existing faculty to address a particular need is of primary importance.

2. Reflecting on the continuum between management and leadership, which of the following statements regarding Mrs. Williams is likely to be true?

   **a.** She may be concerned with the personal and professional development of her staff; however, her actions are out of line.

   **b.** She is receptive to reasonable teacher explanations regarding her request, but is somewhat coercive in her style.

   **c.** She is justified in exercising her authority as principal to see that the new teacher is mentored.

   **d.** She is more concerned with staff cohesiveness than work overload.

3. Which of the following would best serve as justification for the action taken by Mrs. Williams?

   **a.** The quality of the faculty selection and mentoring process needed to be protected.

   **b.** The expertise of the fourth-grade faculty was inconsequential.

   **c.** Completing the task was more important than the quality of the outcome.

   **d.** She lacked the necessary expertise to select and mentor the new teacher without faculty assistance.

4. Mrs. Williams could have possibly influenced the participation of the faculty without making a direct assignment by:

   **a.** reducing the class size of the mentoring teacher.

   **b.** sharing the selection and mentoring responsibilities with the entire fourth-grade faculty.

   **c.** replacing an existing teacher's assignment with the assignment of selecting and mentoring the new teacher.

   **d.** any or all of the above.

5. Given the attitude of the fourth-grade faculty, when moving forward, Mrs. Williams would be well advised to:

   **a.** maintain the autocratic style that appears to have worked effectively.

   **b.** focus on building a learning community within Jacksonville.

   **c.** revert to her initial achievement-oriented style and perfect its use.

   **d.** reassign this group of teachers to other grades.

## DISCUSSION OF THE SOLUTION

1. Initially Principal Williams attempted to use a relationship-oriented leadership style; however, that style proved to be ineffective. She changed her behavior because of the behavior of her faculty members, and the situation dictated that a change was necessary if she were to achieve the desired outcome. Hersey and Blanchard (1982) offer that the leadership style will often depend on the readiness level of followers and when one style proves to be ineffective, contingent on the situation, it may be beneficial for a leader to consider an alternate style. In this instance, faculty members were able but not willing to accept the assignment offered by the principal. Thus, for benefit maximization and to achieve the outcome that was in the best interest of the total school, the principal changed her style. The change was appropriate, as the leader must promote congeniality in pursuit of school goals (Barth, 1990). The suggested response to question 1 is **(b)**.

2. Mrs. Williams expressed confidence in members of the faculty by inviting them to serve on the selection committee and as a mentor to the new teacher. Unfortunately, the teachers had little interest in the inclusion opportunity. They showed little interest in the new position or being included in the selection process. When asked to mentor the new teacher, they attempted to avoid the opportunity. Therefore, Principal Williams used legitimate power vested in the position of the principalship to complete a task she believed to be in the best interest of the school's program. Because of the location of the principal's position in the hierarchy, he/she has legitimate power. It is a mutually accepted perception of both the principal and the faculty that the principal has the right to make such decisions. Principal Williams was within her rights to assign certain tasks to be completed by members of her faculty. Taking such action is part of her responsibility in the area of human resource management and development. The suggested response to question 2 is **(c)**.

3. It is the principal's responsibility to have adequate and appropriate staff in the building. Faculty involvement in the staff selection process is certainly a means of developing staff cohesiveness and indicates the use of democratic principles in school administration (Kouzes & Posner, 1987). In fact, it is a frequently used practice when the site-based management concept is operationalized. However, in this instance, the staff did not willingly agree to participate. Rather, they expressed resistance to participation. Given that the task had to be completed and after expressing concern for the involvement of her staff and listening to their explanations as to why they would not be able to accept additional responsibility, the principal was justified in exercising her legitimate power to assign the task. She then followed up with observations to ensure the job was done in an effective manner. Autocratic decisions are appropriate if decision quality is important and subordinates do not share the leader's concern for task goals (Yukl, 1989). However, as autocratic decisions are made, in instances of this nature, the principal must recognize that a larger problem exists and seek a solution to that problem. The suggested response to question 3 is **(a)**.

4. House (1971) argues that the leader can motivate subordinates and increase their work performance and satisfaction by increasing the payoff they receive from work-goal attainment. He also argues that a leader can increase work performance and goal attainment by removing roadblocks and/or pitfalls that may exist in the path to goal attain-

ment. In that regard, Mrs. Williams could have offered the teachers various incentives or reductions in their existing work assignments. Such actions would likely have been motivational, influencing teacher participation in the selection and mentoring process. Therefore, any one of the alternatives offered in response to question 4 would likely have been of interest and a motivation to members of the faculty. The suggested response to question 4 is **(d).**

5. The behavior of the fourth-grade teachers has signaled a problem more severe than accomplishment of the immediate task. There appears to be a lack of faculty motivation and faculty cohesiveness, and the interpersonal relationship between the principal and members of the fourth-grade faculty is less than what one in a leadership role would desire. Mrs. Williams needs to do more than achieve assistance with the selection and mentoring of a new fourth grade teacher; she needs to focus on building positive interpersonal relationships and building intragroup relationships, which will require new dispositions and ways of thinking. Mrs. Williams will also need to consider leadership strategies that will facilitate the faculty's development of a shared vision, planning together as a team, collaborating, and sharing ideas and resources while working towards an agreed-upon goal. If a shared vision is developed and effectively managed, trust, motivation, and cohesiveness are likely to follow (Bennis, 1995). The suggested response to question 5 is **(b).**

## SUMMARY AND CONCLUSION

Mrs. Williams approached the initial task using relationship-oriented behavior. She shared a goal with the fourth-grade faculty and expressed a desire to have their participation in selecting a new teacher and getting him/her assimilated into the faculty. She also expressed a desire to use a group approach, rather than make an autocratic decision. Such leader behavior showed sensitivity to the needs of a new employee while being considerate of the current faculty members. However, the quality of the interpersonal relations between the leader and members of the fourth-grade faculty is called into question and offers reasons for the lack of effectiveness of the relationship-oriented behavior.

After all members of the fourth-grade faculty refused to willingly participate, Principal Williams' leadership behavior necessarily became task oriented. She was willing to take risks. The fourth-grade position had to be filled; therefore, she made an appropriate assignment, identified the method to be used in completing that assignment, and monitored the work to ensure goal attainment in the most effective and efficient manner possible. In so doing, she made a management decision that would possibly enhance teaching and learning. However, it should be noted that, long term, such behavior could become problematic.

Having taken such action, Principal Williams would be well advised to recognize that a larger challenge exists and should seek a solution to that challenge. To address this challenge, Principal Williams should strive to build faculty cohesiveness. When cohesiveness exists, members of the faculty feel valued and perceive that their input is meaningful in the decision-making process (Greenberg, 1996a). Principal Williams should also recognize the needs of individual members of the faculty, and, to the extent possible, address those needs. She might also give consideration to activities that would enhance the degree of working effectiveness among the fourth-grade teachers. In doing so, she would be advocating and nurturing, which are behaviors that a school leader interested in the success of all students advocates. Such behavior will likely sustain a school culture conducive to student learning and staff professional growth.

## SCENARIO 2
## CHANGING THE WAY WE TEACH SCIENCE

### STANDARD 1

A school administrator is an educational leader who promotes the success of all students by facilitating the development, articulation, implementation, and stewardship of a vision of learning that is shared and supported by the school community.

*In Scenario 2, the characteristics of Standard 1 are exhibited as Principal Johnson works with her faculty to integrate a new science program into the curriculum of the school. She is committed to continuous school improvement, has a vision of high standards of learning, communicates effectively, builds consensus with stakeholders, and allows the vision to shape the educational program.*

### ISLLC Standards Indicators Exhibited in Scenario 2

**Knowledge Indicators**
The administrator has knowledge and understanding of:
▲ Effective communication
▲ Effective consensus-building and negotiation skills
▲ Student growth and development
▲ Applied motivational theories
▲ Curriculum design, implementation, evaluation, and refinement
▲ Diversity and its meaning for educational programs
▲ Adult learning and professional development models
▲ The change process for systems, organizations, and individuals
▲ School cultures
▲ Human resources management and development

**Disposition Indicators**
The administrator believes in, values, and is committed to:
▲ A school vision of high standards of learning
▲ Continuous school improvement
▲ Doing the work required for high levels of personal and organization performance
▲ Professional development as an integral part of school improvement
▲ The benefits that diversity brings to the school community
▲ Taking risks to improve schools
▲ Trusting people and their judgment

▲ Accepting responsibility
▲ Involving stakeholders in management processes

**Performance Indicators**
The administrator facilitates processes and engages in activities ensuring that:
▲ The vision and mission of the school are effectively communicated to staff, parents, students, and community members
▲ The core beliefs of the school vision are modeled for all stakeholders
▲ The vision is developed with and among stakeholders
▲ The vision shapes the educational programs, plans, and actions
▲ An implementation plan is developed in which objectives and strategies to achieve the vision and goals are clearly articulated
▲ Existing resources are used in support of the school vision and goals
▲ All individuals are treated with fairness, dignity, and respect
▲ Professional development promotes focus on student learning consistent with the school vision and goals
▲ Students and staff feel valued and important
▲ Diversity is considered in developing learning experiences
▲ The school is organized and aligned for success
▲ Stakeholders are involved in decisions affecting schools
▲ Responsibility is shared to maximize ownership and accountability
▲ Effective communication skills are used

At the first faculty meeting of the school year, Principal Shirley Johnson informed her faculty that in order to prepare the students for the science competency test that would be given at the end of the next school year, consideration should be given to using a different process of teaching science. She suggested using a hands-on inquiry-based method. Principal Johnson was very persuasive in communicating a need for this type of curriculum. She stated that her goal was to assist all students at Walton Elementary in becoming scientifically literate. She praised the faculty on a job well done in implementing manipulatives into the mathematics curriculum over the past two years and spoke of the dedication and strengths of the Walton faculty. Principal Johnson informed the faculty that moving toward the new science goal would give Walton the opportunity to be in the forefront of changes in science education. She also advised that teachers would be provided professional development, and the district would pay for substitutes.

After sharing her vision of Walton's future in becoming a leader in the new methods of teaching science, she asked the faculty for their ideas on how to make the change work. Comments and questions from the faculty were addressed in detail. Principal Johnson listened to all the concerns and jotted them down on chart paper. Faculty members were given the opportunity to assist in addressing the concerns.

Committees of teachers were formed to discuss the concept and develop instructional plans and implementation strategies. A date (two weeks later) was set for the committees to report, share ideas, and form advisory groups on science topics. Many members of the faculty were enthusiastic about the concept, but not all. Some voiced that it could not be done in a year. As the meeting ended, Principal Johnson carefully noted members of the faculty who appeared uncomfortable with the new concept.

The next day, Principal Johnson invited the teachers who appeared to be uncomfortable with the new concept into her office individually. After listening to the individual concerns, she gave each teacher several articles to read and assigned him/her a specific task that complemented that teacher's strengths. Then she invited members of the faculty who were already teaching science using the "hands-on" approach into her office and asked them for their assistance in developing the concept.

During the next two weeks, Principal Johnson visited classrooms and left numerous positive comments. She put short articles and actual lessons she had found to be helpful to teachers in managing change in their mailboxes. At the end of the two-week period, she waited anxiously to see what the committees would report.

## REFLECTIVE THINKING AND SCENARIO ANALYSIS

1. How would you characterize the approach Principal Johnson used in presenting her vision to the faculty?
2. What theoretical principles can you identify that would inform the manner in which Principal Johnson worked with her faculty?
3. How did Principal Johnson enhance the implementation process by meeting with teachers individually? Which specific powers did she use?
4. Identify Principal Johnson's specific behaviors that contributed to the establishment of a cooperative working relationship with and among her faculty.
5. How much are knowledge of faculty members and interpersonal relations contributing factors to the lack of resistance being experienced by Principal Johnson? Explain your response.

## ADDRESSING THE ISSUES

Select the one best answer to the following questions:

1. Which of the following statements regarding Principal Johnson is likely to be true?
   a. She is being paid to lead so she makes all the decisions.
   b. She believes in one-way communication.
   c. She is a highly skilled, proactive principal who has concerns for production and people.
   d. Once a decision has been reached, there is no changing and she can sell her ideas.

2. Which of the following statements best describes the leadership approach used by Principal Johnson when she informed her faculty that changes needed to be made in teaching science?
   a. She was directive but visionary, motivating the faculty through genuine acts of caring.
   b. She consulted with the faculty and followed their suggestions.
   c. She sought to maintain a pleasant work environment but did not espouse a vision for the science program.
   d. She was highly achievement-oriented, established a set of goals, and challenged the faculty to achieve them.

**3.** Holding conferences with reluctant faculty members was Principal Johnson's way of:

   **a.** making sure the task was completed to her specifications.

   **b.** responding to the low level of motivation of some faculty members.

   **c.** providing professional development.

   **d.** adding structure to the task.

**4.** Which of the following statements provides the best explanation for Principal Johnson's effectiveness as a leader?

   **a.** Principal Johnson managed attention, as she had a vision and the vision was compelling.

   **b.** Principal Johnson managed meaning, as she was able to communicate her vision to the faculty in an understandable manner.

   **c.** Principal Johnson managed self, as she understood her skills and used them effectively.

   **d.** All of the above.

**5.** Which of the following statements provides the best explanation of the process utilized by Principal Johnson?

   **a.** Principal Johnson completed a task using coercive and legitimate power while showing little consideration for the concerns of her faculty.

   **b.** Principal Johnson completed a task using expert and legitimate power while demonstrating a genuine concern for individual members of her faculty.

   **c.** Principal Johnson took explicit and implicit actions and in so doing was very effective.

   **d.** Principal Johnson used a combination of expert and legitimate power to complete a task with little consideration for the concerns of her faculty.

## DISCUSSION OF THE SOLUTION

1. Principal Johnson had a keen vision of the future in science education, and she used a proactive model in presenting that vision to the faculty. Having carefully planned her presentation, Principal Johnson presented it to the faculty and behaved in a flexible manner, diagnosing the needs of the faculty at each phase of the process. The lines of communication were always open, generating a high comfort level between her and the faculty. Her knowledge of the subject area and her personal skills of informing, influencing, and listening enhanced her presentation. A leader who emphasizes high consideration for task completion while maintaining a positive interpersonal relationship with followers has been identified as having a superior style (Blake & Mouton, 1985). The suggested response to question 1 is **(c)**.

2. A principal must have a vision of what is necessary for students to reach the established standards. That vision must be shared by the faculty, staff, students, parents, and the community at large. One of the pivotal leader activities of a principal is to engage constantly in the dynamic process of sharing with the faculty a vision of things to come (Owens, 1991) and getting them to buy into that vision through genuine acts of caring.

Influencing people to assist in the achievement of a vision requires leadership skills that were demonstrated by Principal Johnson. She let her faculty know what was to be done, what was expected of them, and scheduled and coordinated the work. These are characteristics of directive leadership behavior (House, 1971). This is not to suggest that directive behavior is the most appropriate to use, rather, that there are times when a visionary principal might be directive in presenting ideas to the faculty. However, the process followed must consist of genuine acts of caring. The suggested response to question 2 is **(a)**.

3. Hersey and Blanchard (1982) suggest that one's leadership style should be adjusted according to the subordinate's level of maturity. The level of subordinate maturity is one of the factors that dictates whether the leader employs a directing style, a coaching style, a supporting style, or a delegating style. In this instance, some faculty members had a low level of maturity and needed assistance with the task structure. Principal Johnson aligned her style with the maturity level of the faculty. The suggested response to question 3 is **(b)**.

4. Clearly, Principal Johnson was able to work effectively with the faculty to initiate a change in the science program because she managed attention, meaning, and self. She had a knowledge of the program changes that were necessary, the skills to work effectively with the faculty to launch a team effort, and the ability to outline the framework for the changes. These are characteristics of effective leaders (Bennis, 1995), and Principal Johnson effectively demonstrated them. The suggested response to question 4 is **(d)**.

5. In the presentation of her vision for changes in the science curriculum, Principal Johnson displayed several leader behaviors. Her style represents a combination of concern for task, concern for individuals, and interpersonal relations. She clearly outlined the task to be completed, displayed confidence in the faculty, and was sensitive to the personality and needs of each faculty member. Also, she individually assessed each faculty member's knowledge of the new science concept and his/her readiness level to facilitate its implementation.

Principal Johnson never attempted to force involvement, control any members of the faculty, or use the threat of punishment. Rather, she used the knowledge of select faculty members, as well as her own knowledge of the new science concept and her technical, human, and conceptual skills. She took a number of actions to show consideration for her staff and to involve them in the process of changing the science program. She formed committees, provided resource materials, planned professional development activities, and discussed concerns with teachers individually and as a faculty. Over the years, there has been extensive research into "behaviors" of effective leaders. Recent literature based on structured observations of leader behavior shows that effective school leaders use this approach (Newstrom & Davis, 1993). "A true leader is able to influence others and modify behavior via legitimate and referent power" (Lunenburg & Ornstein, 1996, p. 115). The suggested response to question 5 is **(b)**.

## SUMMARY AND CONCLUSION

Principal Johnson had a vision of high standards in science for all students; she wanted to make sure that all students at Walton had the knowledge and skills in science that are needed by today's students. To that end, she effectively communicated a plan to the faculty, acquired their input, and utilized their expertise in its implementation. Utilizing such a process, she demonstrated a knowledge and understanding of how individuals function in a pluralistic society, the need to include stakeholders in the decision-making process, and how the leader can utilize existing resources in support of the school's goals and vision. Principal Johnson is an example of an educational leader who addresses ILSSC Standard 1. She promotes the success of all students by facilitating the development, articulation, implementation, and stewardship of a vision of learning that is shared and supported by the school community.

## SCENARIO 3
## THE NEW PRINCIPAL AT FROST

### STANDARD 1

A school administrator is an educational leader who promotes the success of all students by facilitating the development, articulation, implementation, and stewardship of a vision of learning that is shared and supported by the school community.

### STANDARD 2

A school administrator is an educational leader who promotes the success of all students by advocating, nurturing, and sustaining a school culture and instructional program conducive to student learning and staff professional growth.

### STANDARD 3

A school administrator is an educational leader who promotes the success of all students by ensuring management of the organization, operations, and resources for a safe, efficient, and effective learning environment.

*In Scenarios 3 and 4, Principal Sterling, a new principal at Frost, characterizes Standards 1, 2, and 3 as she manages a reorganization of a school with the intention of improving the instructional program and creating an effective learning environment. Key in this scenario is the principal's knowledge of human resource management and development, as well as processes of developing and implementing strategic plans. Also, crucial to her effectiveness is knowledge of adult learning, principles of effective instruction, and the change process for systems, organizations, and individuals.*

### ISLLC Standards Indicators Exhibited in Scenario 3

**Knowledge Indicators**
The administrator has knowledge and understanding of:
▲ Learning goals in a pluralistic society
▲ The principles of developing strategic plans

- ▲ Theories and models of organizations and the principles of organizational development
- ▲ Organizational procedures at the school and district level
- ▲ Change processes for systems, organizations, and individuals

**Disposition Indicators**
The administrator believes in, values, and is committed to:
- ▲ A school vision of high standards of learning
- ▲ Continuous school improvement
- ▲ A willingness to continuously examine one's own assumptions, beliefs, and practices
- ▲ Doing the work required for high levels of personal and organization performance
- ▲ Taking risks to improve schools
- ▲ Trusting people and their judgments
- ▲ Accepting responsibility
- ▲ Involving stakeholders in management processes

**Performance Indicators**
The administrator facilitates processes and engages in activities ensuring that:
- ▲ A variety of supervisory and evaluation models is employed
- ▲ Operational procedures are designed and managed to maximize opportunities for successful learning
- ▲ Time is managed to maximize attainment of organizational goals
- ▲ Potential problems and opportunities are identified
- ▲ Problems are confronted and resolved in a timely manner
- ▲ Organizational systems are regularly monitored and modified as needed
- ▲ Stakeholders are involved in decisions affecting schools
- ▲ Responsibility is shared to maximize ownership and accountability

Frost Elementary School, with a population of 1,100 students, prekindergarten to sixth grade, is located in the inner city of a large southern, metropolitan area. The ethnic/socioeconomic makeup of the school is African-American and poor. The faculty composition is 45 percent Caucasian and 55 percent African-American. Although the school district has been desegregated for a number of years, Frost's enrollment remains totally African-American.

Scores on achievement tests, which are used to measure student progress and serve as a means of comparison with students in other parts of the city and state, are at an all-time low. They have been some of the lowest scores in the district for a number of years. Mr. Shaw, who served as principal of the school for 15 years, was considered by most faculty members to be an individual who loved children and had their best interests at heart. He was always in the community conveying to parents his interest in the school, community, and the children. Mr. Shaw was quite knowledgeable and worked diligently with the faculty to enhance the school's instructional program. However, in spite of his efforts, achievement scores remained low and incidents of discipline high. During the last five years of his tenure, the average daily attendance of students fluctuated between 84 and 86 percent. Nevertheless, his traditional instructional program was highly supported by the faculty and staff. In addition, the school was several thousand dollars in debt, and fund-raising was virtually nonexistent.

With the appointment of a new superintendent and a push for educational reform and restructuring, Mr. Shaw retired, and Mrs. Sterling was appointed principal. Upon her appointment, she received directions to improve student achievement at Frost using some form of site-based management. During the first week of her assignment, she sent the following memorandum to the faculty and staff:

---

### Frost Elementary School
### MEMORANDUM TO FACULTY AND STAFF

From: Dr. Patricia Sterling, Principal
Re: Task Force for School Improvement
Date: August 21, 2000

I would like to request volunteers to serve on a task force to develop a plan of action to bring about improvements in the instructional program here at Frost. One of the responsibilities of the task force will be to survey the entire faculty and staff for the purpose of ascertaining their ideas, suggestions, and recommendations for program improvements. The work of the task force will be very time consuming; however, the results should propel us into the 21st century and beyond.

Please notify my secretary by September 1, 2000, if you are available to serve. Thank you for your cooperation in this matter.

---

On September 1, Dr. Sterling asked her secretary for the list of volunteers; there were no responses. The word on the grapevine was, "The new principal has considerable work in mind for the faculty, and the faculty is already totally consumed with just maintaining discipline."

### Selecting the Task Force
Receiving no volunteers, the principal invited (selected) one teacher from each grade level to serve on the task force. The individuals selected were not thrilled about being drafted; however, they accepted the principal's invitation and attended the first meeting on September 5, 2000. All subsequent meetings were held once a week (between Principal Sterling and the task force) until the plan was ready for partial implementation on Oct 2, 2000.

### Developing the Plan
The task force met for approximately 40 hours developing the plan. Having read Bradley's *Total Quality Management for Schools,* the principal introduced the task force to the Affinity, Fishbone, and Pareto designs. They used the Affinity Diagram to brainstorm and define the issues that needed to be addressed. The Affinity Diagram allowed her to organize output from the brainstorming session of the task force. Using this design, all of the information could be consolidated. The Fishbone Diagram (cause and effect) was used to get an overall picture of how to move from current reality to the

established goals. Using this design, elements that may be contributing to the problem and their cause-and-effect relationship could be identified. The Pareto Diagram (a simple bar chart) was utilized to identify the pros and cons of various challenging school issues (ranking the problems separating the major ones from the trivial ones) and to ensure that the programs selected for implementation would be effective. Reports were provided to the faculty and staff who, in turn, provided feedback to the task force on their work. Of the issues identified, the most pressing was student discipline. Thus, the task force made the recommendation to the principal that improving schoolwide discipline should be the first issue addressed. Principal Sterling accepted the recommendation, and discipline became the order of the day.

### Implementing the Plan

Realizing that the faculty would need professional development to effectively implement new programs in the area of discipline, Principal Sterling again turned to the task force for an assessment of the professional development program needs of the faculty. By a large majority, the faculty voted to be trained in various methods of assertive discipline, discipline with dignity, and discipline techniques for today's children. In addition, the faculty requested that Principal Sterling formally develop a schoolwide discipline plan and schedule workshops to be held during faculty meetings so teachers could begin to implement various techniques in their classrooms. They also requested that she actively recruit men to serve on the faculty to provide students with male role models. In concluding their work, the task force clearly stated, "For the new programs to be successful, it will be necessary for all faculty and staff to be involved; there can be no exceptions."

In subsequent meetings with the task force, a decision was reached to open the lines of communication between the home and the school so that parents would not feel isolated from the process. Principal Sterling announced an open-door policy and instituted school conferences to inform parents about appropriate and inappropriate behavior. Communication to homes included phone calls, notes from teachers, and monthly informational calendars. An automated phone system was installed to keep parents informed of all school activities and events.

### Results of the Plan

During the first year, discipline was hard and fast; 80 out-of-school suspensions were issued to students. Parents were extremely upset, saying they never had this problem with the previous principal. However, the administration, faculty, and staff held firm. Parent workshops were held on parenting skills and the fair, firm, and consistent policies used by the administration, faculty, and staff. The following year, out-of-school suspensions dropped to 10. Discipline was under control, and the faculty was able to focus on the instructional program.

After improvement in discipline began to occur, Principal Sterling turned to the second item on the list generated by the faculty, "curriculum, instruction, and evaluation." A second time, she asked for individuals to serve on a committee to address instruction. Response was quite different this time, with 16 individuals volunteering to serve on the committee. In her businesslike manner, Principal Sterling accepted all 16, and the committee went to work. After three weeks of discussion, the committee determined that the school had to change and change drastically. Student regression (failure to retain information from the previous year) over the summer nullified any achievement gains the students had made the previous year. Year-round education was determined to be the educational direction for the school to pursue.

### Remaining on the Fast Track

To continue to make improvements at Frost, subcommittees were formed for various initiatives; fund-raising events were held often; teachers were in the community visiting with parents, and instructional planning meetings were continuous. With the planning and implementation of year-round education, Frost became the talk of the educational community. Professors from the local university took an interest in the school and often asked to be allowed to help implement programs. Visitors from other schools in the city, state, and nation frequented the school, and Principal Sterling received and accepted invitations to participate in a variety of local, state, and national conferences. At the end of Principal Sterling's fourth year, discipline had improved, the year-round school concept had been implemented, and most of the faculty was supporting the site-based management concept. However, teacher turnover was above 10 percent. Some of the turnover appeared to be initiated by the principal, and some was teacher initiated.

## REFLECTIVE THINKING AND SCENARIO ANALYSIS

1. What principles regarding developing and implementing strategic plans should Principal Sterling have considered as she made improvements in the instructional program?
2. As principal, if you wanted to maximize ownership and accountability for the attainment of school improvements, how would you have structured the initial memo?
3. What is your assessment of the approach used by Principal Sterling to communicate her vision and mission to faculty, parents, students, and the community?
4. Which applied motivational theories should the leader employ when embarking on a challenge such as the one initially faced by Principal Sterling?
5. What knowledge in the areas of teaching and learning and student development would a school leader necessarily need to inform his/her management decisions in a school like Frost?
6. In the context of this scenario, describe the effects of culture and climate on leader and follower behavior.

## ADDRESSING THE ISSUES

Select the one best answer to the following questions:

1. Which of the following best characterizes the leadership behaviors of Principal Sterling?
   a. She entered the school very energized using a supportive style, changed to a directive style, and then changed again to a participative style.
   b. She entered the school very directive, showing no consideration for the existing programs or the individuals who had initiated them.

    c. She entered the school attempting to delegate the responsibility of instructional improvement to the faculty; however, she changed to a democratic style when the faculty resisted, and after getting their support, she changed to a more directive style.

    d. None of the above really characterizes her leadership style.

2. Principal Sterling's decision to immediately pursue program changes at Frost was:

    a. an aggressive move, filled with flaws.

    b. a necessary move, however, one of high risk.

    c. the normal course of action taken by new principals.

    d. ill advised for a number of reasons.

3. Which of the following would be a logical rationale for the lack of faculty response to Principal Sterling's initial memo?

    a. There was a lack of trust in the new principal.

    b. The morale of the faculty was low.

    c. The faculty was still concerned about the retirement of Mr. Shaw.

    d. All of the above are possible reasons.

4. Which of the following approaches would have possibly enhanced decision quality and acceptance in the reform efforts of Principal Sterling?

    a. She could have spent several weeks assessing the needs of the school, using the acquired information to plan program improvement strategies.

    b. She could have identified and implemented programs that had been effective in schools with the same makeup as Frost.

    c. She could have spoken informally with several members of the faculty, obtaining their ideas on areas needing improvement.

    d. She could have spent several weeks reviewing current school reform literature and selected an approach to use in implementing a reform initiative at Frost.

5. After reviewing Principal Sterling's behavior, which of the following can you accept with theoretical support?

    a. Principal Sterling's directive, coercive, and nonsupportive behavior was inappropriate and would not be acceptable under any conditions.

    b. Principal Sterling's directive, coercive, and nonsupportive behavior was inappropriate but justified by the behavior of her faculty.

    c. Principal Sterling was highly structured and highly considerate in her approach to change at Frost.

    d. Principal Sterling used an authoritarian-type behavior and if she achieves success, this type of behavior will not stand the test of time.

## DISCUSSION OF THE SOLUTION

    1. Principal Sterling entered Frost and attempted to establish a positive and supportive relationship with the faculty. She invited them to become a part of a task force

that was being developed to address the needs and challenges of the faculty, staff, students, and community. However, the faculty was unresponsive. In order to fulfill the directive of the superintendent, Principal Sterling altered her style to one that was more directive. She drafted faculty members to serve on the task force, provided them with specific directions, and closely supervised their performance. After achieving a degree of success and acquiring the confidence, trust, and support of the faculty, she changed her style again, this time to one of a participative nature.

House (1971) theorized that the type of behavior displayed by the leader to motivate and bring satisfaction to subordinates is dependent on the situation. When Principal Sterling arrived at Frost, the faculty was not ready to actively participate in a major change process. Therefore, the supportive style she used was not effective. Making a determination of the readiness level of followers enables the leader to match his/her leadership style to the readiness level of the followers. There was no reason for Principal Sterling to believe that members of the faculty would not cooperate if she asked them to serve on the task force or serve responsibly, once they were members. However, characteristics in the work environment suggested the need for a direct approach. Therefore, selecting members of the faculty to serve on the task force was a viable option. The suggested response to question 1 is **(a)**.

2. Beginning a new assignment as principal can be a very challenging endeavor. Even if the individual is an administrator with extensive experience, challenging circumstances can occur because of the administrator's lack of knowledge of the new situation. Given the normal challenges that will occur for any new administrator, a change process of the magnitude attempted by Principal Sterling during her first month will be extremely difficult to accomplish. This is especially true if it is attempted in the absence of an extensive investigation of the school's internal and external environments.

Without the knowledge that results from investigating the internal and external environments, schoolwide change is a high-risk venture (Fullan, 1993). For effective change to occur, a principal must spend time building a foundation and establishing a capacity for change. Such a foundation consists of personal vision building, inquiry, mastery, and collaboration (Fullan, 1993). Principal Sterling did not build such a capacity, and it is not likely that she would have been able to build this foundation in one month. For this reason, among a number of others, the actions taken by Principal Sterling are ones of high risk. However, much to her credit, she made decisions of quality that were acceptable to the majority of the faculty. The suggested response to question 2 is **(b)**.

3. When Principal Sterling assumed her leadership role at Frost, faculty members had just experienced the loss of a very supportive principal. Even though (under his leadership) the conditions of the school were less than favorable, the faculty had trust and confidence in him. To say the least, he was a known entity. Principal Sterling was an unknown entity; a new principal, under the best of circumstances, is likely to raise the anxiety level of the faculty. The loss of a leader (although ineffective) in which they had confidence and trust, a new principal who is unknown, and the conditions at Frost were collectively problematic enough to influence a low level of morale among the faculty. Fortunately, to her credit, Principal Sterling changed to a directive style, set performance standards, and informed subordinates what had to occur to enhance instruction. The suggested response to question 3 is **(d)**.

4. Although Principal Sterling invited members of the faculty to serve on the task force, she could have demonstrated more consideration for the faculty. Making the determination that seeking solutions to the problems at Frost was timely. Furthermore, establishing the approach that would be used without assistance from the faculty could possibly have been intimidating to the faculty. Seeking the opinion of the faculty regarding the appropriateness of the time and approach could possibly have generated faculty support from the outset.

House (1971) suggests that the leaders should have high expectations of participants in the organization but resist the temptation of programming their work. Owens (1995) advises that a school leader is one who develops the social environment of the school so that the growth of individual participants and groups can be enhanced. Such an environment is best created when the principal has a knowledge of the faculty, and the organization has successfully emerged as a community of learners (Barth, 1990).

Principal Sterling did not take the time to establish the climate for change or prepare the faculty for change. If she had spent several weeks assessing the needs of the school and acquiring knowledge of the faculty's expertise, she would have placed herself in a better position to establish a program of school-based reform. What she needed most was decision quality and decision acceptance. Even though she was successful in her approach, the faculty was in the best position to provide decision quality, and without question, they had to accept the decision outcome if it were to be implemented effectively. The action that occurred is an example of what happens if the principal's vision is ahead of the faculty's vision. The suggested response to question 4 is **(a).**

5. Principal Sterling attempted to implement a process that would address the problematic situation existing at Frost. Focusing directly on school improvements, she formed a task force, gave the task force specific directions, and established lines of communication between the faculty, task force, and her office. She also received reports from the task force, which enabled her to evaluate their work. The leaders of the Ohio State studies characterized such behaviors as initiating structure.

By sending a memorandum to the faculty inviting them to participate on a task force, Principal Sterling demonstrated trust in the faculty members and respect for their expertise. Also, by accepting the initial request of the task force, she demonstrated support for their recommendation and interest in their welfare. Such behaviors were classified in the Ohio State studies as consideration.

From the outset, Principal Sterling was highly structured in her approach to making changes at Frost. However, she was also highly considerate of the faculty, their expertise and the contributions that they could make to the improvement process. Her behavior generated a level of satisfaction among the faculty, considering the faculty's receptivity to the discipline plan and their willingness to serve on the second task force. She was successful in her initial approach, which is often the case when principals use an approach that is high in structure and high in consideration (Hoy & Miskel, 1991). The suggested response to question 5 is **(c).**

# SCENARIO 4
## THE FLOATING COMMUNIQUÉ

*The school improvement efforts of Principal Sterling motivated the writing of an anonymous communiqué.*

### ISLLC Standards Indicators Exhibited in Scenario 4

**Knowledge Indicators**

The administrator has knowledge and understanding of:
▲ Learning goals in a pluralistic society
▲ The principles of developing strategic plans
▲ Theories and models of organizations and the principles of organizational development
▲ Organizational procedures at the school and district level

**Disposition Indicators**

The administrator believes in, values, and is committed to:
▲ A school vision of high standards of learning
▲ Continuous school improvement
▲ A willingness to continuously examine one's own assumptions, beliefs, and practices
▲ Doing the work required for high levels of personal and organization performance
▲ Taking risks to improve schools
▲ Trusting people and their judgments
▲ Accepting responsibility
▲ Involving stakeholders in management processes

**Performance Indicators**

The administrator facilitates processes and engages in activities ensuring that:
▲ A variety of supervisory and evaluation models is employed
▲ Operational procedures are designed and managed to maximize opportunities for successful learning
▲ Time is managed to maximize attainment of organizational goals
▲ Potential problems and opportunities are identified
▲ Problems are confronted and resolved in a timely manner
▲ Organizational systems are regularly monitored and modified as needed
▲ Stakeholders are involved in decisions affecting schools
▲ Responsibility is shared to maximize ownership and accountability

On a warm spring morning as Principal Sterling was preparing to leave home for a professional meeting, she received a phone call from her secretary. The secretary informed her that she wanted to share the contents of a communiqué that was floating around the school. She described it as demeaning to her, the principal, and some members of the faculty and staff. Very much surprised, Principal Sterling inquired as to the contents of the communiqué.

In explanation, the secretary read the following statement: "The principal does not handle the finances of the school properly or openly as monies raised disappear like magic." She further reported, "Specific reference is made to your personal 'social and travel' account." It also contained the statement, "Only young teachers are valued and appreciated; the principal is trying to 'push out' older teachers and experience means nothing." In addition, it was noted that the communiqué contained the statement, "The principal actually recruits men because she is man crazy and feels she can mold men any way she desires."

The secretary further reported that the communiqué made comparisons between Principal Sterling and the previous principal. The previous principal was described as an individual who had a child-centered philosophy. He believed that schools are for children, whereas Principal Sterling's philosophy is self-serving, and the interests of children are secondary. To support this accusation, the writer offered that on National Teachers' Day, the present principal was away, attending a national conference, which apparently was more important to her than being at school celebrating the accomplishments of her teachers.

With a chuckle in her voice, almost a laugh, Principal Sterling asked if the communiqué contained other statements. The secretary responded, "Yes, there are statements about the secretaries and spies." The writer states, "The secretaries are rude and actually run the school; the principal has spies, and the spies report to her the activities of teachers. Using information from these reports, the principal determines who should lose their job or be transferred to another school. A teaching certificate is nothing to this principal; what she wants most are people she can control."

The secretary reported that the communiqué ended with the statement, "Thanks to site-based management, this principal can do anything she wants."

## REFLECTIVE THINKING AND SCENARIO ANALYSIS

1. How significant is such a communiqué to the effectiveness of Principal Sterling?
2. What are some leadership behaviors that might have conveyed the impressions expressed in the communiqué?
3. Can you identify adult learning theories that would inform Principal Sterling's decision as to whether to continue with her plans to attend the professional conference?
4. What effective consensus-building and negotiation skills might Principal Sterling use to respond to the problematic concerns expressed in the communiqué?
5. Accepting the notion that Principal Sterling was ahead of her faculty in terms of a vision for school improvement, what adult motivational theories might inform her behavior?
6. Analyze the communiqué to determine the most damaging statements and prioritize both their potential to disrupt the school environment and any possible repercussions.

## ADDRESSING THE ISSUES

Select the one best answer to the following questions:

1. The reference to site-based management in the communiqué could be a signal that:
   a. the concept is not effectively communicated to the faculty.

b. the concept is not being implemented around a shared vision.

c. there are different perspectives of site-based management among faculty members.

d. any of the above.

2. If Principal Sterling had made a special effort to be in her school on National Teachers' Day, she would have demonstrated the behavior of:

a. a leader who manages meaning and attention.

b. a leader who manages self.

c. a task-oriented leader who was ready to craft a new assignment for the faculty.

d. none of the above.

3. When the writer of the communiqué wrote that Principal Sterling only valued young teachers, the writer may perceive the principal as not being:

a. a leader who sets performance standards and lets subordinates know what is expected of them.

b. a leader who stresses excellence and expresses confidence in the ability of subordinates.

c. a leader who involves the faculty in the decision-making process and works cooperatively with them to achieve the desired outcome.

d. a leader who is considerate, shows concern for the needs and well being of all subordinates while maintaining a pleasant work environment.

4. Which of the following speaks most definitively to the factors that possibly motivated the writer of the communiqué?

a. The faculty was in a frozen state, and change came too fast.

b. The faculty did not have a clear understanding of the reality of the school's condition.

c. Principal Sterling did not include activities in her plan of action sufficient to sustain the motivational level of some faculty members.

d. none of the above.

## DISCUSSION OF THE SOLUTION

1. Site-based management is a concept that has as its basic intent removing decision making from the central office and allowing decisions to be made in the individual schools. The supposition is that the principal, faculty, and staff of schools are in a better position to make the determination of what is best for that school than are individuals in the central office. The comment in the communiqué regarding this concept implies that Principal Sterling was using the flexibility afforded her to fulfill a vision for the school that some faculty members had not accepted and were not willing to work to achieve. The leader must spend time getting individuals to buy into the vision. When there is a shared vision, a clear compelling mission statement can be developed with the involvement of all stakeholders. Then, such a perception as the one motivating the statement in the communiqué is less likely to exist (Senge, 1990). Without a shared vision and mission, any one of the possible responses may have motivated the comment. The suggested response to question 1 is **(d)**.

2. Influencing the behavior of members of the faculty toward the attainment of school goals is a key role of the principal. This happens best when the principal functions as a designer, a teacher, and a steward (Sergiovanni, 1992). "People can suffer emotionally and spiritually under inept leadership" (Senge, 1995, p. 83). This can occur even if the ineffectiveness is only a perception. Therefore, a principal must display understanding, caring, and respect for all members of the faculty. Such would possibly have been the perception if Principal Sterling had been in her school on "National Teacher's Day." Also, leaders must manage attention, meaning, trust, and self (Bennis, 1995, p. 397). When leaders are managing attention through a compelling vision, they bring others to a place where they have never been before; when they manage meaning, they align with their followers (Bennis, 1995). Given that Principal Sterling was frequently out of the building, teachers needed an understanding of the purpose of her absence. If teachers had been made aware, they possibly would have felt connected, and the principal would have built a degree of trust in the process.

The writer of the communiqué did not feel Principal Sterling was a steward, managing self, meaning or attention. The writer saw the principal as someone simply interested in completing tasks for self aggrandizement, rather than to ensure that all students at Frost had the knowledge, skills, and values needed to become successful adults. While they may have viewed her as wanting to involve stakeholders in decisions affecting the school and desirous of making management decisions to enhance teaching and learning, she was not viewed by the writer as supportive or effective in human resource management and development. The leader must be viewed by the faculty as being concerned with them as individuals and as a group. The suggested response to question 2 is **(a)**.

3. In more than one instance, it has been demonstrated that Principal Sterling was somewhat task oriented. At times, she displayed participatory characteristics, but her primary concern was task completion when necessary; she was directive in her style as she worked to achieve the established goals of the school, completing one task and then moving to the next. "A supportive leader is friendly, approachable, and concerned with the needs, status, and well-being of subordinates" (Lunenburg & Ornstein, 1996, p. 137). Perhaps the writer of the communiqué perceived Mr. Shaw in this manner and did not so perceive Principal Sterling. The perception possibly occurred because of the principal's commitment to task completion. The suggested response to question 3 is **(d)**.

4. A number of factors must be considered when determining the motivation for the writing of the communiqué. First is the readiness level of the faculty for change. The faculty was in a frozen state when Principal Sterling arrived, and they indicated a lack of willingness to assume additional responsibility. Hersey and Blanchard (1993) suggest that an individual's motivational level to accomplish a task may be based on the individual's level of ability to perform that task. Conducting an inquiry into the skills and attributes of various faculty members would have assisted Principal Sterling in identifying individuals to serve in various roles on the task force. In addition, acquiring knowledge of the skills and attributes of all members of the faculty would have allowed Principal Sterling to establish the readiness level of the faculty for change.

Secondly, for effective change to occur, a leader must understand the needs of the school and factors in the internal and external environments that influence the transformation process. The leader must acquire an appreciation for current reality in order to assist the faculty in developing an appreciation for what is real (Senge, 1990). Even though individuals agreed to serve on the initial task force, their participation came as a result of legitimate power. Legitimate power can be initially used, but its continuous use often leads to dissatisfaction, frustration, and resistance among faculty members (Lunenburg & Ornstein, 1996, p. 116).

Thirdly, having moved forward with what appeared to be the cooperation of the faculty, Principal Sterling would have been well advised to incorporate into her plan activities that would have sustained the motivational level of all members of the faculty. House (1971) suggests that it is the responsibility of the leader to smooth the path between current reality and the vision and further to reward followers en route. If this had occurred, it is possible that the communiqué would not have been written. The suggested response to question 4 is **(c)**.

## SUMMARY AND CONCLUSION

Principal Sterling entered Frost when student achievement was extremely low, attendance was less than average, and incidents of discipline were high. She attempted to be open and receptive to the needs of the staff while addressing the challenges of the school, the directive of the superintendent, and state requirements. There is no question as to the need for the development of a school improvement plan. However, the Frost faculty was not ready for a change; they seemed somewhat content with current conditions or were not motivated to take on any new challenges. Perhaps, this was because they could not envision what was to be gained from participating as members of a task force pursuing a vision that they had not created, or because professional development was not seen as an integral part of the school improvement plan. Fortunately Principal Sterling's knowledge of the change process for systems, organizations, and individuals was sufficient to complete the reform efforts.

## CHAPTER SUMMARY

In an attempt to establish a theoretical framework for the understanding of leadership over the last century, hundreds of studies have been conducted. Although none of these studies has provided a clear definition of leadership or offered a definitive destination between leaders and nonleaders, several have deepened our understanding of the concept.

From the study of leadership traits, we understand that no one specific set of traits can be used to single out leaders from nonleaders. Also, we came to the realization that the top-down perspective of leadership is not a popular one. Equally important, although there is no single set of traits that can be used to identify effective leaders, we accept the premise that there are some leadership traits that are well received by followers. However, the benefit of any trait appears to be its positive influence on followers.

Other studies on leadership conducted at the University of Iowa, the Ohio State University, and the University of Michigan suggest that leaders tend to be most successful when they exhibit democratic principles, initiate structure, are considerate of followers, and allow them to participate in the decision-making process when appropriate. Building on the foundation laid by these studies, other writers and researchers have identified various cause-and-effect relationships and variables that influence leader behavior. Taken collectively, these studies offer two basic elements concerning effective leadership—concern for people and concern for task completion. Finding the delicate balance between the two appears to be the leadership challenge.

Also, studies have addressed power and its use. Four major types of power have been identified, legitimate, referent, reward, and expert (French, 1993). Though power is often misunderstood and misused, it is a necessary variable in the mix of influencing and persuading individuals to achieve organizational goals. In using power, a combination of legitimate and referent powers has proven to be most effective (Fullan, 1993).

Finally, contemporary researchers and writers in a general sense offer that leaders should create learning communities (Barth, 1990; Fullan, 1999; Goodlad, 1994; Senge, 1990; Sergiovanni, 1992). In such communities, they proffer that individuals should have a shared vision and work collaboratively to acquire that vision. The process should be sensitive to the need for open lines of communication, diversity in the workplace, the values of all individuals, and the need to establish trusting relationships. Writers and researchers who advocate such a process argue that objective ethical reasoning is possible and should be used by leaders of today's schools.

In searching for the characteristics of the most effective leaders of today's schools, one might in summary turn to Bennis (1995), who offers that leaders should have four competencies—management of meaning, trust, attention, and self. They can then use these competencies to ensure that the organization has purpose and structure offering a sufficient amount of freedom for followers. It is this combination that allows people to experience success (Sergiovanni, 1984).

## MOVING INTO PRACTICE

Review the scenarios in Chapter 1. Using the pros and cons of the various situations, identify several approaches that you would use to address the following school-related issues in an actual situation. Project yourself into the role of the principal and take care to formulate a rationale for your selected behavior.

▶ Conduct a comparative analysis of the behavior of Principal Sterling and Principal Johnson, identifying similarities and differences. Cite instances where the differences are justified.

▶ You have served as principal of a large urban high school for eight months. The superintendent advised you when you accepted the job that he expected you to implement a form of block scheduling during your first year. The daily challenges of administering the school have not allowed you to make much progress toward implementing the concept. However, the superintendent is expecting a status report during your annual review, which will occur in four months. Describe your action over the next four months.

▶ Write a description of your leadership style, taking care to make sure it reflects your belief system. From this description, identify various characteristics contained therein and provide a supportive rationale for each.

▶ Devise a set of strategies for use in organizing an effective school program.

▶ Make a list of 10 school situations in which you would delegate the responsibility of completing a task to faculty, staff, or others.

▶ Identify the steps you would use to convince a faculty to accept one of your innovative ideas.

▶ Outline a process you would use to align the strengths of a prospective faculty member with school program needs.

## ACQUIRING AN UNDERSTANDING OF SELF

▶ What are three strengths that you have and can use effectively at all times?
▶ What is the philosophical basis for your style of leadership, and how was it formulated?
▶ Draw a line down the center of a sheet of paper. On one side of the sheet identify challenges that you experience in addressing leadership issues. On the other side, identify the ISLLC Standards Indicators that would be most beneficial in reducing each challenge.

## SUGGESTED READINGS

Bennis, W., & Biederman, P. (1997). *Organizing genius.* Reading, MA: Addison Wesley Longman.

Bennis, W., & Nanus, B. (1985). *Leaders: The strategies for taking charge.* New York: Harper & Row.

Drucker, P. E. (1995). *Managing in a time of great change.* New York: Truman Talley Books.

Fullan, M. (1993). *Change forces.* New York: The Falmer Press.

Gardner, H. (1995). *Leading minds: Anatomy of leadership.* New York: Basic Books.

Greenleaf, R. (1991). *Servant leadership.* New York: Paulist Press.

Ryan, K. D., & Oestreich, D. K. (1991). *Driving fear out of the workplace: How to overcome the invisible barriers to quality, productivity, and innovation.* San Francisco: Jossey-Bass Publishers.

Sergiovanni, T. J. (1992). *Moral leadership: Getting to the heart of school improvement.* San Francisco: Jossey-Bass Publishers.

Smith, D. M. (1997). *Motivating people* (2d ed.). Hauppauge, NY: Barron's Series, Inc.

Walton, S., & Huey, J. (1992). *Sam Walton: Made in America.* New York: McGraw-Hill Inc.

Yukl, G. (1994). *Leadership in organizations* (3d ed.). Upper Saddle River, NJ: Prentice Hall.

# 2

---

# ORGANIZATIONAL INFLUENCES ON LEADERSHIP

## The Influence of Leader Behavior

In today's schools, it is important for the leader to develop and maintain a school organization that promotes the success of all students, is conducive to staff professional growth, and is accepted by the community (CCSSO, 1996). In order to do this, the leader must first understand himself/herself, then proceed to develop an understanding and an appreciation for the individuals who work in the organization, as well as those served by the organization. Effective school leaders manage the organization using leadership skills, strategies, and

**FIGURE 2.1  Organizational influences on leadership**

techniques that influence human behavior in a manner that moves the school toward the attainment of its goals. This process requires knowledge and understanding of how people behave as individuals and members of groups. Equally important is the need for the leader to understand the influences of the forces in the internal and external environments of the school. Attention must also be given to the culture and climate of the school, staff and student motivation, and other factors that influence organizational behavior. These organizational relationships and influences are the focus of this chapter and are summarized in Figure 2.1. The intent is to convey to the reader the type organization that must exist if ISLLC Standards 2, 3, and 4 are to be met.

To adequately address ISLLC Standards 2, 3, and 4, the fundamental question becomes: How can the school leader influence the behavior of individuals and groups in a manner that will ensure the efficient and effective attainment of the school's goals? These standards relate to collaboration, management, and creating an environment that is conducive to teaching and learning, and they respond to the questions raised in Scenarios 5 to 8. Through these scenarios, the reader will be exposed to various approaches a leader uses to understand self, individuals, and groups. In addition, attributes needed by a leader to build organizational capacity and positively influence followers are explored. The knowledge, dispositions, and performance indicators that inform the identified standards precede each scenario. The readers should probe each scenario to identify events, activities, and issues that delineate the indicators preceding them.

# Understanding Self

Before the leader can really develop a clear understanding of the organization and people affiliated with the organization, he/she must first develop an understanding of him/herself. What one values, what one thinks of oneself, what one believes about people, what one believes about children, and what one believes to be the purpose of schools comprise one's disposition, and it is one's disposition that influences leadership behavior.

To achieve self-understanding, an individual must acquire and analyze knowledge about him/herself. It is knowledge of self that helps an individual understand his/her own disposition and why and how he/she responds to people and challenges in the organization (DuBrin, 1996). Often a distinction is made between the self of the leader that individuals affiliated with the organization observe (the public self) and the inner self (private self) of the leader. The public self is what an individual displays to the outside world about himself/herself and the perception others have of that individual. The private self is what the person is in actuality (Snyder, 1988). Knowledge of both the public and private self is an important factor in building relationships in an organization. The leader may not be able to circumvent the influence of his/her values, but being aware of them will allow him/her to monitor their ethical nature. The leader can then formulate a course of action to demonstrate that he/she is sensitive to the needs and concerns of others and is committed to building and sustaining a school culture and instructional program that will challenge all individuals to reach their full potential.

A leader who does not acquire an understanding of self and how his/her behavior affects others is subject to continuous error (Brewer, Ainsworth, & Wynne, 1984). This claim is based on the premise that the success of the leader depends on support from followers. The leader does not function in isolation; his/her ability to obtain required information and acquire resources sufficient to achieve organizational goals is influenced by the type of relationship that exists between the leader, members of the organization, and many other environmental factors (Brewer, Ainsworth, & Wynne, 1984). Then, it seems important for the leader to realize that the actions of people in the organization, functioning as individuals and as members of formal and informal groups, can be positively and negatively influenced by his/her behavior. Given the magnitude of the power and influence of individuals and groups in organizations, the topic will be revisited in a later section of this chapter. First, the organization in which they function will be defined.

# An Organization Defined

An organization can be viewed in a number of ways. Schein (1970) defined an organization as "the rational coordination of the activities of a number of people for the achievement of some common goal, through division of labor and function, and through a hierarchy of authority and responsibility" (p. 9). Katz and Kahn (1978) defined an organization as an open social system that receives resources (input) from its external environment, transforms that input through an internal system (throughput) and returns it to the external environment (output). From another perspective, Hersey, Blanchard, and Johnson (1996) offer that an organization is a social system comprising many interrelated subsystems (administrative, economic/technological, informational/decision making, human/social), which interact with the external environment. The common strand among these definitions suggests that, within an organization, a structure that governs the individuals and groups functioning therein is formulated and offers a sense of predictability regarding their activities and behavior. Schools fall within the realm of this definition and are classified as social systems. The effective school leader manages this structure in ways that channel the energy of self and others into activities that lead to a teaching and learning environment that is safe, efficient, and effective.

Many early theories offering reasons for behavior in organizations have laid the foundation for contemporary ideas about how leaders should function in them. Of the many theories and postulates that address the subject, Classical Organizational Theory, Social Systems Theory, and Open System Theory are most noted for providing a guiding framework for understanding factors relative to leader behavior that should occur in today's schools (Owens, 1995). Several principles advanced by these theories were presented in Chapter 1 as leadership was explored. These theories also offer a rationale for the manner in which individuals and groups behave in organizations. That is the reason we entertain a discussion of the contributions these theories have made to the understanding of organizational behavior. In reviewing them, the reader might find it beneficial to revisit the leadership theories presented in Chapter 1 (interfacing them), as they are closely related.

## Traditional Theories Influencing Contemporary Practice

### Classical Theorists

The classical theorists believe that an organization can be most efficient and effective by employing a set of fixed "principles," two of which are establishing a bureaucratic structure and implementing various systems of organizational control (Owens, 1995).

Classical Theory is often viewed from the perspective of scientific and administrative management. Frederick Taylor (1911), the father of scientific management, theorized that organizations could become efficient by identifying the "one best way" of performing a task and conceptualized scientific management through a series of time and management studies. He theorized that through a careful analysis of jobs in the organization utilizing scientific principles, this "one best way" of performing a job could be identified. After the best approach to performing the job has been identified, the next step is the selection and training of personnel to specifically perform the job. In the third step, management coordination, Taylor suggests that management should coordinate the work to provide assurance that the work is done as prescribed. Finally, he suggested that the work assignments should be divided among managers and workers with managers having the responsibility of planning, organizing, and decision making, while workers perform assigned tasks.

The second perspective, administrative management, focused on the concept of managing the entire organization. Henri Fayol, Lyndall Urwick, Luther Gulick, and Max Weber were major contributors to this perspective of Classical Organizational Theory. Their work addressed the principles of specialization, delegation of responsibility, span of control, and authority. The following section addresses some of the contributions of each of these individuals.

Henri Fayol was the first individual to characterize the continuous process of management. He advocated that all managers perform five basic functions: planning, organizing, commanding, coordinating, and controlling. In addition, he characterized management as a continuous process by emphasizing the chain of command, equity, efficiency, stability, and the allocation of authority through the design of 14 principles of management (Lunenburg & Ornstein, 1996). His notion was that efficiency and effectiveness could be achieved in an organization when these 14 principles were employed. Of these principles, those noteworthy for school leaders are division of labor, authority, discipline, unity of command, order, and equity. Gulick and Urwick (1937) heightened the work of Fayol, expanding his five basic organizational functions to seven: planning, budgeting, reporting, organizing, directing, coordinating, and staffing.

Max Weber (1947) built on the work of both these individuals and in so doing became one of the major contributors in creating a foundation for organizational theory as we view it today. Weber described the concepts of the bureaucratic structure; his work focused on fixed division of labor, hierarchy of positions, rules to govern performance, terms of employment, technical qualities for seeking personnel, and the separation of the personal rights and property of the worker from those of the organization. He theorized that the bureaucratic model was the best structure to use to acquire efficiency in large organizations that are complex in nature and that the use of such a model would influence the behavior of individuals in an effective and efficient manner, enhancing the achievement of organizational goals.

## A Leader with a Classical Perspective

The theorists mentioned above established the basis of classical theory, which has a powerful influence on the organization of today's schools, as well as their leadership. Most school districts currently use some form of the classical model in the operation of their schools (Gorton & Schneider, 1991). When classical leadership is employed, structure is the order of the day, and strict rules and regulations govern the operation of the school and/or school system. The focus is on task completion; little attention is given to the individual or group in the workplace, and the leader is considered to have ultimate authority and responsibility over everything in the system. Experts are employed to function in specialized areas and are grouped according to task specialization. The key concepts are structure, rules, regulations and procedures, organizational control, and efficiency (Gorton, 1987).

A leader who administers a school from a classical perspective would talk about "going by the book" or "running a tight ship" and would assume to have ultimate authority and responsibility over everything that goes on in the school (Hanson, 1991, p. 10). He/she would be specific in actions, very direct, many times displaying autocratic behavior. Problems are not likely to be solved through people, as the leader views himself/herself as the problem solver. Stakeholders may be involved in decisions that affect the school, but such involvement would not be a focus of the leadership, nor would trusting people and respecting their judgment be a primary concern.

## Social Systems Theorists

Another approach that has proven very useful in understanding the behavior of individuals and groups in schools is the study of the theory that explains the organization as a social system. Social Systems Theory has developed over a period of time, building on a number of theoretical concepts. It is defined as a set of interrelated elements that function in a particular manner to achieve a specific purpose. Social Systems Theory provides a way of viewing the organization as a whole, taking into consideration the interrelationships among its parts and its interaction with its internal and external environments (Hanson, 1996).

Within the framework of classical theory, the needs of the organization and the needs of the worker were perceived to coincide; if the company prospered, the worker prospered. However, the social systems theorists take a different point of view. They believe a basic difference exists between the needs of the organization and the needs of the worker. Therefore, the leader of an organization should give consideration to the people who work in that organization. The focus necessarily must be on the whole (the faculty), parts of the whole (members of the faculty), and the relationship among the parts (relationships among faculty members). Hanson (1991) presents their argument in this manner: "If the leader is considerate, uses democratic procedures whenever possible, and maintains open lines of communication, management and workers can talk over their respective problems and resolve them in a friendly, congenial way" (p. 7). The common strand among the definitions of an organization previously presented suggests that a structure that governs the individuals and groups functioning therein is formulated. It also offers a sense of predictability regarding their activities and behaviors. Given the implication of this compilation, it seems appropriate at this point to entertain a discussion regarding the leader's need to recognize the power and influence of individuals and groups in the organization.

## The Power and Influence of Individuals and Groups

Several individuals and groups make up the social system. Within the framework of social systems theory, each individual and/or group in the workplace has the capability of formulating a power base. Using this power base, they can influence the production process to a considerable degree, independent of the demands of management (Hanson, 1991, p. 7). No two individuals in an organization bring the same style or personality to their role. Considering that the personnel makeup of a school is comprised of a wide range of individuals, the implications for school leaders offered by Social Systems Theory are very significant. A school faculty is likely to consist of a variety of individuals from eras that span as many as 50 years. Boyatzis and Skelly (1995) contend that an individual's capability, or competencies, will have significant influence on the effectiveness of that individual's job performance. The beliefs, values, and behaviors an individual brings into the schoolhouse also have that potential and are influenced by the era that individual represents.

Thus, it seems reasonable to assume that if the leader is to support the enhancement of all individuals in the organization, he/she must develop an understanding of their beliefs, ideas, values, and the effect that his/her behavior has on them. Without such an understanding, the development of informal groups is likely to be perpetuated. Table 2.1 contains a representation of individuals who are likely to comprise a school faculty and offers a rationale for the position they are likely to take on school-related issues.

## Informal Groups

Individuals in schools function as members of the faculty (the formal group), as well as members of subgroups (informal groups) that exist within the faculty. They become members of these groups because of common values, shared interests, and a desire to acquire support to achieve individual goals that may be different from the goals being sought by the formal organization (Hanson, 1991). These subgroups often form power bases to assist them in achieving individual and group goals. Because of their makeup, they are often very powerful. Given this, in order to achieve the most productivity from the faculty, the school leader must be very astute in understanding the patterns of behavior of individuals within informal groups. He/she is not likely to be able to

**TABLE 2.1 Individuals functioning in the social system**

| People | Era | Ethic | Value | Dominant Belief | Behavior |
|---|---|---|---|---|---|
| Prebaby-boomer, 49–75 years old 1940–1960 | Economic growth | Self-denial, allegiance to family | Hard work, upward mobility, commitment to the organization | If you work hard and have patience, you will get your turn. Single leadership | Expected obedience and loyalty as repayment of effort on someone's behalf |
| Early baby boomers, 39–48 years old 1960s–1970s | Social fix-it agenda, professional management | Self-fulfillment, people-oriented, protection of the environment | Focus on self and worker happiness | Pluralistic models of how to "beat the system," bottom-up planning, loyalty to one's field, family demands important | Self replaced the organization, did not respond to authority with any automatic respect |
| Late baby-boomers, 29–38 years old 1970s–1980s | Competitive pragmatism | Self-fulfillment, I want mine, get my share | Winning, not losing, self-knowledge, competitiveness | Identifying with an organization through shared beliefs, cost-effectiveness | Cynical of authority, not a team player, get my share |
| The X generation, 20 years old 1990s | Social pragmatism | Empowerment | Personal blended agenda, autonomy and independence, less stressful lifestyle | Belief in technology, personal agenda, health and fitness | Strategic positioning, home-type activities |

SOURCE: Developed from: Richard E. Boyatzis and Florence R. Skelly (1995). "The impact of changing values on organizational life." In D. A. Kolb, Joyce S. Osland and Irwin M. Rubin (eds.), *The Organizational Behavior Reader* (6th ed.), (pp. 1–17). Upper Saddle River, NJ: Prentice Hall.

eliminate these groups, nor should elimination be a primary concern. The critical factor for school leaders is an awareness of their existence and knowledge of their source of power.

The objective of the school leader should be to develop an understanding of the needs and expertise of every individual in the school sufficient to build relationships that will reduce the need for informal groups to exist. According to CCSSO (1996), a school administrator is a school leader who promotes the success of all students, recognizes and values diversity, and is sensitive to the needs of individuals and groups in the school and community. When this occurs, organizational culture conducive to student learning and staff professional growth is likely to be sustained.

## Dimensions of the Social System

As was indicated above, in many instances, the goals and special interests of individuals and sub-groups in schools conflict with the functional goals of the formal school organization. Jacob Getzels and Egon Guba (1957) theorized that the social system could be divided into two dimensions—the institutional dimension and the personal dimension. The institutional dimension depicts the roles and expectations of the formal organization and the way in which individuals in the organization are expected to behave as they pursue its goals. In a school situation, such roles are outlined through job descriptions, and expectations are established through various forms of performance standards.

The second dimension, personal, refers to the nature of the individual and the personality of that individual, as well as his/her need disposition. No two individuals are alike; they react differently to other individuals and in different situations. These differences can be analyzed in terms of the individual's personality because, to some extent, it is determined by the individual's needs. Thus, the personality of an individual predisposes that individual to behave in a certain way in a given situation (Getzels & Guba, 1957).

The values held by an individual working in schools largely determine his/her willingness to work and the amount of effort he/she will exert to be effective in completing an assigned task (Boyatzis & Skelly, 1995). The individual's values set forth his/her commitment to the school and affect relationships with other people who work or receive services there. In essence, the compatibility between the values of the individual in the social system and the inherent values of the culture of the school is the basis for an individual establishing a social contract with the school (Boyatzis & Skelly, 1995). This social or psychological contract reflects an individual's beliefs and assumptions about work and life and establishes the parameters by which the individual functions.

For example, in a school situation, a high school science teacher occupies a given role and is expected to meet certain established standards. However, that teacher has needs that he/she tries to fulfill. These are personal needs and may be quite different from the expectations and requirements of the school or the science department. The difference in the need dispositions can negatively influence the teacher's performance. It is ideal when the needs of the individual and the goals of the organization are compatible; however, this is not always the case and when it is not, conflict between the individual and the organization is heightened (Getzels & Guba, 1957).

The theory advanced by Getzels and Guba (1957) offers that an individual is likely to be most effective when his/her needs and the task to be performed are at the highest level of compatibility. As previously discussed and illustrated in Table 2.1, individuals who make up the social system represent different eras, which gives them a unique perspective of how the system should operate. Therefore, the school leader should acquire an understanding and appreciation of the different eras represented by the faculty and staff. An in-depth understanding of these eras should provide the leader tremendous insight into the behaviors occurring in the school.

## A Leader with a Social Systems Perspective

A school leader with a social systems perspective seeks to employ individuals with a need disposition compatible with the mission and goals of the school, making use of such strategies as compromising, bargaining, retreating, and changing. In both the school and community, he/she strives to maximize the productivity of subgroups that are sometimes hostile and conflicting. The vision of the school is communicated, and clear directions are given without creating hostility. The leader is not an empire builder; rather, his/her primary concern is for the growth of the organization and the people in the organization. Problems are solved through people, as the leader is sensitive to the feelings of others. He/she listens to the ideas and suggestions of others, appreciates their actions, and expresses that appreciation to them.

## Open Systems Theorists

The open systems theorists believe that an organization is a set of interrelated parts that interacts with its environment. The system receives input from the external environment and transforms that input into a product (output) that goes into the external environment and eventually returns to the internal environment as input. Forces in the internal and external environments influence the system's transformation process (Yukl, 1994).

## Schools Functioning as Open Social Systems

Schools function as open social systems because forces in the external environment of the school affect the transformation process inside the school. The leader must give consideration to the entire system, parts of the system, and the interaction that occurs between and among the parts. He/she collaborates with individuals and groups inside and outside of the school, responding to diverse interests and needs, and mobilizing community resources. This inter-action is influenced by the behavior of the leader; the behavior of organizational members functioning individually and as members of formal and informal groups; the manner in which various actions are perceived; motivational levels; the manner in which power is distributed; and the needs of the organization. Such activities are often very challenging; yet, they must be performed (ISLLC, 1997).

The work of individuals and groups is vertically controlled and horizontally coordinated as they strive to reach established goals. The control and coordination, more often than not, are done through a bureaucratic hierarchy governed by rules and regulations that outline job specifications, the chain of command, and the authority and responsibility of all individuals who function as a part of the school organization (the school structure). Such behavior often depicts the culture and climate of the school.

Because forces in the external environment of the school influence its internal transformation process, the leader must remain flexible and be able to continually adjust the internal operations of the school. For example, if the State Board of Education enacts a policy requiring end-of-course examinations, in order to address this new policy it may be necessary for the leader to work with the faculty to change the school's curriculum and/or instructional approach.

## School Culture

The school is viewed as a system in that it consists of interrelated parts (individuals, formal groups, and informal groups) that function to achieve specific ends. These functions are driven by the purpose of the school (school mission, goals, and objectives). The leader (principal) uses various processes to influence movement toward the established goals and objectives (making decisions, delegating, advocating, clarifying roles, and communicating to all stakeholders). The structure is established inside the school (internal organization) to facilitate these activities and to coordinate the behavior of individuals and groups. The interwoven pattern of beliefs, values, practices, and artifacts that specify for faculty members, students, parents, and stakeholders who they are and how they are to function defines the culture of the school (Bolman & Deal, 1997).

## School Climate

The climate of the school refers to the quality of the environment. Indications of the type of climate that exists in a school are such things as the appearance of the building, the mannerisms of the people, and the feelings individuals have about visiting the school and transacting business there (Halpin & Croft, 1963). The climate of a school may be warm and pleasant or it may be hostile and unpleasant. Teachers, students, parents, and others may be treated with dignity and respected as individuals, or they may be disrespected and experience remarks that are in poor taste.

**FIGURE 2.2  Major elements impacting the operation of schools**

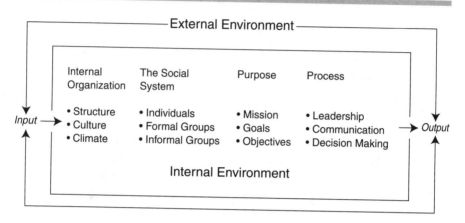

The operation of the school is influenced by factors in the internal and external environments. The school receives input in terms of financial and human resources, conducts a transformation process, and returns a product to the external environment. That product is in the form of students who graduate and other services the school might provide. Figure 2.2 outlines these elements in the context of a school.

## A Leader with an Open Social System Perspective

A leader with an open social system perspective is concerned with compromise and the effective use of human and financial resources. The leader is a comprehensive planner, who concentrates on forming networks inside and outside of the school, attempting to anticipate as much as possible, and striving to be proactive rather than reactive. High visibility and the active involvement of all stakeholders are priorities. Communication is open and continuous; decision making is collaborative; community resources are utilized, and change takes into consideration feedback from the external, as well as the internal environment of the school (Hanson, 1996).

Understanding the structure of the organization and the behavior of individuals and groups that influence inner workings of that structure can help educational leaders manage the organization and its resources in an efficient and effective manner. The theories previously discussed have developed the foundation for this understanding.

## Other Theories Informing Behavior in Schools

Among other theories that offer a rationale for the behavior of people in organizations are McGregor's Theory X and Theory Y, Maslow's Needs Hierarchy, and Herzberg's Motivation-Hygiene Theory. A summary of each follows.

## McGregor's Theory X and Theory Y

Douglas McGregor (1960), the formulator of Theory X and Theory Y, believes that administrative behavior is influenced by two basic assumptions about the nature of people. Following are the main characteristics of this theory:

### THEORY X

1. The average human being has an inherent dislike for work and will avoid it when possible.
2. Because of this human characteristic of dislike of work, most people must be coerced, controlled, directed, and threatened with punishment to get them to put forth adequate effort toward achievement of organizational goals.
3. The average human being prefers to be directed, wishes to avoid responsibility, has relatively little ambition, and wants security above all.

### THEORY Y

1. External control and the threat of punishment are not the only means for bringing about effort toward organizational objectives. People will exercise self-direction and self-control in the service of objectives to which they are committed.
2. The average human being learns, under proper conditions, not only to accept but also to seek responsibility. Avoidance of responsibility, lack of ambition, and emphasis on security are generally consequences of experience, not inherent human characteristics.
3. The capacity to exercise a relatively high degree of imagination, ingenuity, and creativity in the solution of organizational problems is widely, not narrowly, distributed in the population (McGregor, 1960).

It has been found that when leaders differ relative to Theory X and Theory Y, the difference is likely to occur in their attitude toward people. These attitudinal differences are most pronounced related to the manner in which they interact with followers and the extent to which they involve followers in decision making (Owens, 1995). A Theory X leader would likely emphasize policies and procedures, give directions in a blunt and to the point manner, and demand action with the overt threat of punishment. If an error occurs in leader behavior, it is likely to be on the side of task completion. A Theory Y leader would likely function as a facilitator, an individual who is as interested in the process as the product. Decisions would likely be made through people, creating an environment conducive to self-direction and intrinsic motivation. If an error occurs in leader behavior, it is likely to be on the side of consideration and relationship building. The behaviors advocated by ISLLC Standard 2 are most noted in leaders who exhibit Y characteristics.

## Maslow's Needs Hierarchy

Abraham Maslow (1970) theorized that people are influenced by a series of needs that are grouped into five basic categories. The categories begin with the most basic needs of an individual and extend through a hierarchy to self-actualization. The central premise of the theory is that individuals are motivated by a variety of needs. Individuals are first driven by the most basic needs; however, once one's basic needs are satisfied, another will become priority for satisfactorily moving up the hierarchy. Maslow grouped the needs in the following five categories:

1. Physiological needs are viewed as a need for food, shelter, and health.
2. Safety needs are viewed as a desire for protection from danger, attacks, and threat.
3. Social needs are expressed through a desire for belonging and the establishment of relationships.
4. Esteem needs are viewed as being expressed through a desire to feel valued and to value oneself.
5. Self-actualization needs are expressed through an individual's desire to reach his/her full potential.

While addressing the attainment of the goals and objectives of the organization, the effective leader gives careful consideration to the comfort level of individuals who function in the organization, removing any impediments to the satisfaction of their needs. The leader also seeks to always be aware of the needs individuals in the organization are seeking to satisfy. For example, if a veteran teacher has the desire to chair the English Department and teach the Advanced Placement classes, the principal might be sensitive to those needs and not assign such responsibility to a first-year teacher. The first-year teacher is likely to be appreciative, as his/her primary concern is likely getting adjusted and becoming familiar with the school's overall program.

## Herzberg's Motivation-Hygiene Theory

Herzberg (1993) classified the aspects of the work environment into two categories. He categorized those aspects of work that produce job satisfaction as motivators and those that do not provide satisfaction as hygiene factors. Hygiene refers to the work environment and references those factors that Maslow refers to as safety and belonging needs. The motivational level addresses work and consists of what Maslow identified as self-esteem and self-actualization needs. Many inaccuracies have been found in this theory; however, it has proven to be very helpful when leaders choose to use it in increasing the motivational level of workers. The school leader can benefit by developing an understanding of the culture and climate of the school environment and by being sensitive to assignments given individuals. By developing an understanding of the school culture and climate, the school leader can ensure that the school is organized and aligned for success. In so doing, the leader would have met an ISLLC standard. The standard offers that the leader should make assignments in a manner that increases effectiveness and moves the school toward established goals, and at the same time, brings satisfaction to members of the faculty (CCSSO, 1996).

The preceding theories have a rich history and have withstood the test of time. The principles of these theories provide a guiding framework for understanding and predicting many of the behaviors in schools. Without an understanding of these behaviors, leaders are not likely to be able to influence individuals sufficiently to achieve school goals and objectives. Although these theories are products of early thought, they continue to provide a framework for understanding the behavior of individuals and groups in today's schools, and they are the foundation upon which contemporary ideas that currently appear in leadership literature are built.

## Contemporary Postulates Informing Leadership in Schools

In recent years, a number of theoreticians, researchers and writers have addressed the behavior of individuals in organizations from an all-inclusive perspective (Garvin, 1995; Hanson, 1996; Manz & Sims, 1989; Senge 1995). They argue that a school or school district is not administered by a single center of power and authority. Rather, it is administered by a number of power centers that function with semiautonomous power and contribute significantly to the direction the school or district is taking. These theorists suggest that all individuals have value and can make a significant contribution to the growth of the organization. Senge (1995) offers that leaders are responsible for helping individuals expand their capacity to shape their future; in essence, leaders are responsible for subordinate learning. He states, "The old model, 'the top thinks, and the local acts' must now give way to integrating thinking and acting at all levels" (p. 76).

It is also advocated that leaders of today's schools spend time encouraging individuals and groups and helping them to keep up with the changes and demands of the organization, so they might understand the benefits to be derived from achieving the school's vision (Manz & Sims, 1989). In addition, the leader must provide members of the organization with opportunities to learn from failure, and it is critical that when failure occurs, individuals be approached without repercussions. When there are repercussions, barriers to quality work are formed and individuals withdraw, leaving the organization void of their creativity (Ryan & Oestreich, 1991). Organizations that function in the manner described above have been defined in a number of ways; however, they are most commonly referred to as learning organizations.

**FIGURE 2.3  Creative tension in schools**

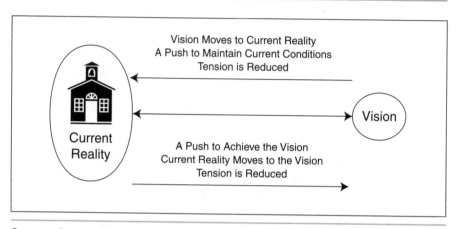

SOURCE: Designed from Peter Senge's definition of creative tension.

## Learning Organizations

"Learning organizations are places where people continually expand their capacity to create the results they truly desire, where new and expansive patterns of thinking are nurtured, where collective aspiration is set free, and where people are continually learning how to learn together" (Senge, 1990, p. 3). In a learning organization, the climate and culture are such that individuals feel valued, respected, and appreciated. The leader facilitates team learning, and the communication process fosters full participation, with everyone feeling a sense of importance relative to making a contribution to organizational growth. The leader seeks a shared vision and serves as a designer, teacher, and steward. He/she utilizes these qualities to ensure that individuals in the organization understand current reality, recognize creative tension, and seek the vision that members of the organization hold.

Creative tension exists when members of the organization have a clear understanding of the current state of the organization, as well as the vision. The gap between the two creates a natural tension (Senge, 1990). Creative tension can be reduced by moving the vision toward current reality or by moving current reality toward the vision. However, having developed an understanding of the internal organization, the interaction of individuals and groups in the social system, and the influences of the external environment, the effective leader selects a process to use in moving current reality toward the vision (see Figure 2.3).

## Schools as Learning Organizations

The research and writings of Bennis and Biederman (1997), Covey (1989), Senge (1990), Sergiovanni (1994), and others indicate that schools can become learning organizations. However, it will be necessary for the leader to devote

**FIGURE 2.4    Thirteen characteristics of nurturing schools**

**Theme A—Student teacher relationships**
- There is mutual trust and positive interaction between teachers and students.
- Teachers have an in-depth knowledge of students' in-school and out-of-school lives.
- Teachers model caring attitudes for students.

**Theme B—Professionalism among administration, faculty, and staff**
- There is a sense of caring among individuals and a collective sense of responsibility for student success.
- The need for self-actualization is respected and encouraged.
- Teachers demonstrate a love for their subject matter and continuously search for competence.

**Theme C—Environment of the school and classroom**
- A sense of community and a sense of family exist in the school, and there is collaboration among professionals.
- Everyone values individual differences, and the self one brings into the environment is respected and nurtured.
- There is recognition of a wide range of talent and the need for the empowerment of all individuals.
- The school draws in the values of the community and involves the community in the education of children.

**Theme D—Students' feelings about themselves**
- Students feel a sense of self-worth and acceptance.
- Students feel safe and involved in their education.
- Students value themselves and others.

SOURCE: Reginald Leon Green, Ed.D. © Copyright 1996. Educational Services Plus. All rights reserved.

time and attention to the structure of the school, the individuals who serve the school, and their relationship with students as well as with each other. Schools that are becoming learning organizations have taken these actions. Green (1997) identified 13 characteristics that exist in such schools. These characteristics cluster into four themes that are consistent with those advocated for a learning organization (see Figure 2.4). In a later study (Green, 1998), it was shown that the magnitude of the existence of these themes may, in some schools, have had a positive effect on student achievement, attendance, and behavior.

Garvin (1995) also described characteristics of schools that are learning organizations. He offers that school leaders who have created learning organizations are fostering participatory governance, using systematic problem–solving techniques, and experimenting with new approaches. Leaders are also learning from their own experience and past history, learning from the experiences and best practices of others, and transferring knowledge quickly and efficiently throughout the organization. In these schools and others that have become learning organizations, leaders are implementing the concept of site-based management, opening lines of communication and allowing all stakeholders an opportunity to participate in the governance of the school. There is openness to a degree that people feel free to express their views and are willing to give and take. There is consistency in words and actions; the message given out is acted upon; and people have developed a sincere belief that they are valued and respected. Everyone receives equal treatment, and the outcome of the school is to advance the welfare of the community (Etheridge & Green, 1998). According to CCSSO (1996), school leaders of today should hold firm to the proposition that all students can learn, view student learning as the fundamental purpose of schooling, and understand diversity and its meaning for educational programs. School leaders who have created learning environments in their schools are meeting these ISLLC indicators.

## Summary

Many writers and researchers use concepts and terms to suggest the behavior that leaders should exhibit in today's schools. In one way or another, most of these suggestions relate to the concepts that are advocated by individuals who subscribe to the creation of learning organizations. These concepts are also supported by ISLLC Standard 3, which advocates that school leaders are administrators who manage the school organization, operations, and resources to ensure a safe, efficient, and effective learning environment. The theories, postulates, and practices presented here and in Chapter 1 support many of the principles that inform leader behavior necessary to meet this standard. The scenarios that follow will allow the reader an opportunity to use these theories, postulates, and practices, as well as others, to assess his/her leadership disposition and provide a rationale for the behavior of individuals functioning in schools.

## The Scenarios

In Scenario 5, the superintendent of schools has requested that Principal Harris complete two tasks during the school year: development of a school improvement plan and establishment of a site-based management team. After allowing the year to elapse without making very much progress toward the completion of either task, Principal Harris takes action to complete both tasks within the requested time frame. The reader will want to pay particular attention to the effects of leader behavior on the environment of the school and subordinates functioning in that environment.

In Scenario 6, the principal addresses an issue involving teachers from different eras. The issue poses a threat to relationships in the environment and could deprive students of a valuable learning experience. The key factor in this scenario is the ability of the leader to influence a change in the attitude of a subordinate.

Scenario 7 moves into the realm of relationships, adult learning, motivation, and collaboration. The scenario indicates the need for the leader to recognize and address various influences in the internal and external environments of the school. Failure to address these influences in an effective manner could possibly inhibit goal attainment.

Scenario 8 addresses two standards, with collaboration and management being the focus. From this scenario, the reader should be able to discern how leadership behavior, the climate and culture of the school district, and influences of the external environment can create a situation that threatens the entire teaching and learning process.

In working through these scenarios, the reader will have an opportunity to review indicators of ISLLC Standards 2, 3, and 4 in practical situations.

## SCENARIO 5

## UNDERSTANDING AND PREDICTING INDIVIDUAL AND GROUP BEHAVIOR IN SCHOOLS

### STANDARD 3

A school administrator is an educational leader who promotes the success of all students by ensuring management of the organization, operations, and resources for a safe, efficient, and effective learning environment.

*In Scenario 5, the focus is on management, assuming responsibility, and effective problem framing and problem solving. Because of a principal's inefficiency in these areas, the climate of the school environment becomes a threat to teaching and learning.*

### ISLLC Standards Indicators Exhibited in Scenario 5

**Knowledge Indicators**
The administrator has knowledge and understanding of:
▲ Applied motivational theories
▲ The change process for systems, organizations, and individuals
▲ School cultures
▲ Theories and models of organizations and the principles of organizational development

▲ Operational procedures at the school and district level
▲ Human resources management and development
▲ Emerging issues and trends that potentially impact the school community
▲ The conditions and dynamics of the diverse school community
▲ Community resources

**Disposition Indicators**
The administrator believes in, values, and is committed to:
▲ Making management decisions to enhance learning and teaching
▲ A willingness to continuously examine one's own assumptions, beliefs, and practices
▲ Trusting people and their judgment
▲ Accepting responsibility
▲ Involving stakeholders in management processes
▲ Professional development as an integral part of school improvement
▲ The benefit that diversity brings to the school community

**Performance Indicators**
The administrator facilitates processes and engages in activities ensuring that:
▲ The school culture and climate is assessed on a regular basis
▲ A variety of sources of information is used to make decisions
▲ Operational procedures are designed and managed to maximize opportunity for successful learning.
▲ Operational plans and procedures to achieve the vision and goals of the school are in place
▲ Time is managed to maximize attainment of organizational goals
▲ Potential problems and opportunities are identified
▲ Effective group-process and consensus-building skills are used
▲ The school is organized and aligned for success
▲ Organizational systems are regularly monitored and modified as needed
▲ Stakeholders are involved in decisions affecting schools

After Principal Harris's appointment, Superintendent Glover advised him that the districtwide strategic plan required the administration, faculty, staff, and parents of each school to develop a site-based management team and implement a plan for instructional improvement that would be aligned with the district's strategic goals. Superintendent Glover then gave him a copy of the district's strategic plan and advised him that he should establish the site-based management team, develop a local school improvement plan, and have that plan in operation within the first two years of his tenure.

As Principal Harris entered the school year and began to carry out his duties, he often thought about the charge he had received from the superintendent and how he would collaborate with the faculty, staff, and community in designing a plan that would be most appropriate for the school. However, the pressures of getting adjusted to a new job and operating a large school were all-consuming, and there never seemed to be time to develop the site-based management team or discuss a new instructional design for the school. He rarely left his office because he was so saturated with paperwork.

As Principal Harris approached the end of his first year, it became clear that unless he took immediate action, the year would end, and the school would not have a site-based management team or a school improvement plan. Therefore, he convened a meeting with his two assistant principals, Alice Harmon and William Johnson. He reviewed the task with them, asking Mr. Johnson to research and formulate a plan that could be used to establish a site-based management team and requesting that Mrs. Harmon formulate the framework for a school improvement plan.

While Mr. Johnson sat silently accepting the assignment, Mrs. Harmon vehemently opposed the assignment. She advised Principal Harris that the time frame was much too short to accomplish the task with any degree of quality, as most of the faculty would not have adequate time to research ideas for program changes this late in the school year. She also spoke against the establishment of a site-based management team, offering that prior to his appointment, many members of the faculty had expressed that unless there was extra pay and/or a reallocation of instructional time, they would prefer not to be engaged in any additional committee work.

Dr. Harris voiced regrets that so much had to be done in such a short period; then he advised his assistants to move forward with the assignments as expeditiously as possible. Mrs. Harmon left the office in a state of anger, voicing her resistance to Mr. Johnson. "We will just see what occurs," she stated. Mr. Johnson made no comments but returned to his office and began to ponder the assignment.

At the next faculty meeting, Principal Harris advised the faculty that the school staff would be implementing a site-based management model and that Mr. Johnson would be providing the leadership for its development. He also advised the faculty that the leadership for the design of a school improvement plan was being provided by Mrs. Harmon. He went on to say that he was sure that the faculty would appreciate the need for these two new initiatives, as they were a part of a districtwide effort to improve student achievement. He asked for the support of the faculty and assured them that they would in turn have the support of his office.

Two weeks later at the regularly scheduled monthly meeting of the subject area department heads, Mrs. Harmon reviewed the request made by the principal with the group. She then asked if anyone had suggestions on how to begin the task. At least three individuals (department heads of English, mathematics, and science) spoke to the time frame and a need to wait until the fall to start any new program initiatives. The social studies department head stated that he believed that if the effort got underway before the end of the school year, the summer could be spent researching and collecting data on new programs. Mrs. Harmon gave a quaint chuckle and asked the question, "Anyone for summer work without pay?" The music department head then spoke up and said, "There are several closing-of-school band activities scheduled, but I can find time to attend a few meetings." "Well, that settles it," replied Mrs. Harmon, "I'll report to Dr. Harris that it is the consensus of the department heads that we delay this activity until the fall." Hearing no opposition, the meeting was adjourned.

Two days later, Mrs. Harmon wrote a memo to Dr. Harris, advising him that she had met with the department heads and that they had expressed a strong desire to postpone any new curriculum efforts until the fall.

During the three weeks that elapsed after the meeting with Principal Harris, Mr. Johnson conducted an extensive literature review on site-based management models. From his review, he developed a list of the pros and cons of various models operating in large urban school districts. He then began to talk with faculty members individually and in small groups. He spoke with the president of the Parent Teacher Organization as well as a number of parents and community leaders. After several meetings in which he

collected the ideas and opinions of many individuals, he formulated a set of recommendations on site-based management for Principal Harris' review.

At the next faculty meeting, Mr. Johnson presented his report and recommendations
to the faculty. After he passed out his report, he described the process he had used to
collect data, explained the content, and provided a rationale for his recommendations.
Then he gave the faculty time to review the report and raise questions.

The faculty appeared stunned at the request but reviewed the material and began to
comment among themselves. At once, Mrs. Harmon spoke to the plan, "Why are there
so many parents on the team? Parents outnumber teachers." Frances Jones, a senior English instructor, noted "Yes, I see a parent is slated to chair the committee, but why can't
a teacher chair the committee?" The chair of the mathematics department then spoke,
"I believe we should all be involved in determining the committee structure." Mrs. Harmon replied, "Yes, isn't that what site-based management is all about?" The English
department head, followed by the science department head, then voiced negative comments. Many other faculty members appeared to want to speak but could not get the
attention of Mr. Johnson, who was stunned by the strong resistance to his report. He had
spoken to all these individuals and whereas they did not voice any strong support for
the concept of site-based management, they did not express any concern with his recommendations. In fact, some teachers had spoken very positively about the concept.
Why didn't these individuals speak up earlier? Then he remembered that several teachers had met with Mrs. Harmon to discuss the concept and its merits.

Dr. Harris then intervened. He thanked Mr. Johnson for his hard work, complimented
him on his recommendations, and told the faculty that some additional work was
needed and that the plan would be discussed further in a later meeting. He completed
the remaining items on the agenda and adjourned the meeting.

## REFLECTIVE THINKING AND SCENARIO ANALYSIS

1. What would be a plausible explanation for the time lapse between Dr. Harris'
   appointment and his definitive action regarding the two required plans?
2. What theoretical principles and models of organizations can you cite that would
   explain Mrs. Harmon's behavior?
3. How would you explain the dynamics of the interpersonal relationship that exist
   between the two assistant principals? What factors in the internal environment
   might be influencing this type of behavior?
4. In this school, what factors can you cite that would permit an assistant principal
   to exhibit the tactics used by Mrs. Harmon?
5. What management decisions would you advise Dr. Harris to use as he proceeds
   in his attempt to enhance teaching and learning? What potential problems and
   opportunities can you identify?

## ADDRESSING THE ISSUES

Select the one best answer to the following questions:

1. Which of the following provides the best explanation for the cause of the dysfunctional behavior in the scenario?

   a. The faculty was resisting control from the leadership.

b. The principal failed to develop an understanding of self and establish a vision for the school.

c. The lines of communication were not effective.

d. The assistant principals did not have an effective working relationship with the faculty.

2. Which of the following would you suggest as being most consequential in this scenario?

a. The expectations the faculty held for the principal and the manner in which he met those expectations.

b. Operational procedures that did not take into consideration the motivational level of the entire faculty.

c. The manner in which Dr. Harris distributed power.

d. Operational procedures that did not take into consideration the power and influence of faculty members functioning individually and as members of formal and informal groups.

3. Which of the following provides the best explanation for the outcome of the work of Assistant Principal Johnson?

a. Involvement of parents and other stakeholders is not a sufficient way to develop models for a faculty to implement.

b. The change process for systems, organizations, and individuals is difficult to implement.

c. Even a well-developed plan with considerable input from stakeholders is difficult to implement if there are strong forces in opposition to that plan.

d. It is not necessary to use a variety of sources to develop a plan in order for it to be accepted.

4. Which of the following actions might Dr. Harris take to ensure the degree of faculty unity and cohesiveness necessary to prevent the type of behavior exhibited by Mrs. Harmon from recurring?

a. Hold a series of workshops on site-based management in order to allow the faculty to develop an appreciation for the concept.

b. Hold a series of meetings wherein the faculty members discuss their values, the mission of the school, and the goals that are to be achieved.

c. Establish the kind of climate that would allow the values, beliefs, and attitudes that are embedded in the faculty to be molded into a culture of productivity.

d. Step forward as principal and take the leadership for the two tasks.

## DISCUSSION OF THE SOLUTION

1. Dr. Harris was appointed principal of a faculty that was well established and appeared to be very knowledgeable about teaching and learning. They were entrenched in a developed culture, and the climate of the school reflected that culture. Dr. Harris's behavior did not positively affect that culture. In fact, his behavior contributed to the lack of organizational effectiveness. He did not influence the emergence

of a central focus around which the faculty could unite. In essence, there was an absence of what Bennis (1995) refers to as the management of self and attention.

When a leader enters a new assignment, he/she should take action to draw individuals to him/her. This is accomplished by managing self and establishing a compelling vision (Bennis, 1995). Dr. Harris took no action that communicated commitment, nor did he provide a thrust around which the faculty could unite. More importantly, his procrastination and lack of planning negatively affected the school climate. When entering a new school situation, it is wise for the leader to examine the existing structure, conditions, and the actions of the faculty. After such an examination, the leadership can move forward building relationships and establishing principles and practices of trust, caring, and collaboration. Everyone can be engaged in conducting a critical inquiry into current conditions. Of all the relationships that exist within a school, none has a greater effect on the quality of life in that school than the relationship between teacher and principal (Barth, 1990).

Dr. Harris also failed to manage self. He did not realize the behavior he was modeling or the influence it had on the behavior of the faculty. Having failed to model the type of behavior he desired from the faculty (intentionally or unintentionally) or to establish an environment in which the school had the capacity to change, he resorted to actions that challenged existing values, ideas, and past behaviors of the faculty. "The ultimate in disrespect of individuals is to attempt to impose one's will on them without regard for what they want or need and without consulting them. Thus treating people with respect is what moral leadership is about, and nothing could be harder. But when there is organizational or social necessity for change, nothing is more practical" (O'Toole, 1995, p. 12). The suggested response to question 1 is **(b)**.

2. People in organizations serve as members of the formal group (the faculty) and faculty subunits (departments), and they often hold membership in informal groups that develop within the faculty. Power and influence can be derived and used in each of these settings. Often, individuals use the power derived from participation in the informal group to influence actions and behaviors in the formal arena, thereby fostering individual and group goals at the expense of the formal organization. Such was the case in this scenario. Mrs. Harmon appears to have built a power base in some of the school's subunits, as well as among several informal groups that exist on the faculty, and in each, her power base appears to be very strong. As a result of her power in these settings, she was able to divert the faculty from the goal it was attempting to achieve. Examples of such behavior were evident in her meeting with the department heads and were reflected in the manner in which she directed the behavior of the group. Although some members were reasonably receptive to the task, she managed to direct the group's final decision in a manner that was in line with her personal way of thinking.

Informal work groups within the workplace create and reinforce their own standards and codes of behavior (Lipham, Rankin, & Hoeh, 1985). Considering this factor, it is important for school leaders to be knowledgeable of individuals in the organization and aware of the power they hold and the influence they might exert both as individuals and as members of informal groups. It is also extremely helpful when the leadership can predict the manner in which individuals will use their power and influence. When a leader is knowledgeable of the informal groups and can predict the behavior of individuals who function in these groups, operational procedures can be put into place to effect positive outcomes. In this instance, Mrs. Harmon's behavior functioning individually and as a member of various informal groups was very consequential in the faculty's efforts to achieve school goals. The operational procedures of the leader did not offset this type of behavior, nor did Principal Harris employ effective conflict-resolution skills. The suggested response to question 2 is **(d)**.

3. When the leader of a school attempts to bring about change, it is important for him/her to be advised by motivational theories. Before the change is attempted, it is wise to assess the culture and climate of the school in order that operational procedures can be put into place to ensure that the change will occur in an effective manner. When this does not happen, even though some members of the faculty may support the change and work hard to make it a reality, sufficient forces may exist to prohibit the change. Even though Assistant Principal Johnson conducted a process that included all of the correct steps, it was not successful because of other forces in the school. Process is very important to goal attainment, for it is through the process that organizational influences are addressed. Decision quality alone is not sufficient. It must be accompanied by decision acceptance. The suggested response to question 3 is **(c)**.

4. The school climate suggests a need for the use of democratic principles, open lines of communication, positive interpersonal relationships, and faculty acceptance of decisions that are reached. Dr. Harris failed to explain to the entire faculty why it was necessary to develop a school improvement plan or to involve the faculty in activities that would enable them to develop an appreciation for the concept of site-based management. At the first faculty meeting, he informed the faculty of the task at hand as opposed to influencing or persuading them to get involved. He did not do an effective job of managing attention.

In addition, he failed to express an appreciation for Mrs. Harmon's concerns. Being empathetic would possibly have assisted greatly. Simply telling assistants to develop a framework for changes of the magnitude described is not sufficient; the faculty will need to change their behavior, and only a change in attitude is likely to lead to a change in behavior (DuBrin, 1996). Individuals in organizations have personalities, values, and goals that may be different from the goals of the organization. The faculty may have little control over whether the school moves to site-based management or develops a plan for school improvement; however, they do maintain control over their actions and the manner in which they carry out directions. Therefore, it is wise for the leadership to acknowledge their concerns and build the type of interpersonal relationships that would allow them to be influenced and persuaded.

In order to prevent the behavior exhibited by Mrs. Harmon from recurring, it will be necessary for Dr. Harris to motivate the faculty to discuss their values and develop a shared mission for the school. It will also be necessary for him to involve them in the identification of a process that can be used to establish site-based management and develop a school improvement plan. Therefore, he will have to develop positive interpersonal relationships between him and his associates and among the faculty at large. If the faculty develops positive interpersonal relationships and participates in developing the framework for the two initiatives, they are likely to support their implementation, and the type of behavior exhibited by Mrs. Harmon is less likely to be effective. The suggested response to question 4 is **(c)**.

## SUMMARY AND CONCLUSION

Dr. Harris met with challenges only after he failed to plan and organize his responsibilities in a manner that would allow tasks to be completed efficiently and effectively. New challenges surfaced when he delegated assignments to his assistant principals and failed to consider the organizational influences that had to be addressed. He took too narrow a view of his responsibility and did not manage attention or self. In addition, he did not acknowledge the context in which the faculty functioned and disregarded the influence of the informal groups of the organization. Unless a leader can think flexibly about the organization and see it from multiple angles, he/she will be unable to envision the full range of issues that is likely to surface.

Dr. Harris was able to view the needs of the organization. However, he failed to take into account the personality of the individuals with whom he was working or their desires and goals. Leaders are constantly making decisions that involve people and their relationships in the organization. Developing an understanding of these individuals sufficient to enable one to effectively predict their behavior is a key factor in the leader's effectiveness. The better an administrator is at predicting the behavior of people, the better he/she is likely to be in achieving the goals and objectives of the school. If the school leader can identify the goals of individual members of the faculty and groups affiliated with the school, he/she can align those goals with the objectives of the school.

As was illustrated in Chapter 1, individuals in schools need to feel important, valued, and treated fairly with dignity and respect. A basic skill to be mastered by the leader is one of managing interpersonal relations. Once acquired, this skill can become a powerful tool to be used by the leader to advocate nurturing and sustain a school culture and instructional program that are conducive to student learning and professional growth.

## SCENARIO 6
### ADDRESSING DYSFUNCTIONAL THINKING

### STANDARD 2

A school administrator is an educational leader who promotes the success of all students by advocating nurturing and sustaining a school culture and instructional program conducive to student learning and professional growth.

*In Scenario 6, the principal works with faculty members to ensure that student learning remains the fundamental purpose of the school. In the process, several indicators of Standard 2 are addressed. The focus is on the indicators of fairness, respecting the expertise of faculty members, and the need for all individuals to feel valued and important.*

## ISLLC Standards Indicators Exhibited in Scenario 6

### Knowledge Indicators
The administrator has knowledge and understanding of:
▲ School cultures
▲ Adult learning and professional development
▲ Diversity and its meaning for educational programs
▲ Theories and models of organizations and the principles of organizational development
▲ Operational procedures at the school and district level
▲ Human resources management and development
▲ Emerging issues and trends that potentially impact the school community
▲ The conditions and dynamics of the diverse school community
▲ Community resources

### Disposition Indicators
The administrator believes in, values, and is committed to:
▲ Student learning as the fundamental purpose of schooling
▲ The benefits that diversity brings to the school and community
▲ Making management decisions to enhance learning and teaching
▲ A willingness to continuously examine one's own assumptions, beliefs, and practices
▲ Trusting people and their judgment
▲ Involving stakeholders in management processes
▲ Professional development as an integral part of school improvement

### Performance Indicators
The administrator facilitates processes and engages in activities ensuring that:
▲ All individuals are treated with fairness, dignity, and respect
▲ Students and staff feel valued and important
▲ Barriers to student learning are identified, clarified, and addressed
▲ Diversity is considered in developing learning experiences
▲ Lifelong learning is encouraged and modeled
▲ Student and staff accomplishments are recognized and celebrated
▲ Curricular, cocurricular, and extracurricular programs are designed, implemented, evaluated, and refined
▲ Problems are confronted and resolved in a timely manner
▲ Human resource functions support the attainment of school goals
▲ A variety of sources of information is used to make decisions
▲ Operational procedures are designed and managed to maximize opportunity for successful learning
▲ Operational plans and procedures to achieve the vision and goals of the school are in place
▲ Potential problems and opportunities are identified
▲ Effective group-process and consensus-building skills are used
▲ Stakeholders are involved in decisions affecting schools
▲ Diversity is recognized and valued
▲ Opportunities for staff to develop collaborative skills are provided

Oakview High School is located in a large urban city with a student population that reflects its community. Until this year, the faculty of the school was comprised of veteran teachers who had spent 5 to 10 years at Oakview. In the fall of 1999, a large number of new faculty members were assigned to the school. Many of them were first-year teachers who were anxious to practice their newly learned techniques and eager to make a difference in the lives of their students. However, the veteran faculty members were somewhat defensive and resistant to new faculty, often labeling them as inexperienced and refusing to offer assistance or camaraderie. In fact, there was talk that central administration was attempting to save money by pushing veteran teachers out and employing faculty with less experience.

For the first time this year, Oakview has been chosen to participate in the citywide annual Wordsmith contest, a prestigious competition among honor students in English. The contest attracts community support, and one company traditionally awards $10,000 for computer equipment to the winning school. Ms. Farmington, a new faculty member, is experienced in Wordsmith competition and has demonstrated her ability to work well with the students, as well as her competence in English and literature. Nevertheless, Mrs. Douglas, a veteran teacher at Oakview, is opposed to appointing a "neophyte" to chair such an important event. Although she is not desirous of working with the Wordsmith competition, Mrs. Douglas feels that an experienced faculty member could supervise the students more effectively and get assistance from teachers who have previously participated in Wordsmith events.

Mrs. Douglas is a "faculty favorite." She chairs the homecoming program and shares after-school tutoring duties with other faculty members. She also meets regularly with several faculty members who are affiliated with her sorority. Discussion in each of these arenas often centers on school events and activities.

The principal, Gerald Carroll, feels that Ms. Farmington would make an excellent chair for Wordsmith. However, he is aware of Mrs. Douglas's concerns, and she has requested a meeting with him to discuss the assignment.

## REFLECTIVE THINKING AND SCENARIO ANALYSIS

1. What actions must Principal Carroll take in order to get the support of Mrs. Douglas?
2. What influence might the composition of the faculty have on the divisiveness that exists among faculty members?
3. What leadership strategies might Principal Carroll employ to address this dilemma in a manner that will promote cooperation and positive relationships while making maximum use of the talents of both junior and senior faculty members?
4. What is likely to be the difference between the need disposition of Ms. Farmington and Mrs. Douglas? Why might this difference be a factor for Principal Carroll to consider?
5. What are some assumptions being made by Mrs. Douglas?
6. What necessarily has to be reflected in the leadership style of Principal Carroll?

## ADDRESSING THE ISSUES

Select the one best answer to the following questions:

1. In the context that student learning is the fundamental purpose of schools, the primary concerns of Principal Carroll must be:

    **a.** Acknowledging and utilizing the expertise of Ms. Farmington without diminishing the support of Mrs. Douglas.

    **b.** Obtaining the funds from winning the contest and enhancing the exposure of students.

    **c.** Reducing the possibility of Mrs. Douglas utilizing her power in a negative manner.

    **d.** both a and c.

**2.** Which of the following would be a plausible course of action for Principal Carroll to take in meeting with Mrs. Douglas?

    **a.** He could discuss aspects of mentoring and nurturing new personnel and utilizing the talents and attributes of all individuals.

    **b.** He could take a firm stance indicating that teacher assignments are within his domain.

    **c.** He could reverse himself and yield to her perspective.

    **d.** He could discuss the formation of a committee to be chaired by Mrs. Douglas for the purpose of making the decision.

**3.** If Principal Carroll's actions are informed by adult motivational theories, which of the following is true?

    **a.** Mrs. Douglas is likely seeking a sense of belonging.

    **b.** Ms. Farmington is likely seeking self-esteem.

    **c.** There is "no one best" way to motivate all individuals on the faculty.

    **d.** Mrs. Douglas and Ms. Farmington are likely seeking self-actualization.

**4.** Which of the following must be given consideration by Principal Carroll?

    **a.** He must consider potential problems that could occur.

    **b.** He must trust Mrs. Douglas and her judgment.

    **c.** There must be opportunities for the faculty to develop collaborative skills.

    **d.** all of the above

## DISCUSSION OF THE SOLUTION

1. A leader advocating, nurturing, and sustaining a school culture and instructional program conducive to student learning and staff professional growth (ISLLC Standard 2) would likely take the human relations approach to addressing issues that caused dysfunctional thinking in the organization. He/she would listen to the ideas of all individuals involved and express an appreciation for their position. To further understand an approach to addressing such issues, the reader might consult the group decision-making techniques discussed in Chapter 4. Displaying high consideration behavior, the leader would demonstrate that all individuals have value and are needed for the school to effectively address the needs of all students. This factor must be emphasized, as the interpersonal relationships of Mrs. Douglas and Ms. Farmington are of paramount importance to the school climate and future school projects. The leader must understand diversity and how it affects the development

of learning experiences. Using effective group-process and consensus-building skills, he/she must advocate nurturing and sustaining a school culture that will foster student learning and professional growth of both faculty members. Such actions will maximize the motivational level of both Ms. Farmington and Mrs. Douglas. The suggested response to question 1 is **(a)**.

2. In this instance, Principal Carroll is likely to be most successful by taking a compromising approach to obtaining a solution to the issue. First he could talk with each of the teachers individually, providing them with a rationale for his position, then proceed to acquire the opinion of each teacher as to an acceptable solution, and conclude with a persuasive argument that would foster the involvement of both teachers. He might invite the two teachers to be partners in this and all school activities. Perhaps Mrs. Douglas could serve as a mentor to Ms. Farmington or even cochair the activity. Regardless of the approach taken by Principal Carroll, each teacher must leave this situation feeling that she has been treated professionally and her talents and attributes are respected. The suggested response to question 2 is **(a).**

3. Mrs. Douglas is likely seeking self-esteem whereas Ms. Farmington is likely seeking a sense of belonging. The environment of the school must foster success for both. For this to occur, the leader must acquire knowledge of the values, desires, and aspirations of both individuals. Through a diagnosis of the situation, he should realize the differences in their desires. There is no one best approach to motivating all employees; realizing this factor will assist him in addressing the situation in an appropriate manner. The suggested response to question 3 is **(c)**.

4. The Wordsmith contest holds considerable meaning for the students at Oakview. It also places Oakview in a position to benefit from the resources in the community. Therefore, Principal Carroll must consider a number of factors. He must consider the potential problems that could occur as a result of any decision he makes. He must also trust Mrs. Douglas's judgment and motivate her to become actively involved in the total school program. Of major importance is getting her to realize that student learning is the fundamental purpose of schooling, and often it is necessary for the faculty to collaborate in order for effective and efficient programs to be implemented. The suggested response to question 4 is **(d).**

## SUMMARY AND CONCLUSION

In a school, relationships are very important, and the leaders should influence positive relationships between and among all individuals and groups affiliated with the school. People have to work with each other, and the work environment must be one that allows each individual to have his/her needs met and acquire personal desires and goals. When the leader has an understanding of the needs and concerns of each individual, motivational and learning theories that foster the desired organizational climate can be applied. Therefore, the leader must be creative, using his/her position to open the lines of communication so people will bond, embrace the culture of the school, share ideas, provide assistance to one another, and take pride in being a part of a team that successfully achieves its goals.

# SCENARIO 7
## THE NEW PRINCIPAL AT EVANS MIDDLE SCHOOL

### STANDARD 2

A school administrator is an educational leader who promotes the success of all students by advocating, nurturing, and sustaining a school culture and instructional program conducive to student learning and staff professional growth.

*In Scenario 7, the principal is faced with the challenge of building a capacity for change. She is perplexed as to how a shared vision can be acquired. The critical question is: How does a principal implement change, address organizational influences, and respect diversity, while maintaining an environment that is conducive to student learning?*

### ISLLC Standards Indicators Exhibited in Scenario 7

**Knowledge Indicators**
The administrator has knowledge and understanding of:
▲ School cultures
▲ Adult learning and professional development
▲ Diversity and its meaning for educational programs
▲ Theories and models of organizations and the principles of organizational development
▲ Operational procedures at the school and district level
▲ Human resources management and development
▲ Emerging issues and trends that potentially impact the school community
▲ The conditions and dynamics of the diverse school community

**Disposition Indicators**
The administrator believes in, values, and is committed to:
▲ Student learning as the fundamental purpose of schooling
▲ The benefits that diversity brings to the school and community
▲ Making management decisions to enhance learning and teaching
▲ A willingness to continuously examine one's own assumptions, beliefs, and practices
▲ Trusting people and their judgment
▲ Involving stakeholders in management processes
▲ Professional development as an integral part of school improvement

**Performance Indicators**
The administrator facilitates processes and engages in activities ensuring:
▲ All individuals are treated with fairness, dignity, and respect
▲ Students and staff feel valued and important
▲ Barriers to student learning are identified, clarified, and addressed
▲ Diversity is considered in developing learning experiences
▲ Lifelong learning is encouraged and modeled

▲ Problems are confronted and resolved in a timely manner
▲ Human resource functions support the attainment of school goals
▲ A variety of sources of information is used to make decisions
▲ Operational procedures are designed and managed to maximize opportunity for successful learning
▲ Operational plans and procedures to achieve the vision and goals of the school are in place
▲ Potential problems and opportunities are identified
▲ Effective group-process and consensus-building skills are used
▲ Stakeholders are involved in decisions affecting schools
▲ Diversity is recognized and valued
▲ Opportunities for staff to develop collaborative skills are provided

Janice Freeman has served as principal of Evans Middle School for three months. When she accepted the assignment, the superintendent informed her that the enrollment at Evans was increasing an average of 15 students per grade level each year. However, budget constraints would not allow additional staff. He also stated that he was aware of her creativity and felt that she would be able to design a program plan to serve students at Evans in a manner that would allow achievement to continue at the level of excellence that parents had come to expect.

Principal Freeman, challenged by the information received from the superintendent, began to ponder how to deliver the same quality of service with additional students and no additional staff. As she deliberated the issue, many ideas came to mind. The one that seemed most appropriate for the situation was team teaching. She thought that by implementing this concept she could capitalize on the strengths of each teacher, have larger classes, and thereby address the increase in enrollment. Also, this concept would allow teachers to select a schoolwide theme and work together in departments, thereby easing the workload. More to the point, team teaching was a concept that she loved, had worked with as a teacher, and had always stated she would implement if she became principal.

Although energized by the notion of implementing the concept, Janice is somewhat concerned about how the faculty will react to her plan. She realized from past meetings that several factions exist within the faculty. There is a core group of influential teachers who seem to be somewhat skeptical of her ideas. In addition, there is a group that has no ambition, always needs directions, and has to be coerced to teach their classes. She wonders if this group will be able or willing to take on the challenge of implementing such a concept in the time allotted.

Principal Freeman is also aware of a parent group that is not particularly fond of new instructional program ideas; they feel it is unsettling to the children. Then there is the union. As she pondered the concept she thought, "Maybe I can just direct the teachers to implement the concept; after all, the superintendent is expecting me to come up with a new program. I do have one group of teachers who has really been supportive and seems to be enthusiastic and eager for new program ideas. I can depend on them to assist me."

Nevertheless, she realized that it is important for new ideas to be presented in a way that will gain the most support and leave the entire faculty with a positive outlook for the school year. Her basic concern is how best to approach the faculty in the upcoming meeting.

## REFLECTIVE THINKING AND SCENARIO ANALYSIS

1. What barriers to student learning are identifiable in the scenario?
2. Do the concerns expressed by Principal Freeman indicate a particular theoretical persuasion? What management decision must she make if her primary concerns are teaching and learning?
3. What are some reasons you would give for advising Principal Freeman to consider the feelings of teachers prior to presenting the concept in an open faculty meeting? What adult learning and professional development models might she consider?
4. What are some strategies that you would recommend for Principal Freeman to use in establishing an effective working relationship between the various groups of teachers? Base your response on factors that are relevant to a principal desirous of formulating faculty teams and using professional development as an integral part of school improvement.

## ADDRESSING THE ISSUES

Select the one best answer to the following questions:

1. Which of the following approaches is likely to be of least benefit to Principal Freeman?

    a. Developing an in-depth knowledge of group interaction before the next faculty meeting.

    b. Utilizing her position as principal to ensure that the concept of team teaching is accepted by the entire faculty.

    c. Identifying the forces in the external environment of the school that may affect the implementation of the team teaching concept.

    d. Engaging the teacher groups in an open dialogue regarding the concept of team teaching.

2. Which of the following should be a critical factor for Principal Freeman to consider relative to having the faculty support the attainment of school goals?

    a. Completing tasks and fostering her ideas.

    b. Understanding that what is good for the organization is good for the employee.

    c. Realizing that each teacher is a valuable member of the school faculty.

    d. Not being a proponent of the bureaucratic system.

3. Which of the following is likely to produce the most success for Principal Freeman?

    a. Utilizing expert power, as she appears to be very knowledgeable about team teaching.

    b. Utilizing legitimate power, as the maturity level of the faculty suggests that such power is warranted.

    c. Utilizing a combination of expert and charismatic power, as this combination would allow teachers to acquire knowledge about the process of team teaching while developing a level of acceptance of a new instructional approach.

    d. None of the above.

**4.** If Principal Freeman were to encourage parents and individuals from the local business community to join teachers in the exploration of her new idea, engaging them in goal setting, planning, and problem solving, which of the following would best describe her leadership behavior?

   **a.** Practicing a leadership approach advocated by individuals who seek to solve problems quickly in a very definitive manner.

   **b.** Practicing a leadership approach advocated by individuals who seek to build a learning community and solve problems working with others.

   **c.** Practicing a leadership approach advocated by individuals who are autocratic and directive in administering organizations.

   **d.** None of the above.

## DISCUSSION OF THE SOLUTION

1. Evans Middle School has a number of known informal groups within the organization. One is a core group made up of long-standing, valuable members of the faculty, another an enthusiastic, more eager group of first- and second-year teachers. Both groups, as well as others, will voice their own ideas regarding the new program. Knowledge of group interaction is and will continue to be of tremendous benefit to Principal Freeman. Therefore, she should have a working knowledge of the interaction that is likely to occur between the groups.

Implementation of a team teaching model will require a large number of individuals to work cooperatively, both inside and outside the organization. The faculty, which influences the transformation process, will play a major role in the successful implementation of the new program, and parents will have to accept the instructional concepts. Principal Freeman seems to recognize these factors and is greatly concerned with two-way communication, which will assist her in establishing a bond between the teacher groups and communicating the team teaching concept to the larger community. She is likely to be very effective if she opens the lines of communication between the groups, conducts some bonding activities, and gets them collectively involved in the decision-making process. Identifying and respecting the forces of the external environment are also likely to prove to be beneficial as decision acceptance inside and outside of the school is vital to the success of the program.

The principles of classical theory are not likely to lead to effective implementation and should not receive the attention of the principal. If Principal Freeman uses a classical approach in this situation, she would likely utilize her position as principal to ensure that her ideas are implemented. Because she is the principal, she can use position power to force implementation of the concept. Bureaucratic principles are based on a hierarchy, top-down management, strictness in policy and following established rules, and advocating a very controlled environment (Lunenburg & Ornstein, 1996). However, this structural approach is least likely to work at Evans, as the change proposed is an instructional one that requires teacher acceptance and cooperation for effective development and implementation. The suggested response to question 1 is **(b)**.

2. Principal Freeman seems to be somewhat concerned about task completion. However, it does not appear to be her major concern. There is no evidence to suggest that

she is putting the organization before members of the faculty. True, she has made a program selection (team teaching) without the involvement of the faculty, but she does not project the attitude that "what is good for the organization is good for the employee," a principle of Classical Theory. Instead, as she prepares to introduce this new program concept, she displays concern about the interaction and welfare of the faculty, individually and collectively. Teaching and learning appear to be her primary concern.

The principal also appears to be aware of the informal groups that exist in the school, as well as their receptivity or lack of it. She is obviously concerned about human relations and the effect the influence of individuals and informal groups will have on the success of the team teaching program. If a difference is to be made in the school's program, it will be necessary for her to make some basic assumptions and carefully consider how logical the connections are between those assumptions and the behavior of the people in the organization. Her selection of the team teaching program indicates that she has made a basic assumption, and now she is assessing her options relative to making a connection between her assumptions and the behavior of the people in the organization, an excellent approach for an effective principal to use.

Each teacher is a valuable member of the faculty, even those who are not receptive to the new ideas of Principal Freeman. Therefore, the principal should be as concerned about the emotional state of those individuals as she is about the plan she wants to implement. After all, in the final analysis, all teachers will be asked to implement the program, and its success will depend on their attitudes and actions. The fact that teachers in a learning organization are leaders in their own right is a critical factor for Principal Freeman to consider. The suggested response to question 2 is **(c)**.

3. In the implementation of the team teaching plan, Principal Freeman might use several sources of power: legitimate, charismatic, or expert power. However, to be successful, she must choose a source of power and leadership approach that reflect her knowledge of the situation and the forces of resistance to her ideas. When change is introduced, it often meets with resistance. This resistance might occur at an organizational level and/or an individual level. The resistant forces occurring at either level must be analyzed and factored into the implementation process if the change is to be effective. We saw evidence of this possibility in the behavior of Mrs. Harmon in Scenario 5.

Principal Freeman should avoid using legitimate power, as the maturity level of one of the groups suggests that such an approach would not be effective. She would be using her legitimate power if she goes into the next faculty meeting and tells the faculty that they are going to begin team teaching and using themes, regardless of their concerns. She would be exercising her bureaucratic authority to impose her agenda on the faculty. If she does that, the faculty might change only because their supervisor is telling them to do so, and the effectiveness of the plan is likely to be compromised. Legitimate power-type actions tend to minimize human relations and rationality (French, 1993).

Motivating the teachers toward implementing the team teaching instructional plan appears to be the challenge. Therefore, the approach used by Principal Freeman should be inclusive, one that develops congruence among the elements of the system, and as many segments of the school family as possible should be involved. The greater the congruence, the greater will be the degree of effectiveness. Principal Freeman's behavior seems to demonstrate that she has a cognitive and humanistic perspective on motivation. The cognitive perspective suggests that we are motivated from within to make sense of the world as we perceive it, stay in control of our life, and establish an inner direction (Owens, 1995). Principal Freeman is likely to achieve the greatest success using a combination of charismatic and expert power. The suggested response to question 3 is **(c)**.

4. A program change of this magnitude is a major departure from present conditions and is best undertaken with a great deal of faculty involvement. Teachers need a high level of participation. Committees consisting of individuals from all segments of the faculty could be formed. The formation of committees would open the lines of communication between groups on the faculty, as well as those in the community. In this way, the entire school community would feel involved in the planning process, and Principal Freeman would be well on her way to establishing a learning organization at Evans.

Participation in the decision-making process allows the staff to develop a feeling of belonging, meet esteem needs, and develop ownership for decisions made. When all stakeholders take ownership for a decision, they are likely to support the implementation of that decision. Individuals who must assume responsibility for the implementation of a decision, as well as those who will be affected by the decision, should participate in reaching that decision. The suggested response to question 4 is **(b)**.

## SUMMARY AND CONCLUSION

Principal Freeman is concerned about how to approach the Evans Middle School faculty regarding the implementation of her team teaching plan. Having presented ideas in previous faculty meetings, she is aware that, on the surface, the faculty is comprised of a number of informal groups and that one of the groups is not very receptive to her ideas. As a result of this assessment, she has developed concerns about the possible faculty reactions to her plan. Her concerns are justified inasmuch as informal groups form power sources that can positively or negatively impact the actions taken by the formal leadership.

Conflict between the institutional elements and the individual elements often influences the behavior of people in the organization. Therefore, Principal Freeman must be keenly aware of the effects of the use of her power, the influence of the experienced faculty members, and the behavior they may display as a result of any decisions that are made. She must apply motivational theories that inform approaches that can be used in removing barriers to faculty resistance and/or success in the team teaching approach. Operational plans and procedures must be outlined and managed to maximize opportunity for successful implementation of the team teaching program.

One activity that is likely to be necessary is the implementation of a professional development program that provides the assurance that all team members are compatible and have the skills necessary to implement the team teaching concept. Another is inclusion of parents in the planning process. Considering that student learning is the primary purpose for implementing the concept, the school leader must manage the process to ensure the involvement of all stakeholders. Then learning occurs in a productive environment.

## SCENARIO 8
## ONE OF THE BUS CONTRACTS HAS BEEN CANCELED

### STANDARD 3

A school administrator is an educational leader who promotes the success of all students by ensuring management of the organization, operations, and resources for a safe, efficient, and effective learning environment.

### STANDARD 4

A school administrator is an educational leader who promotes the success of all students by collaborating with families and community members, responding to diverse community interests and needs, and mobilizing community resources.

*In Scenario 8, Superintendent Wallace is challenged with a situation that seems to escalate with each decision. The reader will want to carefully note Superintendent Wallace's leader behavior as it relates to management of self, trust, meaning, and attention. The influences in the internal and external environments of the district on leader behavior should also be given attention.*

### ISLLC Standards Indicators Exhibited in Scenario 8

**Knowledge Indicators**
The administrator has knowledge and understanding of:
▲ School cultures
▲ Adult motivational theories
▲ Management, evaluation, and assessment strategies
▲ The change process for systems, organizations, and individuals
▲ Legal issues impacting school operations
▲ Community resources
▲ Community relations and marketing strategies
▲ Diversity and its meaning for educational programs
▲ Theories and models of organizations and the principles of organizational development
▲ Operational procedures at the school and district level
▲ Human resources management and development
▲ Emerging issues and trends that potentially impact the school community
▲ The conditions and dynamics of the diverse school community

**Disposition Indicators**
The administrator believes in, values, and is committed to:
▲ Student learning as the fundamental purpose of schooling
▲ The benefits that diversity brings to the school and community
▲ Making management decisions to enhance learning and teaching

▲ Taking risks to improve schools
▲ Accepting responsibility
▲ Schools operating as an integral part of the larger community
▲ Collaboration and communication with families
▲ Families as partners in the education of their children
▲ Resources of the family and community needing to be brought to bear on the education of students
▲ A willingness to continuously examine one's own assumptions, beliefs, and practices
▲ Trusting people and their judgment
▲ Involving stakeholders in management processes
▲ Professional development as an integral part of school improvement
▲ An informed public

**Performance Indicators**
The administrator facilitates processes and engages in activities ensuring that:
▲ All individuals are treated with fairness, dignity, and respect
▲ Students and staff feel valued and important
▲ Barriers to student learning are identified, clarified, and addressed
▲ Diversity is considered in developing learning experiences
▲ Lifelong learning is encouraged and modeled
▲ Problems are confronted and resolved in a timely manner
▲ Human resource functions support the attainment of school goals
▲ A variety of sources of information is used to make decisions
▲ Operational procedures are designed and managed to maximize opportunity for successful learning
▲ Operational plans and procedures to achieve the vision and goals of the school are in place
▲ Potential problems and opportunities are identified
▲ Effective group-process and consensus-building skills are used
▲ Stakeholders are involved in decisions affecting schools
▲ Diversity is recognized and valued
▲ Opportunities for staff to develop collaborative skills are provided

On July 1, 1997, Alice Wallace became superintendent of the Arrowhead School District. She began her tenure by establishing a good relationship with the entire community, her administrative staff, and the teachers in the district. Her opening presentation to district administrators was received with a thunderous standing ovation. She followed that meeting with a visit to each school. During her visit to the schools, she engaged in dialogue with the principal, PTA members, and other individuals who were available. Then she held town meetings in each section of the community, met with the leadership of each bargaining unit, and hosted a luncheon for political, religious, and business leaders of the larger community. Everyone expressed great expectations for her as the new superintendent. In fact, one could sense that people throughout the district were charged with newfound positive energy.

The new school year was fast approaching, and she had planned well. Everything was in order. The media had indicated that the district was poised for a successful opening. Then, on August 3, just four weeks before the first day of the 1998–99 school year, the director of transportation advised Superintendent Wallace that a bus-contracting agency that serviced 27 bus routes had canceled their contract. The bus routes in question provided service to students from the areas of the district where people felt they never received equitable treatment. At once, Superintendent Wallace took charge of the situation. She advised the Arrowhead Board of Education of the problem and assured them that a new contract would be obtained prior to the opening of school. A similar announcement was made to the community.

Superintendent Wallace then contacted the contracting agency in question and asked them to reconsider, but to no avail. She contacted other contracting agencies and attempted to enter into a contractual agreement with them, but because of the late notice, they were unable to offer the district bus services. Contacts with the State Department of Education and other districts in the state yielded no positive results. Over the next three weeks, she held several meetings in the community, assuring parents that a solution was being sought and that the problem would be resolved before the first day of school. However, as the first day of school approached with no solution in sight, the community meetings grew increasingly hostile. Even though the director of transportation was very knowledgeable about transportation issues and had served the district for a number of years, he had very little involvement in the community meetings. Principals of affected schools also attended the meetings; however, they were not invited to participate in the discussions.

Often the superintendent held meetings with the director of transportation to obtain status reports, and the results were always the same, "We are working on getting additional buses, and we will have them by opening day." Weekly the superintendent made a similar report to the board and community.

After three weeks passed with no additional buses being secured, the superintendent developed an alternate plan. The plan required a double schedule for some buses to return middle-school students to their homes as late as 5:30 P.M. This was an acceptable practice until the fall ended, and students were reaching their homes after dark. Parents throughout the district, even those not affected, demanded a change in the bus schedule. The newspaper reported that the district was returning to its past practices.

## REFLECTIVE THINKING AND SCENARIO ANALYSIS

1. What are the major leadership issues facing Superintendent Wallace? Relate your response to the leadership skills and attributes presented in this chapter, as well as in Chapter 1.
2. What, if anything, was flawed in the statement Superintendent Wallace made to the board and community? What statement(s) would you have made?
3. What are the leadership issues pertaining to Superintendent Wallace's involvement (micromanagement) in the day-to-day operations of the district?
4. What are some of the emerging issues that could potentially impact the total school community? Provide a rationale for your response.
5. How important are community relations strategies and practices in a situation of this nature? Explain your response.
6. What role should various principals and central office administrators play in resolving an issue of this nature?

## ADDRESSING THE ISSUES

Select the one best answer to the following questions:

1. Which of the following leader behaviors most likely produced the unsuccessful outcome experienced by Superintendent Wallace?

   a. She was highly structured and provided specific directions to her staff, keeping in control of the situation and closely supervising subordinates.

   b. She was highly structured in her approach, but she was not very directive. She personally handled the situation from beginning to end, only collaborating with subordinates when necessary.

   c. She displayed trust, respect, and concern for her subordinates, and she was highly structured in her approach to completing the task.

   d. She displayed trust, respect, and concern for her subordinates, allowing them to utilize their expertise in reaching a solution to the bus issue.

2. In order to maintain the positive energy that has been generated and to positively influence the internal and external forces of the organization, which of the following skills and/or attributes would be needed most by the Arrowhead superintendent?

   a. Interpersonal skills sufficient to mobilize community resources.

   b. Communication skills sufficient to collaborate with the board of education, staff, and parents in the community.

   c. Personal motivation sufficient to take the necessary steps in addressing a difficult challenge.

   d. All of the above.

3. Which of the following descriptions of the superintendent's response to organizational influences best describes the appropriate leader behavior?

   a. The superintendent enthusiastically sought a resolution to the problem.

   b. The superintendent did not effectively utilize the expertise of her staff.

   c. The superintendent took the appropriate actions with all district personnel.

   d. The superintendent displayed task-oriented behavior in seeking a solution.

4. Which of the following approaches would have been most appropriate for the superintendent of the Arrowhead School District to utilize in addressing the contractual issue?

   a. Remain in the background and delegate the task of finding a solution to staff.

   b. Personally assume responsibility for finding a solution.

   c. Work cooperatively with staff in finding a solution and refrain from getting directly involved.

   d. Take legal action against the contractor who canceled.

5. Which of the following actions taken by Superintendent Wallace was ill advised?

   a. The communication approach used.

   b. The content of the communiqué.

    c. The meetings held with the director of transportation.

    d. The decision-making approach.

6. Which of the following solutions would not be plausible?

    a. Impacting the starting times of schools that were not affected by the canceled contract.

    b. Impacting any school necessary to reach a workable solution.

    c. Refraining from impacting the starting times of schools not affected by the canceled contract.

    d. Changing the opening and closing times of all schools in the district sufficient to afford students impacted by the canceled contract the necessary bus service.

## DISCUSSION OF THE SOLUTION

1. Superintendent Wallace was highly structured in her approach, but she was not very directive with her subordinates. She personally handled the situation from beginning to end, only collaborating with subordinates when necessary. It is obvious that she deemed the issue to be very important, as she immediately took charge of the situation. When she was made aware of the problem, she responded quickly, feeling she had to find a solution. Her first action was to call the President of the Board of Education and advise him of the matter. Then she directed the staff to schedule a meeting with parents in the affected community. She met frequently with the director of transportation and kept all members of the board informed of progress being made toward a solution. Nevertheless, the manner in which she responded caused additional problems. She focused on the needs of the organization and task completion, giving little consideration to individuals on her staff.

    In addressing the issue, Superintendent Wallace did not effectively involve members of her staff. The director of transportation was very knowledgeable about transportation issues and had served in the district for years, but he was not charged with the responsibility of finding a solution to the problem. Principals of affected schools attended the community meetings, but they were not invited to participate in the discussions. In a learning community, all individuals participate in the decision-making process. There is a sense of shared responsibility for the success of the organization.

    Superintendent Wallace took charge of the situation without considering and utilizing the expertise of members of her staff. She was so focused on the goal that she failed to realize the benefit to be derived from the involvement of others. The superintendent, whether intentional or not, employed tactics that were deeply rooted in Classical Theory. She took control of the situation in order to reach the desired goal, but demonstrated a lack of trust in the ability of subordinates and displayed the belief that she knew the best way of solving the problem. In some ways, her approach to finding a solution to the problem magnified the problem. Perhaps she should have given more consideration to the skills and attributes of members of her staff. Leaders who are high on both initiating structure and consideration tend to be rated as effective by subordinates (Halpin, 1956). The suggested response to question 1 is **(b)**.

    2. Although district personnel and the community showed support for their new superintendent, the support was based on perception. True support will only come

after she has demonstrated effective leadership skills. Perceptions are sometimes short lived. To truly be accepted and respected as the educational leader of the Arrowhead community, she will need to utilize all three skills.

Her communication skills will need to be exceptional; constantly communicating to the staff and community in a manner that will influence the development of a shared vision will be necessary. Her interpersonal skills will need to be strong. Constantly interacting with a variety of individuals and groups, she will have to present herself in a manner that will convince all concerned individuals that she is fair and can be trusted to make decisions that are in the best interest of all students. Personal motivation will be needed because she is functioning in an unknown community, which already is a major challenge.

The transportation issue is the first real issue in which the superintendent will have an opportunity to demonstrate her true leadership skills to the community. Through her handling of this issue, she will also have an opportunity to state in an action-oriented manner the value of the staff and how they will be involved in her administration. The suggested response to question 2 is **(d)**.

3. The superintendent did not effectively utilize the expertise of her staff. She enthusiastically sought a resolution to the problem and shifted all the accountability to herself. Specifically, she did not effectively assess the external organizational influences or utilize the services of the director of transportation and building principals. Principals could have assessed community sentiment and facilitated a calm atmosphere. Also, they could have been asked to generate suggestions to resolve the problem. This is the type of involvement that exists in a learning organization. The leader creates a feeling of shared decision making and shared ownership of the problem. One must consider those most affected by the problem. Being new to the district and an unknown entity, the superintendent getting involved in such a direct manner isolated principals.

The behavior of principals may have been somewhat guarded, as they had not had time to build a relationship with the new superintendent. It is possible that they could have felt as if they were not a vital part of the new administration. The superintendent missed an opportunity to influence individuals who had established contacts in the community to take the lead in solving a problem that affected them. Such an action may have yielded better results. The Director of Transportation could have taken the lead; the principals could have served as liaisons, and the superintendent could have served as a support system to both. Increased productivity results from a participative leadership style (Lewin, 1951). The suggested response to question 3 is **(c)**.

4. Although the superintendent should have been very concerned with finding a solution to this problem, her approach should have been one of working cooperatively with the staff in finding a solution and refraining from getting directly involved. Superintendent Wallace put herself too close to the line of fire in attempting to resolve the bus issue and failed to give her subordinates the opportunity to perform their assigned tasks. The leader should become knowledgeable of his/her strengths and weaknesses, as well as those of his/her staff, and manage them effectively. If this is not the case, the staff is likely to feel that their opinions are not valued and will be reluctant to share information or participate in reaching decisions. Superintendent Wallace appears to have excellent leadership qualities but failed to share the leadership role with members of her team. At the outset, she should have trusted the expertise of members of her staff

and allowed them an opportunity to perform their responsibilities as team members. The suggested response to question 4 is **(c)**.

5. Superintendent Wallace is an administrator with considerable confidence in herself. However, many issues that are out of the control of the superintendent and his/her staff will arise in school situations. It is for this reason that an effective leader manages self. Superintendent Wallace should never have given an assurance to the board and community that the bus problem would be resolved by the first day of school. She projected a solution to a problem issue in which there were unknown variables over which she had no control. She promised something that she could not deliver. When addressing a situation of this nature, information should be provided based on facts, not assumptions or hopes. The suggested response to question 5 is **(b)**.

6. In seeking a solution to this problematic situation, Superintendent Wallace is going to have to appeal to the entire community and push for unity. Any plan crafted will necessarily have to affect the entire district and be viewed across the district as a plan that benefits the district as a whole. The superintendent must work cooperatively with representatives from all four communities and secure their assistance in acquiring acceptance of a workable plan. Engaging members of all areas of the district would allow any decision reached to become a districtwide decision.

It would not be plausible to refrain from impacting the schools not affected; such a plan would send a message that would not be well received in some sections of the district. Such a solution would, most assuredly, further polarize the communities complaining of past inequities. The suggested response to question 6 is **(c)**.

## SUMMARY AND CONCLUSION

Superintendent Wallace seemed to have had good intentions from the very beginning of an admittedly difficult job. Her behavior, though somewhat problematic, is understandable; she really wanted to resolve the transportation issue. She knew that individuals were supportive of her from the outset, and she was perhaps threatened by the notion of allowing an incident so early in her tenure to damage that confidence and trust. Also, she was aware of the expectations that were being held for her and intended to manage the attention and trust of the people. Consequently, she resorted to position power and an authoritarian style of leadership.

Her plan failed to take into account the culture of the district or the state. Not fully aware of the culture of the district or the state, she was unable to accurately assess the actions of others. At best, she could only apply practices that had worked well in the past and trust that people would do the right thing. Unfortunately, the approaches utilized were not effective, and the influences in the external environment prevailed.

It is important that school leaders make decisions that will positively affect both the organization and the people the organization serves. In order to do this, leaders must be aware of the culture and internal and external influences and be able to predict the behavior of people. This is extremely difficult for any leader, but particularly difficult for one who is new to a district. The central issue of concern is the fact that Superintendent Wallace took too much of a role in resolving the busing situation. She made the right contacts with her staff and the public, but she failed to factor the human side of the equation into her efforts. The results were community meetings from which the public left angered and without a solution. The staff, namely school principals, felt they did not have a voice, and therefore, they did not actively work toward the goal. Also, the skills of the director of transportation were ineffectively utilized.

## CHAPTER SUMMARY

The organization is a system in which people function to achieve established goals. The effective leader manages this system in ways that allow the organization to achieve its goals while the needs of employees are being met. However, in an organization there are many factors that influence the manner in which individuals and groups behave and the extent to which they achieve the established goals. Among these are leader behavior, environmental conditions, and motivational influences. In order to provide effective leadership, the leader needs to acquire knowledge and understanding of these factors and influences. To some extent, he/she can obtain this knowledge and understanding from theories. The principles embedded in early traditional theories (Classical, Social System, and Open Systems) have laid much of the groundwork for understanding leadership practices that are advocated for leaders of today's schools.

Classical theorists focus on the organization and the task the organization is desirous of performing. Little attention or consideration is given to the worker or the needs of the worker. Problems are not solved through people, but rather by the leader who views himself/herself as the problem solver. Production in an efficient and effective manner is the charge.

Following the principles of another early theory, Social System, the leader gives more consideration to the worker and recognizes the presence of informal groups that function in the organization and the power and influence of these groups. This theory views the organization from a holistic perspective, in part, and considers the interrelationships between and among the parts. To address these entities in an effective manner, leader behavior changes to a more considerate style because leaders recognize that production depends on the worker and the extent to which the worker is motivated to complete a given task. Democratic principles and open lines of communication guide leader behavior.

Then there is Open Social Systems Theory, which calls to our attention the fact that influences from the external environment of the organization affect the transformation process inside the organization. In order for the goals of the organization to be attained, the leader must be able when necessary to adjust the internal transformation process to the forces in the external environment.

The above-mentioned theories, coupled with several others that speak to organizations being two dimensional (institutional and individual), the motivation of followers (desire to work and individual needs), and the type of behavior exhibited by the leader (assumptions about self and others) have provided a foundation for the development of current leadership practices. For the most part, they have led us into an era that focuses on the learning organization.

Leaders functioning in learning organizations operate with a shared vision and a compelling mission, acting on the accepted notion that collaboration is essential to their success and the success of the school. Time and attention are devoted to establishing and building relationships with teachers, students, parents, other professionals, and members of the community. The disposition of the leader illustrates a belief that student learning is the fundamental purpose of schools, professional development an integral part of school improvement, and collaborative relationships with all stakeholders essential to organizational effectiveness. Leaders of today's schools must have knowledge and understanding of the influences that impact organizational behavior and be able to apply these management principles.

## MOVING INTO PRACTICE

Review the scenarios in Chapter 2. Using the pros and cons of the various situations, identify several approaches that you would use to address the following school related-issues in an actual situation. Project yourself into the role of the principal and take care to formulate a rationale for your selected behavior.

- Describe the process you would use to formulate a set of goals with individual faculty members, an entire faculty, and/or members of various community groups.
- Describe the approach you would use to acquire the support necessary to resolve an issue similar to the bus contract cancellation in Arrowhead.
- Describe a process in which you would take leadership in enhancing the role of teachers and parents in designing curriculum and implementing an effective instructional program.
- Formulate a list of school characteristics that are negatively impacting the teaching and learning process in a school where you are principal, and identify an organizational structure that you would advocate for that school. Take care to provide a theoretical base for your selection of the organizational structure.
- Cite four ways in which the school and community serve one another as resources.
- Describe a school environment where you would feel pleased to serve as principal.
- Describe the issues from the cases that offer you the best opportunity to utilize your leadership skills and attributes.

## Acquiring an Understanding of Self

▶ What do you believe about schools?
▶ What do you believe about children?
▶ What do you believe about people in general?
▶ How do you behave in your current role? How does that behavior compare with the expectations individuals hold for the role?

## Suggested Readings

Barth, R. S. (1990). *Improving schools from within: Teachers, parents, and principals can make a difference*. San Francisco: Jossey-Bass.

Bennis, W., & Biederman, P. (1997). *Organizing genius*. Reading, MA: Addison Wesley Longman.

Greenberg, J. (1996). *Managing behavior in organizations*. Upper Saddle River, NJ: Prentice Hall.

Senge, P. M. (1990). *The fifth discipline*. New York: Doubleday.

Sergiovanni, T. J. (1994). *Building community in schools*. San Francisco: Jossey-Bass.

Short, P., & Greer, J. (1997). *Leadership in empowered schools: Themes from innovative efforts*. Upper Saddle River, NJ: Merrill/Prentice Hall.

# 3

COMMUNICATION IN TODAY'S
SCHOOLS

## The Importance of Effective Communication

In today's schools, the importance of communication practices cannot be overemphasized. Through effective communication, relationships are built, trust is established, and respect is gained. When the leader is an effective communicator, the vision and mission of the school can be effectively shared with staff, parents, students, and the larger community. "In the areas of leadership there is no talent more essential than one's ability to communicate" (Guarino, 1974, p. 1). "Communication is the lifeblood of the school; it is a process that links the individual, the group, and the organization" (Lunenburg & Ornstein, 1996, p. 176).

As the leader seeks to share the vision of the school and achieve the agreed upon goals and objectives, he/she is constantly advocating, nurturing, delegating responsibility, and developing the potential of followers. He/she also seeks their cooperation to sustain a school culture and instructional program conducive to student learning and staff professional growth (ISLLC, 1996). In carrying out these activities, the leader uses various forms of communication.

In the daily operation of the school, leaders not only communicate messages, but they receive, monitor, and seek them. Studies indicate that school leaders spend up to 80 percent of their time involved in communication with other members of the organization, parents, and members of the community (Kmetz & Willower, 1982; Sobel & Ornstein, 1996). Therefore, tantamount to the school operating in an efficient and effective manner is the leader's ability to communicate with people. A leader who is sensitive and uses a reliable network of communication patterns with which members of the organization are familiar and comfortable is not only likely to be effective, but he/she will also transform the climate of the school into a pleasant place to work.

The purpose of this chapter is to emphasize the need for school leaders to be effective communicators. In so doing, the communication process will be described, barriers to effective communication will be identified, and the relationship of communication to select ISLLC Standards will be demonstrated. In addition, the importance of listening skills will be stressed, and strategies that reduce defensive barriers to communication effectiveness will be identified. In substance, communication will be viewed as the link that ties together the leadership processes of decision making, conflict management, and change.

The scenarios in the chapter, which characterize ISLLC Standards 1, 2, and 3, serve a twofold purpose; they offer examples of how communication effectiveness can enhance the progress of the school, moving it toward its vision and mission and how the lack of it can prove to be problematic. Analyzing these scenarios, the reader will be able to experience, through practical school situations, the importance of communication in terms of both the content of a message and the feelings being conveyed by the sender of the message.

## The Communication Process

The communication process involves transmitting information from a person (the sender) to another person or group (the receivers) and may occur verbally or nonverbally. When a message is transmitted using spoken language face-to-face, over a public address system, in a telephone conversation, in a memo, in a letter, or electronically, verbal communication is occurring. Any form of communication involving the use of words, oral or written, is considered verbal.

When a message is transmitted without the use of words, the form of communication is considered nonverbal. Nonverbal behaviors are very important to the communication process, for more than half of what is communicated is

**FIGURE 3.1   The communication process**

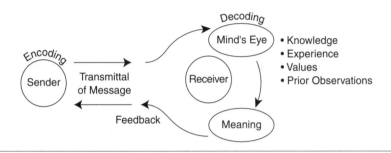

not conveyed by words but by body language (Sobel & Ornstein, 1996). The manner in which the leader hesitates in his/her speech can reveal much about how he/she is feeling relative to a situation and so can the tone of voice. Certain ideas may be expressed in a loud tone, whereas others may be expressed in a mumbled tone. Hand movements, eye movements, and facial expressions are all actions that help to convey a message. Any activity that conveys a message between individuals is considered communication (Myers & Myers, 1982). Figure 3.1 graphically depicts the communication process.

Given that both words and nonverbal actions can insult, injure, and/or exalt, all of which interferes with the communication process, school leaders need to be aware of what they say and the way they portray themselves and be cognizant of actions that can make or break a situation. Body language and tone of voice should transmit the message in a manner that clearly indicates that both the meaning and feeling behind it are understood and appreciated.

## Transmitting the Message

In transmitting messages, the leader must realize that meaning is not in the words of the sender, but rather in the mind of the receiver. Meaning is not transmitted; the receiver gives the message meaning. The receiver gives meaning to the message based on his/her background, knowledge, experience, values, and prior observations. In some instances, because of differences in these areas, the same words hold different meanings for different people, causing a problem in semantics. Considering this factor, the sender must strive to encode the message, using symbols that will be most familiar to the receiver. The greater the agreement regarding the meaning of the symbols, the greater the probability of understanding existing between the two parties when the receiver decodes the message (Gibson, Ivancevich, & Donnelly, 1976).

The agreement on the meaning of the message can be enhanced through two-way interactive forms of communication and repetitiveness. Such is the case with face-to-face meetings where both verbal and nonverbal clues are a

part of the transmittal process. Television presentations, videotape presentations, and telephone conversations also allow the type of interaction that
enhances the possibility that the receiver will give the message the meaning
that is intended by the sender. Letters, memoranda, and other one-way forms
of communication do not allow verbal and nonverbal clues to assist in the
transmittal process, and therefore, the message is subject to interpretation. It is
advisable in most school situations to use multiple forms of communication, as
repetitiveness improves effectiveness.

Rogers and Farson (1995) offer several other suggestions in this arena. They
suggest that the leader must be available, approachable, and able to listen intel-
ligently and carefully to others, conveying the feeling that he/she is as concerned about them as the situation that is being addressed. Further, they offer
that the leader must be attentive to both the content of the message and the
feelings of the sender. The feedback given the sender must make clear that the
message was appreciated in terms of both its meaning and the feelings with
which it was conveyed. More specifically, to be an effective communicator, the
leader must be an active listener, acquiring the total meaning of the message
and observing the underlying feelings of the message, while noting and being
sensitive to all verbal and nonverbal clues displayed by the sender. One way for
the leader to become an active listener is to view communication as a people
process, rather than a language process (Gibbs, 1995), and develop a clear
understanding of the networks used in a social system to transmit messages. To
provide a deeper understanding of the need for the leader to be an active listener and to assist in that process, some active listening skills are summarized
in Table 3.1.

## Transmitting Messages in a Social System

Information in schools (open social systems) is transmitted through formal and
informal networks. Formal networks are the means of transmitting messages
sanctioned by the organization in accordance with its hierarchy. Informal networks emerge as individuals in the organization interact with each other in
ways that do not reflect the organization's hierarchy. Such an approach is likely
to be taken by the informal groups discussed in Chapter 2. The leader must be
knowledgeable of both networks and recognize that the network being used
to transmit information is essential to goal attainment. The following are examples of how these networks function in school settings.

If the principal holds a faculty meeting and shares information regarding the
new reading program, the formal communication network is being used. The
formal network is also being used when the principal receives a message from
the superintendent and passes the message to teachers who, in turn, pass it to
students. However, members of the faculty interacting personally may use the
informal network. If Jackie (a science teacher at Weaver High School) advises

**TABLE 3.1   The active listener**

| OBJECTIVE OF THE LISTENER | ACTIVITY PERFORMED | IMPLICATIONS OR END RESULT |
| --- | --- | --- |
| Understand the message | Grasp the facts and feelings | The sender of the message is assisted in presenting the message. |
| Demonstrate respect for the potential worth of the speaker | Demonstrate a positive attitude toward the sender of the message and for its content | The sender is less defensive, more democratic, less authoritarian, and more open to experiences. |
| Listen with sensitivity | Demonstrate the willingness to change | Information is acquired about people; positive relations are built, and attitudes are constructively altered. |
| Reduce any threat that might exist | Create a climate that is not critical, evaluative, or demoralizing | Defensiveness is reduced, and the individual feels safe enough to address new values and experiences. |
| View the issue in an objective manner | Refrain from being directive and influencing a position | One can listen with understanding and be open to change. |
| Listen for total meaning and remain sensitive | Seek to understand the content of the message and the feeling underlying the message, noting the nonverbal actions or cues of the speaker | Positive relationships are enhanced and the climate is supportive. |
| Convey interest in the speaker, respect for his/her position, and the fact that it is valid from his/her perspective | Demonstrate respect for the speaker through behavior | A tone is set for positive interaction to occur. |
| See the world from the speaker's perspective | Reflect on what the speaker seems to mean by his/her words | The climate is less emotional. |

SOURCE: Constructed from the readings of Carl Rogers and Richard E. Farson's "Active Listening" in David A. Kolb, Joyce S. Osland, and Irwin M. Rubin, *The Organizational Behavior Reader,* pp. 203–214.

her friend Betty (the school's reading coordinator) that a new reading program is going to be announced by the principal and Betty shares the information with James (who teaches reading), the informal network is in use.

Both networks have their place in the organization and, if effectively utilized, can enhance communication. However, the informal network, often referred to as the grapevine, does have some negative features, of which the most noted are distortion and rumors (unsubstantiated information). When the needs of faculty and staff are not met, rumors tend to spread and may signify that the leader is not meeting the informational needs of the faculty and staff. Although it is somewhat difficult and may be virtually impossible for a leader to eliminate all rumors, his/her knowledge of them can prove to be very beneficial.

The positive aspects of the grapevine are flexibility and speed in disseminating information. If used in a positive manner, the grapevine can help keep subordinates informed, give administrators insight into subordinates' attitudes, and provide a test arena for new ideas. However, in a school system, the objective of the communication process is to provide a means for the flow of information so that activities regarding goal attainment can be coordinated. Therefore, the formal network should be as effective as possible.

## The Flow of Communication in Schools

Communication in schools or school districts flows in several directions: downward, upward, horizontally, and diagonally. Downward communication often involves sending messages down the chain of command of the hierarchical structure. It is not atypical for school district personnel to use downward communication to keep employees informed, provide a sense of mission, impart information to subordinates regarding their performance, and orient new employees to the system. Upward communication occurs when individuals in subordinate roles send messages up the chain to their superordinates. Such communication is often in response to messages that have come down the chain of command. The receiver is providing feedback to individuals at a higher level. Upward communication is perhaps the form of communication that is most prone to filtering (sharing only select portions of a message). Sometimes subordinates resist providing leaders with unpopular or negative information. In such instances, there is a breakdown in communication as the message is modified, and the leader is only provided information that subordinates believe will be well received (Barge, 1994).

When individuals communicate with other individuals of the same status in the organization, horizontal communication is occurring. If individuals at one level in the organization communicate with individuals at another level in a different division or department, then the communication flow is considered diagonal. Communication in an organization can also be described as vertical. The term *vertical* is not used here to refer to the direction of the communication; rather, it describes a pattern that focuses on combining upward and downward communication, making leaders more visible through face-to-face contact. It is the effective flow of communication in schools that provides task coordination and furnishes emotional and social support among peers. The direction of the communication flow in a school district appears in Figure 3.2.

Each of these directions provides a means of effectively transmitting a message of a specific nature. Therefore, if breakdowns in communication are to be avoided, it is important for the leader to clearly understand which direction is most appropriate for use in any given situation.

**FIGURE 3.2  The flow of communication in a typical school district**

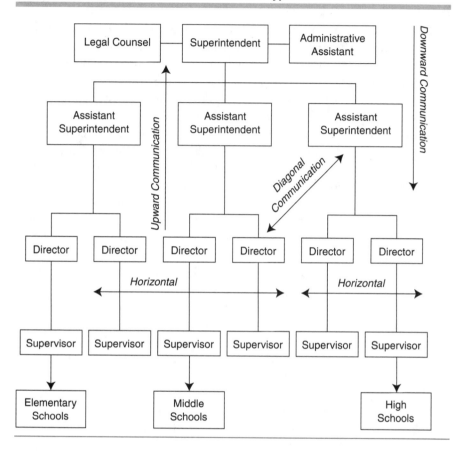

## The Participation of Individuals in the Network

In a social system, individuals have various means of exchanging information. Another pattern of communication flow in schools is the communication network connecting senders and receivers. The network system consists of five patterns, described as star, wheel, chain, circle, and Y, that illustrate degrees of centralization and structure that can occur between senders and receivers (Lewis, 1987). The most structured and centralized of the patterns is the wheel network. The wheel structure would allow the principal to discuss a curriculum issue with each teacher on the fourth-grade curriculum team.

The chain network, the second most restrictive, characterizes two people who communicate with each other and then with one other person. If the principal gets a directive from the superintendent regarding the curriculum issue previously discussed with members of the fourth-grade curriculum team and communicates that directive to the department chair of the fourth grade, then the chain network is operable.

Two-way communication and open accessibility to all network members best characterize the star network. This type of network is likely to be practiced in a learning community because status is not an issue, and the benefit to be derived is high faculty morale. If all fourth-grade curriculum team members communicate with each of the others regarding the development of the new curriculum, the star network would be operable.

With the circle pattern, there is also flexibility in the flow of communication as an individual communicates in two directions (right and left), there is equal communication, and each individual is considered a decision maker. This pattern might also be found in a learning community.

The last network in the pattern is the Y network, which allows communication similar to that of the chain. A principal may get directions from the superintendent to complete a task and give directions to each of two assistant principals who may be part of his staff. In such an instance, each assistant principal could discuss the task with the principal but not with each other or the superintendent.

Regardless of the pattern, it is important for the leader to have a communication plan that can be used to clearly articulate objectives and strategies that will achieve the vision and goals of the organization. This plan must be one that allows him/her to demonstrate a sense of understanding, trust, and respect for the potential worth of the individuals affiliated with the organization (ISLLC, 1996).

To reach the ISLLC Standards addressing the process of communication, school leaders must acquire accurate pictures of how they are perceived as communicators and constantly assess those pictures to refine their communication skills (Stech, 1983). It is also necessary that the leader acquire an understanding of the individuals with whom he/she works and be willing to continuously examine his/her own assumptions, beliefs, and practices (ISLLC, 1996). As was illustrated in Chapter 2, individuals who make up a school faculty can represent many different eras. To enhance communication effectiveness, it is important for the leader to recognize the variety of ideas, values, and cultures of people from these different eras. This is critical if leaders want followers to act on what is being transmitted, for every message sent by the leader will be given meaning by the receiver, based upon his/her characteristics and the conditions under which the message is being received (Barge, 1994).

Because of the above-mentioned factor, barriers can form, and depending on the nature of the situation, barriers can interfere with the effectiveness of the transmittal process and cause a breakdown in communication. By being sensitive to the barriers that exist and knowledgeable of strategies that can be employed to eliminate them, the leader enhances his/her communication

**FIGURE 3.3   Common barriers that frequently interfere with effective communication in schools**

**Information overload:** A situation wherein an individual receives more information than he/she can cognitively process in the given period.

**Status difference:** A situation wherein the free flow of information between personnel at different levels in the organization is inhibited because of their position. Note: The greater the disparity in status, the less likelihood that communication will occur openly and effectively.

**Semantics:** A situation wherein the spoken word has a different meaning for the receiver than the sender. Note: This is likely because of the varied backgrounds, knowledge, and experience of individuals in the organization.

**Filtering:** A situation wherein the message from the sender is altered (intentionally or unintentionally) or partially transmitted to the receiver.

**Paralanguage:** Situations wherein stress, the speed of speech, grunts, sighs, and other such clues that are vocal but not really verbal are displayed.

**Interpersonal relationships:** The quality of the relationships of the individuals interacting and the interpersonal style of the parties in a relationship.

effectiveness. A list of barriers that can interfere with effective communication in schools appears in Figure 3.3.

## Reducing Barriers to Communication

Leaders can often remove barriers, prevent breakdowns in communication, and improve communication effectiveness by:

1. establishing effective interpersonal relationships;
2. managing position power;
3. acquiring feedback; and
4. displaying empathy.

Using these strategies, the leader can safeguard against communication barriers while benefiting from a variety of ideas, values, and cultures as he/she works to influence the type of school climate that enhances decision quality and acceptance.

## Interpersonal Relationships

In a learning environment of the type suggested by the ISLLC Standards, to acquire information necessary to effectively administer the school, leaders have to interact and communicate with individuals inside the school, as well as in the larger school community. Therefore, interpersonal relations skills are very important, and barriers in this area certainly should be removed.

The interpersonal style of the parties in a relationship can be a significant determinant of the quality of the relationship. The manner in which individuals interact creates an emotional climate that characterizes their interaction and determines whether or not communication problems emerge (Rogers & Farson, 1995). For example, if the principal has a poor relationship with teachers, and they do not respect his/her judgment, the quality of the information he/she receives from them may not be sufficient to adequately address school issues. The quality of decisions, to a large extent, depends on the information used to make them. Poor information results in poor decision quality. Therefore, the leader can ill afford to have poor interpersonal relations with his/her faculty. Barth (1990) offers that no relationship in a school has a greater effect on the quality of life in that school than the relationship between teacher and principal.

## Position Power

Another factor that must be given consideration by the leader is the position that he/she holds and the power (position power) that is associated with that position. Because leaders are in a position to reward or punish, individuals will sometimes refrain from providing them information, or to say the least, they will filter the information if it is negative. When one holds power over another (status difference), there is the possibility that fear can be invoked. Ryan and Oestreich (1991) reported accounts in schools of subordinates who were reluctant to speak out about certain issues because of possible leader behavior. If the behavior of the leader places fear in the school, a barrier to effective communication will occur. It is extremely difficult to have a high level of quality in the organization when people are afraid (Deming, 1986).

When the leader enters a room, he/she should not enter demonstrating power; rather he/she must realize that everyone in the room has some type of power (expertise, charismatic, or position) and can use that power to negatively or positively influence the attainment of school goals. Such was the case in Scenario 5, Chapter 2, when the principal gave Mrs. Harmon an assignment. He was very directive and used position power to influence her behavior. This type of behavior proved to be ineffective. The leader has to place himself/herself in a collaborating position in order to influence and facilitate the implementation of a vision of learning that is shared and supported by the entire school community (ISLLC, 1996). If individuals in the internal or external environment refrain from communicating with the leader, this standard will be extremely difficult to reach.

## Acquiring Feedback

The leader can reduce the likelihood of position power interfering with effective communication by creating the type of support environment that was discussed in Chapter 2 (a learning environment). Such an environment promotes effective communication because there is a feeling that individuals listen to one another, welcome comments, and respect and appreciate each other. In this type of environment, leaders can anticipate meaningful feedback regarding their behavior.

Feedback is literally defined as the information provided to the sender by the receiver conveying how the message was received and acted upon (Cusella, 1987). It is a process that can be used to give individuals and groups important information about their level of performance, and its skillful use is critical to leaders' successful management of relational obstacles (Barge, 1994). It is also important in defining roles, motivating and empowering individuals, and managing conflict. Feedback can involve the leader in actively seeking opinions and concerns of followers and in providing a comfort level for followers to express their true feelings regarding the message being communicated. However, it cannot be overemphasized that for feedback to be provided in a manner that fosters effective communication, the climate must advance a sense of equity, allowing participants to feel trust, acceptance, and warmth.

In such a climate, individuals feel safe enough to be open and share true feelings and concerns. If the climate is hostile or threatening, emotions can become a factor, resentment might exist, and defensiveness builds, making it difficult for the parties to communicate effectively. To openly address an issue, individuals must feel that there is no need to fear exposure of themselves to members of the group. If this fear is removed, the individual is likely to speak freely and openly.

## Displaying Empathy

Also, individuals are less likely to communicate openly when others (especially leaders) convey a feeling of superiority in position, power, wealth, and intellect or arouse some type of defensive position. Such defensive actions interfere with the communication flow, making it difficult for the leader to move the agenda effectively, solve problems, and make decisions using the best data available. Simply put, it causes a breakdown in communication. Subordinates tend to be receptive to leaders who display empathy in the communication process. Empathy is best described as the ability of the sender of a message to put himself/herself in the position of the receiver (Stech, 1983). An important aspect of empathy involves conveying to the receiver that his/her feelings are acknowledged and understood and that both the meaning and feeling behind what is being said are appreciated. It is a way in which the leader can demonstrate a spirit of genuine respect for the potential worth of the individual, conveying the notion that the individual has rights and can be trusted to be self-directed. Most definitely, a leader in a learning community would be an individual who showed empathy in appropriate situations.

# Summary

Communication is very pervasive in schools; it is the lifeblood of relationships, which are a lifeline to accomplishing the goals of the school. When members of the school team communicate effectively, they feel connected, understood, valued, trusted, and respected. Messages are transmitted, and the organization moves toward goal attainment. When people do not communicate effectively and are not in the communication channel, they often feel unappreciated, misunderstood, defensive, hostile, frustrated, or distressed (Sobel & Ornstein, 1996). Therefore, it is important for the school leader to be skilled in the process of communication.

# The Scenarios

The scenarios that follow hold implications for how ineffective communication prohibits the establishment of the type of educational community supported by ISLLC Standards 1, 2, and 3.

In Scenario 9, the lack of effective communication skills becomes a roadblock to the implementation of a new professional development plan. The reader will want to particularly note the activities ongoing in the administrative meeting and the consequences of a communication system that does not afford the leader the benefit of appropriate feedback.

In Scenario 10, ineffective communication, the climate of a school, and emotions contribute to a fatal incident.

Scenario 11 allows the reader to view position power and its effects when inappropriately used in the communication process.

## SCENARIO 9
## THE NEW PROFESSIONAL DEVELOPMENT PLAN

### STANDARD 1

A school administrator is an educational leader who promotes the success of all students by facilitating the development, articulation, implementation, and stewardship of a vision of learning that is shared and supported by the school community.

*In Scenario 9, this standard was clearly not met. What happened? What went wrong, and what could have been done differently? These are the underlying questions to which the reader might seek an answer. Also, the reader will be able to see what can happen in a school district when communication is ineffective and the vision is not shared. In reviewing the responses to the multiple-choice questions, the reader will be able to assess a variety of communication approaches that can be used in a school situation.*

## ISLLC Standards Indicators Exhibited in Scenario 9

### Knowledge Indicators

The administrator has knowledge and understanding of:

▲ Information sources, data collection, and data analysis strategies
▲ Effective communication
▲ Operational procedures at the school and district level
▲ The change process for systems, organizations, and individuals
▲ Effective consensus building and negotiation

### Disposition Indicators

The administrator believes in, values, and is committed to:

▲ A willingness to continuously examine one's own assumptions, beliefs, and practices
▲ The inclusion of all members of the school community
▲ Trusting people and their judgment
▲ Importance of a continuing dialogue with other decision makers affecting education
▲ Accepting responsibility
▲ Involving stakeholders in management processes
▲ Professional development as an integral part of school improvement
▲ The benefit that diversity brings to the school community

### Performance Indicators

The administrator facilitates processes and engages in activities ensuring that:

▲ The vision and mission of the school are effectively communicated to staff, parents, students, and community members
▲ The vision and mission are communicated through the use of symbols, ceremonies, stories, and similar activities
▲ Progress toward the vision and mission is communicated to all stakeholders
▲ Barriers to achieving the vision are identified, clarified, and addressed
▲ Effective communication skills are used
▲ The school culture and climate is assessed on a regular basis
▲ A variety of sources of information is used to make decisions
▲ Operational plans and procedures to achieve the vision and goals of the school are in place
▲ Potential problems and opportunities are identified
▲ Effective group-process and consensus-building skills are used
▲ The school is organized and aligned for success
▲ Organizational systems are regularly monitored and modified as needed
▲ Stakeholders are involved in decisions affecting schools

Dr. Georgia Edwards is superintendent of Oakville, a large metropolitan school district. Her central staff recently developed a new set of instructional goals and outlined an ambitious professional development program. This new professional development program was the topic of discussion at the April administrative meeting, which included principals who were not members of the superintendent's central office staff. After considerable discussion of the program, Dr. Edwards asked the principals to share the program concepts with their faculties and to promote their implementation.

The assistant superintendents and departmental directors expressed a great deal of excitement about the new program and agreed to share the program with their staffs. The principals, on the other hand, did not seem as excited about the program, but nevertheless agreed to promote its implementation.

Three weeks later at a parent meeting, Dr. Edwards was talking with teachers from several of the buildings and found that they knew little or nothing about the new professional development program. In fact, a number of them complained that they rarely heard anything from her office other than rumors. "Unless there is a problem or a new mandate from the Board of Education, we do not hear from your office," one teacher advised. The teachers also expressed frustration over the lack of opportunities to share their opinions about issues that affected them and their classrooms.

Dr. Edwards is unsure how to proceed. Until now, she was confident that the channels of communication were open—both those leading to and from her office. "Why didn't principals share the new program as they promised they would? Why am I not receiving teachers' opinions? How can I open the channels of communication?"

## REFLECTIVE THINKING AND SCENARIO ANALYSIS

1. Based on your knowledge of effective operational procedures at the district level that influence effective operational procedures at the school level, which approach would you suggest Superintendent Edwards use in facilitating the development, articulation, and implementation of her vision for a professional development plan?
2. What are some consensus-building and negotiation skills that might prove to be helpful to Dr. Edwards in this situation? Support your response with indicators from ISLLC Standard 1.
3. Based on the indicators of ISLLC Standard 1, how did Superintendent Edwards compromise the implementation of the professional development plan?
4. Giving consideration to components of implementation plans that enhance goal attainment, what strategies and objectives could Dr. Edwards have used to improve the flow of information, data collection, and analysis?
5. Giving consideration to the formal communication network, if teachers felt comfortable in voicing their concerns to the superintendent, what other problems might Dr. Edwards find to exist in Oakville? If Dr. Edwards is interested in demonstrating that she is professionally ethical, how should she have responded to the teachers?
6. As superintendent, how important is it to maintain a continuous dialogue with other decision makers regarding the implementation of a new program plan? Justify your response with principles of effective communication.

## ADDRESSING THE ISSUES

Select the one best answer to the following questions:

1. In her approach to implementing the new professional development plan, how did Dr. Edwards minimize its success potential?

   a. She failed to communicate an implementation plan in which objectives and strategies to achieve the vision and goals were clearly articulated.

   b. She failed to establish procedures to receive feedback on the implementation process.

c. She did not sufficiently identify and clarify the vision for principals.

d. any one of the above.

2. Dr. Edwards was fortunate to receive such open feedback from the teachers, as communication between superintendents and teachers is often affected by barriers. Which of the following barriers might have affected communication between Dr. Edwards and the teachers?

a. The teachers' lack of interest in the new professional development plan.

b. The teachers' attitude toward the district's communication system.

c. The difference in the status of the superintendent and the teachers.

d. none of the above.

3. Which of the following methods would least likely improve the flow of communication in the district?

a. The adoption of a communication plan for all administrators to utilize.

b. A plan for the superintendent to release information on a need-to-know basis.

c. The implementation of a program that required the superintendent to make quarterly visits to each of the schools in the district.

d. Implementation of a plan that required the superintendent to conduct regular meetings with the assistant superintendents, departmental directors, and principals and encouraged them to do the same with their staff.

4. Which of the following modes of communication would least likely assist Dr. Edwards in disseminating her message regarding the professional development plan?

a. Establishing an open-door policy as a means of enhancing communication.

b. Establishing a television program to inform teachers and the general public of the new program and the need to enhance the skills of teachers sufficiently to meet the needs of all children.

c. Establishing a series of meetings at the building level that included all members of the school community.

d. Disseminating a newsletter on the program inclusive of a statement that indicated that she was willing to re-examine her plan.

5. Which of the following is likely to be the most serious among the communication problems being experienced by the superintendent?

a. Lack of feedback from the principals.

b. The superintendent's failure to display empathy for the concerns of the principals.

c. Failure of the principals to share the plan with teachers in their buildings.

d. Failure on the part of the superintendent to acknowledge the nonverbal communication of the principals.

## DISCUSSION OF THE SOLUTION

1. Communication within organizations flows in four directions: downward, upward, diagonally, and horizontally. In this scenario, the flow of communication is initially downward,

in a direct manner. Even though there was considerable discussion in the meeting, the superintendent did not clearly articulate an implementation process. In the final analysis, she simply instructed principals to communicate to their faculties information regarding the implementation of her program. Her vision was not clear nor did the principals share it. In fact, the principals were not very receptive to the plan, and little effort was made by the superintendent to acquire feedback about their lack of interest, the implementation approach that would be used, or an evaluation of the success of the implementation process. An effective communication system contains each of these components, and the absence of any one of them is likely to contribute to communication ineffectiveness. The suggested response to question 1 is **(d)**.

2. At the parent meeting, status differences could have been a restrictive barrier to communication between the superintendent and teachers. The superintendent, at a very high level in the organization, received information from individuals (teachers) at a different level, which was much lower. Dr. Edwards, as well as the teachers, would be especially prone to status differences because of their positions in the organization. However, in this instance, the superintendent was a sensitive listener. She did not display a sense of power nor indicate in any manner that she was superior in position or intellect. Therefore, the teachers focused on the message they wanted to deliver, rather than the person to whom the message was being delivered. They described their attitudes regarding the district's communication system and their lack of knowledge about the plan. The superintendent created the climate for this to occur; if there had not been an acceptable comfort level between the teachers and the superintendent, status would have become a barrier, and free exchange would not likely have occurred. Nevertheless, this process of communication does not replace the operational procedures that must govern the formal communication process at the school and district levels. The suggested response to question 2 is **(c)**.

3. Dr. Edwards was using a form of communication that involves the transmission of information from people at higher levels to people at lower levels (downward communication). This type of communication is frequently plagued with difficulties because information provided is incomplete, and no effort is made to evaluate the accuracy of the message (Sobel & Ornstein, 1996). In regard to the implementation of the new plan, a form of communication that would generate evaluative data sufficient to analyze the success of the implementation process should have been utilized. Once Dr. Edwards received feedback data, any necessary changes could have been made, and all administrative personnel could have been informed of the changes.

In this instance, the communication process did not facilitate data collection and analysis from all sources. Dr. Edwards could make several changes to improve the flow of communication in the district, three of which are listed among the options to question three.

(a) Adopting a districtwide communication program would improve the flow of communication. Processes that would assist individuals in understanding messages communicated between all administrators could be put in place. The program might also focus on the development of active listening skills that require participation, openness, and receptivity. It is more than just keeping quiet, smiling, and hearing someone else's words; rather, it means actively participating and providing meaningful feedback to the sender of the message (McPhee & Thimpkins, 1985).

(b) Dr. Edwards might also improve communication by implementing quarterly visits to each school. Information could be transmitted on a firsthand basis, and misunderstandings could be discussed immediately. Sometimes employees need face-to-face contact with superiors to feel respected and informed. Dr. Edwards might find the practice of "management by walking around" to be an effective way of keeping in touch with all employees and promoting an effective communication system. Certainly, visibility on the part of the superintendent, principal, or any key administrator can lead to the development of a positive and trusting relationship throughout the entire district.

(c) Conducting regular staff meetings, with agendas disseminated well in advance of the meeting, is another way of providing information and receiving meaningful feedback. These meetings could assist an administrator in identifying, analyzing, and solving problems in collaboration with staff members. Members of the faculty and staff are more inclined to voice opinions when they have had an opportunity to research agenda items.

The method that is not likely to improve Dr. Edwards' system of communication is the release of information only on a need-to-know basis. When administrators hold back information, directions can become unclear, vague, and open to different interpretations and rumors. Individuals often feel unappreciated, misunderstood, defensive, hostile, frustrated, or distressed (Sobel & Ornstein, 1996). This method also suggests a lack of trust and confidence in employees. Subordinates are more likely to lose faith in the integrity of the communication channels when information does not flow freely. The suggested response to question 3 is **(b)**.

4. The initial administrators' meeting was a good start in introducing the program information; the problem developed when the information did not continue down the chain. As a mode of communication, the verbal mode, or speech, tends to be spontaneous, be flexible, and permit an immediate response (Stech, 1983). It was commendable that there was considerable discussion regarding the new program in the April administrative meeting. However, often after a period of reflection, new insight into a message may be acquired and need discussion and reinforcement through a form of repetitiveness. Such reinforcement will improve communication effectiveness (Barge, 1994). In this instance, a districtwide newsletter, in addition to the original meeting, may have assisted greatly in dissemination of the message. Also, a written mode of communication is more permanent and involves more thought and preparation; it could have served as a point of reference throughout the implementation process.

In addition, Dr. Edwards could have improved the dissemination of information regarding her plan by establishing building level employee meetings that included representatives of all role groups in the community. In so doing, she would have been able to enhance program implementation by assessing the extent to which information was being disseminated, the accuracy of communication, and other relationship concerns. Also, her presence at the meetings would have emphasized the importance of the program. McCaskey (1979) advises that face-to-face contact is very important in the communication process, as senders of messages are able to look the receiver in the eye and enhance the impact of their presentation. As a follow-up to her on-site visits, information obtained could have been used to systematically evaluate districtwide communication effectiveness. Principal Johnson of Scenario 3 in Chapter 1 was very effective in using repetitiveness in her communication process.

Using an open-door policy is another effective way to receive feedback from messages communicated. This practice can either be implemented anonymously through unsigned letters, or it can be done through personal visits by the faculty to the office of the superintendent. However, in order to have an effective face-to-face open-door procedure, the leader must take care to practice active listening and demonstrate nonverbally that employees' thoughts are valuable and that there will be no retribution for negative feedback (Bormann & Bormann, 1972).

Because the principals did not communicate the reason for their lack of enthusiasm, it is unlikely that they would have taken advantage of an open-door policy to express their concerns. The teachers advised the superintendent that they had never heard of the program; thus, the open-door policy would have generated results only if an individual was there about another matter and discussion of the plan occurred by chance. Whereas all the approaches mentioned have merit, in this instance, an open-door policy would least likely assist Dr. Edwards. The suggested response to question 4 is **(a)**.

5. Communication cannot be considered effective just because the leader delivers a message. Individuals who receive the message must understand it and be willing to act on it in an efficient and effective manner. To ensure that this occurs, the leader might take several courses of action, among which are being sensitive to nonverbal messages, showing empathy, taking actions to avoid filtering, and securing feedback sufficient to evaluate communication effectiveness.

Empathy requires the superintendent to put herself in the position of the receiver in order to predict how the message is being received. Had Dr. Edwards done so, the results might have been different. Empathy, in this case, might have been negatively affected by position power because Dr. Edwards's statements reflected dominance and assertiveness, whereas questions from staff were more submissive. Status differences might also have made it difficult for Dr. Edwards to put herself in the place of the principals.

The superintendent gave the principals a complete explanation of the plan. However, the principals may not have had a clear understanding of the content and purpose of the information they were directed to give to their staffs. Nevertheless, the principals did not transmit the message about the plan to their faculties. Thus, a communication void existed at the building level between the principals and teachers.

A leader can ill afford to have subordinates ignore directives, as was the case in this scenario. Such action strongly impedes goal attainment and signals a serious organizational problem. Failure to show empathy in the meeting, failure to acquire adequate feedback, failure to acknowledge the nonverbal behavior of the principals, and the communication void between the principal and teachers were all problems in Dr. Edwards' communication chain. However, the most serious of these occurred at the building level. The suggested response to question 5 is **(c)**.

## SUMMARY AND CONCLUSION

Dr. Edwards made the professional development program a priority in Oakview. The program plan was introduced in a manner that conveyed to the principals that it was the superintendent's plan, designed to implement a new set of goals, which they may or may not have supported. Quite clearly, even though the principals agreed to implement the plan, they had not bought into it. The total school community did not share the vision. The principals' lack of excitement, tone of voice, mumbling, and hesitation in the exchange of information transmitted this message. In the communication process, these are clues that the effective school leader must be able to identify and consider. The transmission of nonverbal messages is very prevalent in school systems; often half of the messages communicated are nonverbal (Covey, 1989).

The real challenges for Superintendent Edwards are listening with feeling, showing empathy for staff, and creating a climate that fosters the kind of feedback from her staff that will inform the decision-making process. Superintendent Edwards' decision lacked quality that could have been acquired from the involvement (in the planning stage) of individuals knowledgeable of teacher needs. It lacked acceptance that could have been obtained by initially involving the people who would ultimately have to implement the plan. Both decision quality and acceptance can be improved through effective communication. With these improvements, Dr. Edwards would take a major step toward becoming a school administrator who is an educational leader who promotes the success of all students by facilitating the development, articulation, implementation, and stewardship of a vision of learning that is shared by the school community.

# SCENARIO 10
## "THE TARDY POLICY KILLED KATO"

### STANDARD 2
A school administrator is an educational leader who promotes the success of all students by advocating, nurturing, and sustaining a school culture and instructional program conducive to student learning and staff professional growth.

*In Scenario 10, many issues are at hand. Among them are school climate, culture, and barriers to student learning. These characteristics as they exist in Merry High School are the focus of this scenario. The reader is challenged to identify others.*

### ISLLC Standards Indicators Exhibited in Scenario 10

**Knowledge Indicators**
The administrator has knowledge and understanding of:
▲ School cultures
▲ The values of the diverse school community
▲ Models and strategies of change and conflict resolution as applied to the larger political, social, cultural, and economic context of schooling
▲ The dynamics of policy development and advocacy under our democratic political system
▲ The importance of diversity and equity in a democratic society
▲ Information sources, data collection, and data analysis strategies
▲ Effective communication

▲ Operational procedures at the school and district level
▲ The change process for systems, organizations, and individuals

**Disposition Indicators**
The administrator believes in, values, and is committed to:
▲ Trusting people and their judgment
▲ Involving stakeholders in management processes
▲ Collaboration and communication with families
▲ Families as partners in the education of their children
▲ Development of a caring school community
▲ Importance of a continuing dialogue with other decision makers affecting education
▲ Accepting responsibility
▲ Involving stakeholders in management processes
▲ The benefit that diversity brings to the school community

**Performance Indicators**
The administrator facilitates processes and engages in activities ensuring that:
▲ The vision and mission of the school are effectively communicated to staff, parents, students, and community members
▲ The vision and mission are communicated through the use of symbols, ceremonies, stories, and similar activities
▲ Progress toward the vision and mission is communicated to all stakeholders
▲ Barriers to achieving the vision are identified, clarified, and addressed
▲ Effective communication skills are used
▲ Time is managed to maximize attainment of organizational goals
▲ High visibility, active involvement, and communication with the larger community are priorities
▲ Effective media relations are developed and maintained
▲ The environment in which the school operates is influenced on behalf of students and their parents
▲ A variety of sources of information is used to make decisions
▲ Operational plans and procedures to achieve the vision and goals of the school are in place
▲ Potential problems and opportunities are identified
▲ Effective group-process and consensus-building skills are used
▲ The school is organized and aligned for success
▲ Stakeholders are involved in decisions affecting schools

Kato, a senior at Merry High School, is a recent immigrant and star athlete. He makes friends easily and is very well liked by his teachers and peers. His class work is average, and discipline is not a problem for him. Unfortunately, Kato has been tardy for his first-period class (English, Mrs. Clark) three times this quarter (tardy 1—overslept, late 5 minutes; tardy 2—Mom drove him to school, late 10 minutes; tardy 3—left a book at home and had to return to get it, late 8 minutes).

On November 11, when Kato came to his first period class 8 minutes late, his third tardy, Mrs. Clark advised him that he would have to report to the On Campus Suspension Class (OCS). Kato begged and pleaded with Mrs. Clark, saying, "I really want to be in class because the midterm examination in this class is scheduled for next week, and I want to be prepared." Mrs. Clark, thinking about the last faculty meeting and the strong emphasis that Principal Johnson placed on strict adherence to the new tardy policy, politely stated the consequences and directed Kato to OCS. Kato refused to go to OCS and was sent to the principal's office.

When Kato reached the office, he spoke with Mr. Martin, Vice Principal at Merry High. Kato explained, "Mr. Martin, I really do not want to go to OCS; I must get ready for midterm. Please allow me to return to class. I don't want to miss a day out of class!"

"You know the rules, Kato. This is your third tardy. I am going to insist that you serve your time in OCS during your first period."

"Mr. Martin, I want to go to class. If you will not permit me to go to class, then I refuse to go to OCS."

"Then, Kato, if you refuse, I will have to send you home."

"Fine, Mr. Martin."

"Fine, then that's what we will do, Kato."

Mr. Martin filled out the necessary paperwork and sent Kato home. Kato did not have a car, so he had to walk home. As Kato walked out the door, Mr. Martin headed toward the phone to contact Kato's parents. On the way to the phone, his office assistant advised him that a fight was in progress in the quad, and he was needed out there at once. Mr. Martin headed to the quad without intending to break the district's rule that parents must be contacted when a student is suspended.

One hour later, Mr. Martin found out that Kato had been killed.

Apparently, Kato was on his way home when an older "gang member" friend, Serge, drove by and offered Kato a ride home. Kato accepted because he did not want to walk the two miles home. As the boys drove to Kato's home, Serge saw a rival gang member walking on the sidewalk, pulled up next to him, and starting talking "trash." The rival gang member pulled out a gun, fired it at Serge, missed, and hit Kato, killing him instantly.

The media got the story right away. They asked, "Why was Kato going home? Who authorized his dismissal from school, and why were his parents not contacted? Is it true that he was killed because he was tardy three times?" Final message to the public: **The Tardy Policy Killed Kato.**

## REFLECTIVE THINKING AND SCENARIO ANALYSIS

1. Looking at the big picture, was Mr. Martin's behavior representative of an educator who influences an environment that focuses on the needs of students and their families? What evidence can you provide to support your conclusion?
2. If you were making management decisions to enhance teaching and learning, what action would you have suggested to Mrs. Clark? In your response, give consideration to the concept of trusting people and their judgment.
3. In your judgment, which is more important, meeting the needs of individual students or following the letter of policy? Provide a rationale for your response.
4. If it is true that administrators, faculty, and staff should develop a caring community in schools, were the consequences created by the tardy policy too severe for the offense? If so, why? If not, why not?
5. Given that school leaders should view families as partners in the education of their children, in what ways could school personnel collaborate and communicate with families to prevent a situation of this nature from occurring?

**6.** How could the tardy policy be changed to serve the same purpose, but allow some flexibility for teachers and assistant principals to reflect their judgment in its implementation?

**7.** What kind of message would be sent to the larger community (parents, students, teachers, and citizens) if the administration of the school completely dropped the tardy policy?

## ADDRESSING THE ISSUES

Select the one best answer to the following questions:

**1.** As a school leader desirous of assessing the learning environment for the purpose of improving its effectiveness, which of the following would you identify as the factor that most influenced Mrs. Clark's behavior?

**a.** The leadership of the organization did not foster the proposition that all students can learn.

**b.** The communication process of the organization did not foster collaboration with families.

**c.** The organizational climate was not one of nurturing.

**d.** All of the above.

**2.** Which of the following may have contributed to communication ineffectiveness in the faculty meeting?

**a.** The communication process used by the principal to stress policy importance likely reduced feedback from the faculty.

**b.** The leadership style of the principal did not reflect a willingness to continuously examine one's own assumptions, beliefs, and ideas.

**c.** There was a lack of feedback from the faculty regarding the negative effects of placing a strong emphasis on the tardy policy.

**d.** All of the above.

**3.** Which of the following factors likely influenced the manner in which Mrs. Clark communicated with Kato?

**a.** The dynamics of policy development and implementation.

**b.** Making a decision that enhanced teaching and learning for Kato.

**c.** The need to develop a caring school community.

**d.** An examination of her personal and professional values.

**4.** Which of the following barriers to communication most likely influenced Mr. Martin's behavior?

**a.** The pressures placed on him to respond to the situation in a timely manner.

**b.** Failure to use effective communication skills that removed the barriers to achieving the vision of the tardy policy.

**c.** The lack of involvement of Kato's family in his education.

**d.** The conditions and environment of the school, which did not allow school personnel to communicate the mission of the school to all stakeholders.

**5.** Mr. Johnson would be well advised to:

    **a.** Review board policy to determine action steps.

    **b.** Contact members of the Board of Education and inform them of Kato's death.

    **c.** Call the superintendent and collaborate with him or his/her designee regarding the death of Kato.

    **d.** Be concerned with developing and maintaining effective media relations and responding to the questions of the media, then calling the superintendent.

## DISCUSSION OF THE SOLUTION

1. School climate is a relatively enduring quality of the school environment that refers to people's perception of the general work environment. The formal organization, informal organization, personalities of participants, and organizational leadership influence this perception. The quality of the environment of the school can have a major effect on the behavior of people who work in the schools (Lunenburg & Ornstein, 1996). It is the responsibility of the school leader to develop a school climate that is nurturing and caring. The design and implementation of policies, procedures, and programs must take this factor into consideration.

The development of a new tardy policy tends to suggest that tardiness is a problem at Merry High School. In the last faculty meeting, the principal's action of emphasizing strict adherence to a new tardy policy tends to suggest that attention is being given to resolving the problem. The manner in which a principal communicates new policy and emphasizes its importance denotes a style of organizational leadership (Hoy & Miskel, 1991), and the leadership style of the principal contributes to the climate of the school. Therefore, it is necessary for the principal to continuously examine the effect his behavior has on personalities in the school.

Organizational leadership must influence the climate in a positive manner in order to assure decision effectiveness (McPhee & Thimpkins, 1985). For this to occur, the principal must possess three general skills: (1) diagnosing—understanding the problem situation, (2) adapting—altering behavior and other resources to meet the contingencies of the situation, and (3) communicating—interacting with others in a way that they can easily understand and accept the decision (Gorton & Schneider, 1994). The leadership style of the principal, the manner in which the decision on the tardy policy was communicated to the faculty, and the climate of the school are all possible contributors to the problems and concerns at Merry High School. The suggested response to question 1 is **(d)**.

2. The communication medium used by a principal to convey to the faculty a message concerning the implementation of a new policy may pose advantages and/or disadvantages for the effective implementation of that policy (Cunningham & Cresco, 1993). In a situation such as the one occurring at Merry High School, the type of communication used to convey the policy to the faculty likely influenced the manner in which the policy was implemented. It determined, to a large degree, the flexibility each faculty member elected to use in the implementation process.

The directive from the principal to strictly adhere to the tardy policy presents itself as a downward or top-down, authoritarian communication approach. This approach can create barriers because members of the faculty decoding the principal's message do not provide feedback on their understanding of the message (McPhee & Thimpkins, 1985). Faculty members are likely to view the directive based on their perceptions of the principal's character, personality, motivation, and style and give these factors priority as they implement the policy. Once again, we note that the leader must be aware of the influence his/her behavior has on the faculty.

In school settings, different situations warrant different actions, and whereas policies must be followed, the faculty often needs room to make judgments. Therefore, the mode of communication used to emphasize the new policy should have been one that allowed interaction and feedback from the faculty, providing the principal an opportunity to check for understanding, expectations, and level of comfort in the implementation process. The suggested response to question 2 is **(d)**.

3. Mrs. Clark was unable to see beyond the rule. Her primary concern became implementation of the policy as directed by the principal. Following the rule was more important than identifying a cause of the problem. Mrs. Clark's perception of what was best for her, Kato, and the school was to some extent influenced by her perceptions of the principal's character, personality, motivation, and style. She gave these factors priority as she implemented the policy. Under different circumstances, she might have taken different actions. Kato expressed concern with missing out on the review in class. His expressed intentions were not to avoid On Campus Suspension Class, but to attend English class. Mrs. Clark exercised no flexibility in policy implementation. The school climate at Merry High appeared to have influenced the behavior of Mrs. Clark. The suggested response to question 3 is **(a)**.

4. Mr. Martin took the same position as Mrs. Clark—follow the rules. He never considered any alternatives to On Campus Suspension Class. Very seldom, if ever, should a rule be so hard and fast that an alternative cannot be considered (Hersey & Blanchard, 1993). When this occurs, the lines of communication often close, and the situation turns into one of confrontation. An effective school leader never allows this to occur. The situation with Kato should never have progressed to the confrontation stage; an either/or situation is rarely, if ever, in the best interest of effective problem solving and decision making (Bormann & Bormann, 1972). The emotions of both individuals became a barrier to effective communication. Both parties became defensive, and neither was willing to set aside his concerns and be understanding of the other's concerns.

Time pressure was also a problem for Mr. Martin. He did not take the time to advocate, nurture, or make Kato feel valued and important. Also, he failed to call Kato's parents. The policy and the climate of the school were the guiding factors as opposed to the problematic concerns of Kato. Failure to call Kato's parents was a policy violation on Mr. Martin's part, even though it was unintentional. Pupil personnel policies should be designed to meet the needs of students and their families, and the implementation procedures should foster the same.

As we view the key issues in this scenario, quite clearly the major barrier that most likely prevented Mr. Martin from reaching a different solution to Kato's problem was his failure to use effective communication skills that removed the barriers to achieving the vision of the tardy policy. Barriers to achieving the vision were not identified, clarified, and addressed. The dialogue that occurred between Mr. Martin and Kato became confrontational and defensive, creating still another communication barrier. The suggested response to question 4 is **(b)**.

5. A well-informed principal is likely to be knowledgeable of board policy that governs situations of this nature. In the absence of such knowledge, a quick policy review

might prove to be helpful—but just that, helpful. The real solution lies in decision making, where alternatives are identified, consequences are assessed, and the best alternative is selected. All the right people must be involved in the decision-making process, and decisions must be made within the bounds of policy.

In most situations of this nature, the first action would be to inform the superintendent of the occurrence. Once the superintendent becomes informed, he/she can assist in the decision-making process. Effective media relations must be developed and maintained, and more often than not, those relations are governed by central procedures designed to handle situations of this nature. Relationships with the general community must be nurtured through a carefully designed process. It tends to serve the best interest of the district if the superintendent informs the board. The suggested response to question 5 is **(c)**.

## SUMMARY AND CONCLUSION

The climate at Merry High School forced strict compliance to the policy in an authoritarian manner. The end objective (enforcement of the tardy policy) was achieved while the needs of the student went unattended, creating a more challenging situation. Although it is understandable that policies are needed and must be enforced, one must also recognize that a school administrator is an educational leader who promotes the success of all students by advocating, nurturing, and sustaining a school culture and instructional program conducive to student learning and staff professional growth (ISLLC, 1996). This is not occurring at Merry High School. In schools where students are nurtured, rules, regulations, and procedures are matched with the needs, personality, and desires of the student (Greenberg & Baron, 1997). Student learning is the fundamental purpose of schooling; thus, the school has to be organized and aligned for success (ISLLC, 1996).

Once Kato reached the office, he reinforced his desire to remain in school and attend class. However, the policy and strict adherence to the policy again became the dominant issues. Mr. Martin failed to address Kato's real concern—missing class. His position of strict adherence to the policy and the rules of the school provoked a confrontational win/lose situation.

An assistant principal has legitimate power. Mr. Martin could have utilized legitimate power in a manner consistent with good human relations. Consistency in leadership does not mean taking the same position all the time; it may mean taking the position appropriate for the follower's level of readiness in a manner that allows the follower to understand why a particular behavior is occurring (Gorton & Schneider, 1994). In school situations, it is often helpful to try and see the other person's point of view, to be open to influence, and to be prepared to alter one's position (Bormann & Bormann, 1972).

When school personnel are nurturing, they show concern for the unique problems of their students and a willingness to assist them in finding solutions to their problems (Greenberg & Baron, 1997). Mutual trust exists, and finding the cause of the problem is more important than enforcing the policy (Arnold & Feldman, 1989). After all, a school administrator is an educational leader who promotes the success of all students by advocating, nurturing, and sustaining a school culture and instructional program conducive to student learning and staff professional growth (ISLLC, 1996).

## SCENARIO 11
### COMMUNICATING A PERSONNEL CHANGE

#### STANDARD 3

A school administrator is an educational leader who promotes the success of all students by ensuring management of the organization, operations, and resources for a safe, efficient, and effective learning environment.

*In Scenario 11, a decision has been made that is in the zone of concern of teachers, parents, and administrators, none of whom were involved in the decision-making process. Their judgment was not trusted, nor was their dignity respected, which is an indication that ISLLC Standard 3 was not met.*

### ISLLC Standards Indicators Exhibited in Scenario 11

**Knowledge Indicators**
The administrator has knowledge and understanding of:
▲ Effective communication
▲ Principles of effective instruction
▲ The change process for systems, organizations, and individuals
▲ Human resources management and development
▲ Information sources, data collection, and data analysis strategies
▲ Operational procedures at the school and district level

**Disposition Indicators**
The administrator believes in, values, and is committed to:
▲ A willingness to continuously examine one's own assumptions, beliefs, and practices
▲ Making management decisions to enhance learning and teaching
▲ Involving stakeholders in management processes
▲ Development of a caring school community
▲ Importance of a continuing dialogue with other decision makers affecting education

**Performance Indicators**
The administrator facilitates processes and engages in activities ensuring that:
▲ Curriculum decisions are based on research, expertise of teachers, and the recommendation of learned societies
▲ Effective communication skills are used
▲ Human resource functions support the attainment of school goals
▲ The vision and mission of the school are effectively communicated to staff, parents, students, and community members
▲ The vision and mission are communicated through the use of symbols, ceremonies, stories, and similar activities
▲ Barriers to achieving the vision are identified, clarified, and addressed
▲ The environment in which the school operates is influenced on behalf of students and their parents
▲ A variety of sources of information is used to make decisions

▲ Operational plans and procedures to achieve the vision and goals of the school are in place
▲ Potential problems and opportunities are identified
▲ Effective group-process and consensus-building skills are used
▲ Stakeholders are involved in decisions affecting schools

The results of a recent study of the district's instructional program in the Greenfield School District identified deficiencies in instructional delivery at some schools and a number of inconsistencies in personnel assignments across the district. This finding motivated the Board of Education to suggest to the superintendent that inconsistencies be corrected and the district's instructional program be improved.

After studying the report, the superintendent determined that the instructional program was not being implemented consistently across the district. However, a review of the staffing formula indicated that inconsistencies in staffing only existed in two schools, Northside High and Eaton High. Applying the staffing formula fairly and equitably at these two schools appeared to be the major issue.

Realizing that the issue surfaced first in the Northside community, the superintendent made the determination to first address the challenges there, report to the Board that staffing was equitable across the district, then move to address instructional improvement in all schools.

While speaking with Bob Jones, principal of Northside, the superintendent discovered that both Northside and Eaton had vocational education programs that utilized an applied academic component and could share teachers in that area. If the teachers were shared between the two schools, the problem could be solved without layoffs or the cost of employing three additional teachers. The applied academic component included applied mathematics, applied communications, and support services, which could be scheduled at different times during the school day. The superintendent was very energized about an idea he referred to as "the best of all worlds."

The sharing idea was not well received by Principal Jones, and when he attempted to voice his concerns, the superintendent responded, "Let me handle this one, Bob. I am getting pressure from the Board, and I need to make these changes as soon as possible." Having made that statement, the phone conversation ended without additional comments from Principal Jones.

The superintendent then called Mr. Sims, principal at Eaton High School and indicated that Eaton was overstaffed. He stated that a determination had been made to address the issue by having three of the vocational teachers assigned to Eaton share their services with Northside. He quickly added that the alternative was the elimination of three teachers from the Eaton faculty. The superintendent stated, "John, I want you to ask each of the teachers in the applied academic component of your vocational program to submit a letter indicating that he/she is volunteering to share time between the schools. In that way, the plan is likely to be accepted by the Board."

After hearing the superintendent's directive, Mr. Sims indicated that he had misgivings concerning the implementation of the directive. The suggested solution would cut back on teaching time for all involved, and the teachers would have logistical problems getting back and forth between the two schools. The schedules of the teachers would require that they travel between the two schools several times each day. He also raised the question as to which principal would supervise the teachers.

Mr. Sims shared with the superintendent that he believed the teachers would cooperate in order to keep their jobs; however, he feared that this would be a delicate situation to explain to each person involved, as well as to other members of the faculty. Finally, he advised that it would be difficult to get the teachers to write a "voluntary" letter if they perceived their jobs were in jeopardy. The superintendent gave no reply to the comments made by Principal Sims, ending the conversation with the comment, "I trust you will handle this, John; in fact, I expect you to handle this situation." Hanging up the phone, Principal Sims muttered, "Advising the superintendent is like talking to a brick wall."

## REFLECTIVE THINKING AND SCENARIO ANALYSIS

1. What is your assessment of the management decision made by the superintendent? Provide a justification for your response, allowing the enhancement of teaching and learning to be the primary concern.
2. Identify the concerns that a school leader interested in effective human resource management and development would have with the series of events that occurred.
3. How would you characterize the effectiveness of the communication skills utilized by the superintendent? In your response, identify some of the barriers that are inherent in this mode of communication. Also, develop a rationale for your position, taking into consideration best practices of teaching, learning, use of power, and instructional effectiveness.
4. What problem and/or challenges might Principal Sims anticipate when he approaches the teachers in question?
5. What medium of communication would you advise Principal Sims to use in communicating the superintendent's message to the faculty at Eaton? In formulating your response, reflect on your understanding of principles of effective interpersonal skills and human resources management and development.
6. If Mr. Jones did not feel good about the decision and/or the process that was used to arrive at the decision, what actions might he have taken to influence the superintendent to reexamine the decision? What are the implications from an ethical and political perspective?

## ADDRESSING THE ISSUES

Select the one best answer to the following questions:

1. Which of the following statements best characterizes the ineffectiveness of the communication approach utilized by the superintendent?

   a. The communication flow was downward in the form of a directive with no opportunity for feedback from Principal Sims.

   b. The communication flow was downward in the form of a directive; two-way communication existed, but the communication medium was inadequate.

   c. There was two-way communication; however, the decision had already been made, and a mandate was issued.

d. The communication flow was downward; the communication medium was inadequate and was not likely to enhance human resource development.

2. If Principal Sims is concerned with principles of interpersonal skills and effective human resources management and development, which of the following approaches should he use to communicate the changes to the faculty at Eaton?

a. Principal Sims should outline the changes in writing, including an explanation for the changes, and disseminate them to the faculty.

b. He should outline the changes in writing and review them with each of the individuals directly affected, inclusive of an explanation for the changes. Then he should make a presentation to the faculty in a meeting called for that purpose, allow time for questions and answers, and remain available after the meeting for further assistance.

c. Principal Sims should simply make a general announcement in a regular faculty meeting and allow time for questions and answers.

d. He should invite the superintendent to a faculty meeting and allow him to make the announcement.

3. The manner in which the decision was communicated to Principal Sims by the superintendent suggests that he:

a. is superior in position and does not have empathy for the principal.

b. has reached a decision and does not want feedback from the principal.

c. does not understand the benefits that can be derived from effective two-way communication.

d. all of the above.

4. Which of the following statements best depicts the communication assumptions made by the superintendent when he uttered the statement, "I trust you will handle this John; in fact, I expect you to handle this situation."

a. His objective could be achieved without difficulty.

b. Principal Sims would give the message the same importance that the superintendent gave it.

c. It was not necessary for a reexamination of the feasibility of his communication objective.

d. He was superior in position power and intellectual ability.

## DISCUSSION OF THE SOLUTION

1. It is highly questionable as to whether or not a decision of this magnitude should flow downward in the manner that occurred. The decision was communicated in the form of a directive. A number of problems can be generated as a result of communicating a decision with such broad ramifications in a downward directive manner. The process tends to suggest that the leader is not sensitive, has a lack of concern for the individuals involved, and is not trusting of his/her support staff. It also conveys a sense of superiority on the part of the leader.

If the leader wants to ensure an effective learning environment, he/she must be sensitive to principles of interpersonal relations and effective human resources management and development. Principal Sims, Principal Jones, and the faculties at Eaton and Northside should have had an opportunity to discuss the issue and to provide input into the decision before it was reached. Team members want to be perceived as valued individuals with special worth. In the absence of such involvement, the superintendent would have been better advised to use a different medium to communicate the decision to Principal Sims.

The decision came by telephone, which is not the richest medium of communication. It did not afford the superintendent the benefit of visual clues, which is a form of feedback that can be used in assessing how the decision will be received and implemented (Greenberg & Baron, 1997).

Whereas there was an attempt on the part of Principal Sims to give the superintendent feedback, the feedback was not well received; thus, two-way communication was not very effective. The superintendent was not practicing active listening, nor did he give any indication that he understood the importance of human resource functions in the attainment of school goals. He showed no empathy, and his tone communicated a sense of neutrality and superiority that likely motivated the defensive attitude of the principal. The suggested response to question 1 is **(d)**.

2. Changing the work assignment of employees can be very disruptive. Nonetheless, in school administration, disruptions cannot always be avoided. However, when they are unavoidable, the means of conveying the change requires much thought. If the message is communicated effectively and followed up with appropriate actions, the effects of the disruption can be minimized (Fullan, 1993). The leader must assess the possible effects and impact that his/her procedures and practices will have on the individuals involved. People in the organization want to feel that they are treated fairly, equitably, and with dignity and respect.

Principal Sims is likely to be most effective in communicating the change at Eaton if he uses multiple mediums because redundancy increases the richness and the accuracy of the message being delivered (Greenberg & Baron, 1997). Also, it provides various means of demonstrating fair treatment and equitable practices.

To ensure that the change is understood, an explanation might be outlined in writing and followed up with several other actions. Principal Sims could present the changes and the rationale for them orally in a meeting specifically called for that purpose. The oral presentation would give the changes importance, allow the faculty to ask questions and clarify concerns, and afford Principal Sims an opportunity to be supportive and nurturing. In a face-to-face meeting, the faculty would have an opportunity to provide Principal Sims with feedback. This feedback would likely come in verbal and nonverbal forms, affording the principal an opportunity to assess the faculty receptivity to the changes and predict possible faculty actions. The suggested response to question 2 is **(b)**.

3. The superintendent was very direct in providing instructions to Principal Sims. He displayed an attitude of superiority and provoked a sense of defensiveness. There was no empathy shown, and the lack of it could be observed in the responses of Principal Sims. In addition, empathy on the part of the superintendent would have possibly raised the trust level between the two administrators and prevented the resentment that seemed to develop after Mr. Sims hung up the phone. When the speaker appears to

the listener to be transmitting the message from a position of superiority and with a lack of empathy or concern, the listener is likely to become defensive.

The superintendent got his message across but in a risky manner. He did not respond to Principal Sims' concerns, nor was he receptive to the feedback being provided, which is vital to the achievement of the outlined goal. The superintendent showed no empathy, displayed poor listening skills, and was not receptive to the feedback offered by Principal Sims. Such behavior is not likely to enhance a learning environment that is efficient and effective. The suggested response to question 3 is **(d)**.

4. The superintendent had an objective that he was attempting to achieve, and he assumed that his objective could be achieved with little difficulty. A portion of his objective could likely be achieved with little difficulty (informing the teachers); however, there is a second portion, which could prove to be somewhat problematic (convincing the teachers not to take additional action).

Considering the circumstances, the superintendent would have been well advised to have welcomed feedback from Principal Sims. The feedback would have enabled him to reexamine his approach and its feasibility, as well as to establish a framework for moving forward. An effective leader does not assume that objectives communicated will be achieved without difficulty or that the individual receiving the message will have the same attitude as he/she does regarding its importance. Rather, to maximize communication effectiveness, he/she thinks about the characteristics of his/her message, the manner in which it will be received, the circumstances, and the possible repercussions. The suggested response to question 4 is **(d)**.

## SUMMARY AND CONCLUSION

When change occurs, the effective leader strives to minimize the unpleasantness of the change. Realizing that the quality of the relationship will influence to a large extent the level of communication and outcome effectiveness, he/she should approach the change process with a focus on people and process as opposed to strictly focusing on product and outcome.

At Eaton, effective communication between the superintendent and the building principal was impeded. However, this ineffectiveness does not have to continue. The principal, who is at the next level in the chain of command, can assure effective communication moving forward. He can implement the directive, making sure that the message is understood and acted upon appropriately by all parties involved. The principal, to the extent possible, can allow the individuals involved to participate in decisions that remain. Such actions would give faculty members a feeling of control over what is about to happen to them. School leaders who manage the school in an efficient and effective manner take these actions.

## CHAPTER SUMMARY

Communication is the lifeblood of the school. It is the glue that holds the other administrative functions together. Through effective communication, the school family can work collaboratively to achieve the vision of the school, openly identifying problems and seeking solutions, while trusting, respecting, and valuing the diversity that comprises the school family.

The form of communication can be verbal or nonverbal. When the leader uses words, either written or oral, he/she is using a form of verbal communication. A school leader uses verbal communication in faculty meetings, staff conferences, parent meetings, and when discussions are held with students about various matters of teaching and learning. This type communication is two way and very effective, as it allows for interaction to occur between the sender of messages and the receiver of messages. Also, verbal communication is being used when the leader sends out newsletters, parent notices, and other written materials. However, this form of communication is one way and often does not generate instant feedback. Its effectiveness lies in conveying information that needs to be retained and used as a point of reference or for directions. When the faculty, staff, students, parents, and others need information regarding the implementation of policies, procedures, and directives, the written mode of communication tends to work well.

When a message is transmitted without the use of words, the form of communication is considered nonverbal. Nonverbal behavior is very important, as more than half of what is communicated is conveyed by body language. More often than not, the feelings of the sender are conveyed nonverbally. Therefore, for the dynamics of communication to have the greatest impact, both the content of the message and the feelings of the sender must be considered. Communication has to occur with the sender giving the highest level of attention to the feelings that underlie the content.

The school has both a formal communication network and an informal one. The formal network is directed by the structure of the organization, and individuals who function in the organization direct the informal network. Both networks serve a meaningful purpose, and the school leader should be knowledgeable of both and the manner in which they function. The major function of the formal network is to convey information sanctioned by the system. Members of the organization use the informal network to convey messages of interest often called rumors. The leader should be aware of rumors, as they can be detrimental to goal attainment.

Information flows in several directions—upward, downward, horizontal, and diagonal. The flow is very important, as it provides task coordination and furnishes emotional and social support. However, regardless of the flow, barriers interfere with communication effectiveness and must be removed. Barriers can be removed by managing the use of power, eliminating fear, encouraging feedback, and establishing a climate of openness and trust.

When people effectively communicate, fear is removed from the workplace, and creativity comes alive, as positive emotions stimulate creativity. Then the communication process can be used as a catalyst for creativity. When this occurs, not only do children benefit, but the entire community functions at a more productive and self-actualizing level. However, ineffective communication can become a usurper of the creative process. Negative emotions inhibit creativity, and, in essence, deprive children of the highest level of teaching expertise.

## MOVING INTO PRACTICE

Review the scenarios in Chapter 3. Using the pros and cons of the various situations, identify several approaches that you would use to address the following school-related issues in an actual situation. Project yourself in the role of the principal and take care to formulate a rationale for your selected behavior.

> ▶ Select a local school district policy that addresses school attendance and tardiness and relate the requirements of that policy to the ones in the policy at Merry High School.
> ▶ Hold a mock press conference and explain the Kato incident to the media and the general public.
> ▶ Talk with a principal in your school district about the superintendent's directive to Principal Sims and discuss how he would have handled such a directive.
> ▶ How can the school climate problem that is likely to exist as a result of Kato's death best be addressed? What community resources would prove valuable?

## ACQUIRING AN UNDERSTANDING OF SELF

> ▶ What does your body language communicate to individuals?
> ▶ How do you assess the manner in which people perceive you?
> ▶ Are you communicating the message that you want to convey to people? What evidence do you have to support your conclusions?

## SUGGESTED READINGS

Barge, J. K. (1994). *Leadership communication skills for organizations and groups*. New York: St. Martin's Press.

Greenberg, J., & Baron, R. A. (1997). *Behavior in organizations*. Upper Saddle River, NJ: Prentice Hall.

# 4

---

# DECISION MAKING: QUALITY AND ACCEPTANCE

## The Importance of Decision Making

In today's schools, decision making is one of the primary leadership functions. Leaders are continuously making decisions about individuals, groups, school structure, the instructional program, and many other factors that ultimately determine if schools function effectively. If the process is not conducted in an effective manner, the entire school stands to be negatively impacted. Therefore, understanding the decision-making process and how to improve it should be very beneficial to school leaders.

The primary purpose of this chapter is to examine the process of decision making in schools. The reader is first provided with a definition of decision making. Within the definition, three elements are presented: (1) choice (choosing between two or more options), (2) process (electing to make the decision independently or involving others), and (3) purpose (the results or desired outcome). The definition is followed by a general overview of several approaches school leaders can use to select alternatives that lead to decision quality and acceptance. A discussion is then held on the involvement of sub-ordinates and other stakeholders in the decision-making process. Barriers and traps that inhibit decision effectiveness are also presented.

The chapter concludes with three scenarios that address ISLLC Standards 5 and 6, providing the reader an opportunity to practice selecting appropriate decision-making strategies and involving subordinates and other stakeholders in the decision-making process. In working through the scenarios, the reader will want to note instances of fairness, ethical practices, and situations when the characters, especially the leader, act with or without integrity.

# A Definition of Decision Making

Decision making is defined as a systematic process of choosing from among alternatives to achieve a desired result (Kamlesh & Solow, 1994). Selecting among alternatives often involves providing resources to some individuals and groups while denying them to others. A choice has to be made, and making choices in schools has far-reaching implications. For example, if a principal in a school with multiple grade levels only has enough financial resources to pur-chase computers for one grade level, a decision must be made as to which grade level receives the computers. When the principal makes that decision, some faculty members will receive resources that others do not, thus conflict that negatively affects the instructional program might result. Therefore, in making such a decision, the school leader should seek to minimize negative consequences and maximize positive outcomes. The possibility of achieving this objective can be enhanced if the leader makes informed choices and acts with integrity and in an ethical manner (ISLLC, 1996). Informed choices are likely to be made when the leader has a thorough understanding of decision processes and uses that knowledge to select and implement alternatives that result in decision quality and acceptance. Figure 4.1 summarizes a basic model that many researchers and writers offer for use in making decisions (Barge, 1994; Gorton, 1987; Hoy & Tarter, 1995; Yukl, 1994). From this model, the reader can understand the complex nature of problem analysis, selecting a solu-tion to that problem, and effectively implementing the solution.

## A Model of Decision Making

In the first step, the leader identifies the problem. The next step is to analyze the problem to determine the real issues. A thorough analysis is needed to iden-tify a satisficing alternative. The analysis should take into account individuals who are affected, situations that are impacted, and the type and sources of data that are needed to select an appropriate solution.

In the third step the leader develops problem solution alternatives. A note of caution at this juncture is that the alternatives seldom appear in an either/or manner. If the problem is carefully analyzed as described in step two, the leader

**FIGURE 4.1   Steps in the basic decision-making model**

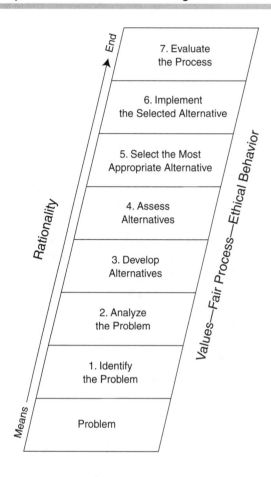

will likely come to the realization that several alternatives exist. Also, in some instances, leaders have a tendency to resort to past experiences in applying an alternative. This temptation should be resisted, as problems may seem alike but in actuality are different, thus warranting a different alternative. Therefore, it is advisable for the leader to explore all possible alternatives.

Once the alternatives have been identified, they should be assessed in terms of their match with the problem. Simply put, determine which one of the generated alternatives will most effectively address the problem (decision quality) and which one will produce the least amount of conflict (decision acceptance). After assessing all alternatives, step five—selecting the most appropriate alternative—is taken.

The sixth step involves the implementation of the alternative. This step should be carefully planned, as decisions of high quality serve no meaningful purpose if they are not implemented effectively and in a manner that is acceptable to stakeholders.

Finally, step seven is an evaluation of the process used to make the decision. The entire process should be assessed, and the decision alternative implemented should be monitored to determine if the problem is being addressed adequately. The leader needs to know that the decision alternative selected solved the problem and that the process used to identify it was not flawed. If the leader fails to evaluate the process and the success of the alternative chosen, flaws in the process, if any, will not be identified and are likely to be repeated.

## The Leader's Disposition

Simply following the sequential steps of the decision-making model is not sufficient. Effective decision making also depends on the disposition of the leader. School leaders make selections from various alternatives as individuals and/or as members of groups. In so doing, they reveal their preferences for particular values, interests, and beliefs (Barge, 1994). It is extremely difficult for leaders to behave in a manner that is different from what they believe or to remove all biases that may exist. Given this factor, the school leader has to be concerned with the biases, values, interests, and beliefs that he/she brings to the decision-making process, as they are likely to be reflected in the consequences of any decisions and actions. A section of Chapter 2 focused on the leader's understanding of self and the need for leaders to assess the influence of their values on their behavior. As we continue our exploration of decision making, a review of that section, as well as the constructs in Figure 1.2 of Chapter 1 may be beneficial.

# Approaches to Decision Making

Several writers and researchers (House & Dessler, 1974; Maier, 1963; Yukl, 1994) have noted that there is no one best way to make effective decisions. The complexity of school situations and time frames that demand decisive actions often influence leader behavior in a manner quite different from that suggested by theory and research. More often than not, making good decisions in schools is contingent on the nature of the situation and the process used by the leader.

Although there is no one best way to make decisions, there are a number of theoretical models that, if appropriately applied, can improve one's decision-making capability. In applying theoretical models, the leader may elect to use either a normative (rational) or a descriptive (nonrational) one. "These two theories of the nature of decision making have dominated social science thinking about the topic" (Gorton, 1987, p. 3). Each presupposes that the decision maker will reach a decision by proceeding through a series of steps like or similar to those outlined in Figure 4.1. Given the popular use of these two models, a summary of each is presented in the following section.

## The Normative Models

If a normative model is used, leaders follow a series of prescribed actions. They begin with a problem that is logically addressed by engaging in a series of sequential steps that leads to an effective problem solution (Gorton, 1987). Using a normative model in a school situation, the principal would identify the problem and its causes, analyze it, develop alternatives or possible solutions, evaluate the alternatives, select the alternative that seems most satisfactory for implementation, then evaluate the outcome. In utilizing a normative model, varying degrees of rationality are available to the decision maker. These models are often referred to as rational models because the steps taken in reaching a solution are sequential, and it is assumed that the leader will be rational in following them (Gorton, 1987). "Decisions are rational if there is a reasonable connection between the means and ends, that is, if decision makers choose wisely the appropriate means for achieving the goals" (Hoy & Tarter, 1995, p. 3). The Classical, Administrative, and Mixed Scanning theoretical decision-making models are popular normative models that vary in their degree of rationality.

## The Descriptive Models

Commonly used descriptive models are the Garbage Can, Political, and Incremental models. If the leader chooses one of these models, the focus is on the manner in which the decision is *actually* reached, rather than how the decision *should* be made. Descriptive models are somewhat nonrational and tend to simply describe the process the leader follows in reaching the decision. Individuals who support this theory question whether the complex nature of school problems and the lack of leader control over elements in the environment of the school permit decision making in a rational sequential manner (Gorton, 1987).

Both the normative and descriptive models presuppose that certain actions and situations will apply. In the following section, we identify the characteristics of the six models previously mentioned and note situations in which they can be appropriately used.

## The Classical Model

The Classical Model is completely rational and has as its prime objective maximizing achievement of the goals of the organization by finding the best solution from among all possible alternatives. The process, which presupposes that all alternatives are identifiable, consists of a series of sequential steps that begin with problem identification and end with the achievement of the desired outcome. Most accounts of the model in the literature on decision making suggest that it is unrealistic for use by school leaders, as complete rationality in school decision making is not possible (Bolman & Deal, 1997; Hoy & Tarter,

1995; Yukl, 1989). School leaders never have access to all the information relative to an issue, nor are they able to identify all the possible alternatives. However, the model does offer school leaders a rational plan of action that is preferable to arbitrary and biased responses.

Given that one of the primary objectives of the school leader is to make management decisions to enhance learning and teaching (ISLLC, 1996), finding satisfactory solutions to multifaceted issues in an efficient and effective manner is desirable. However, if complete rationality is not possible (Classical Model), where can the school leader turn? What is an acceptable alternative that is suited for issues that occur in the day-to-day operation of schools? To some extent, Herbert Simon (1982) answered these questions when he presented the strategy of satisficing, which is reflected in the Administrative Model.

## The Administrative Model

The Administrative Model offers a systematic process to enhance the identification of the appropriate alternative when competing alternatives exist. It is an acceptable alternative to the classical process when a strategy of satisficing is employed. Simon (1982) theorized that there are instances when a decision alternative that does not reflect everything desired by the decision maker is selected. If this alternative is not totally unsatisfactory, a form of satisficing comes into play. Because leaders do not have all the data necessary to find the one best alternative to complex issues, they may settle for what is known as "bounded rationality." In such cases, the leader uses a rational sequential process to find the most satisfactory solution possible. The process consists of distinct phases: (1) recognition and definition of a problem, (2) analysis of difficulties, (3) establishing criteria for success, (4) development of an action plan, and (5) the appraisal of the plan. Using such a process, administrators can, more often than not, obtain wise solutions to problems using sound decision-making strategies. Decisions can be reached, using a means-ends analysis; in this process, the administrator selects a means to reach a desired end. Although the solution reached may not be optimal, it is satisfactory.

On some occasions, the school leader finds problems that are very complex in nature—so much so that decision outcomes are difficult to predict. In such instances, the leader may turn to the nonrational incremental decision-making model.

## The Incremental Model

Hoy and Tarter (1995) describe the Incremental Model as one that allows the school leader to make changes in small increments to avoid unanticipated negative consequences. The means-end analysis found in rational decision making is inappropriate. Decision objectives and alternatives are intertwined, and alternatives are selected when they are only slightly different from current reality and lie between current reality and the desired goal. Outcomes of decisions made are assessed and compared to the desired direction or what is accepted before other decisions are attempted. Lindblom (1959), who refers to this type of decision making as the "science of muddling through," argues that administrators are able to only muddle through many issues because of their complexity, uncertainty, and the amount of conflict that is likely to be provoked. Therefore, they make small decisions, and evaluate the consequences of each, proceeding until they reach the ultimate desired alternative. Because of the pressure of time and the void that exists within the information base, school administrators often turn to this descriptive model of decision making.

## The Mixed Scanning Model

The Mixed Scanning Model offered by Etzioni (1967) allows the school leader to combine the flexibility of the incremental model with the rationality of the satisficing model. By responding to the questions, What is the basic mission of the organization? and What incremental decisions will move the organization in that direction?, the leaders can make decisions and stay within the realm of the organization's mission and policies. Problems can be surveyed, difficulties analyzed, and a tentative action plan initiated; if it fails, something new is attempted. The school leader who meets the ISLLC Standards will have to be willing to take risks in the pursuit of the school's vision, and that seems acceptable as long as personnel are perceived as placing student success first and acting with integrity, fairness, and in an ethical manner. The Mixed Scanning Model seems appropriate to meet those ends, as the approach guides the decision process allowing the school leader to remain focused while reflecting on consequences of the selected alternative and the common good.

## The Garbage Can Model

The Garbage Can Model and the Political Model are often used in school situations. March (1982) reasons that the Garbage Can model allows individuals to act before thinking an issue through, an action that should be infrequent in its occurrence, but is sometimes necessary. In such instances, rather than beginning with a problem and ending with a solution, decision outcomes are products of independent streams of events. As problems occur and alternatives are formed, they are deposited into what is referred to as a garbage can. When the solution, the problem, and the participant just happen to connect, making a fit, the problem is solved. If the solution does not fit, then the problem remains unsolved (Cohen, March, & Olsen, 1972). This model relies on chance and provides an explanation for the actions of school leaders who appear to make decisions in an irrational manner.

## The Political Model

The Political Model is used when organizational goals are replaced by personal influence, and power is the overriding force (Kanter, 1982). Most organizations have defined goals, which they strive to achieve. However, in some instances, the power and influence of individuals and/or groups suppress organizational goals. In such instances, personal perspectives and preferences influence decisions in the organization. Individuals and/or groups maneuver to influence organizational outcomes so that objectives they favor might be achieved, rather than the objectives of others in the organization. The prevailing order of the day is manipulation. Conflict, bargaining, and game playing are intensive and pervasive. Satisficing organizational decision making gives way to influence, power, and persistence (Kotter, 1985).

As one might realize, selecting a model to utilize in reaching a decision of quality and acceptance takes considerable thought on the part of the leader. In addition to selecting an approach, the leader must also determine whether to make the decision independently or to invite assistance. We now turn to a discussion of the styles leaders might use. Two noteworthy styles are autocratic and participatory.

# Participatory or Shared Decision Making

In addition to determining whether to use a normative model or a descriptive one, the leader must determine whether to involve others in the process (participatory) or make the decision independently (autocratic). The determination can be a challenging decision within itself. Also, if the incorrect approach is selected, it can prove to be quite problematic.

If the leader chooses an autocratic approach and makes the decision with little or no involvement of subordinates, contingent on the situation, decision quality and acceptance could become problematic. If the situation is reversed and the leader chooses to involve subordinates and/or other stakeholders and such involvement is not warranted, the decision reached could also be of poor quality and not well received. The leader should not conclude that an autocratic decision will always be either inferior or superior. The goal should be to involve subordinates in the decision-making process when their involvement will improve the quality and/or acceptance of the decision. In other instances, the leader should make the decision independently. Choices range from totally autocratic behavior to joint participatory behavior. These choices, as described by Yukl (1994), appear in Figure 4.2.

In recent years, with the widespread acceptance of the reform movement, shared decision making has increased in importance. Involving subordinates in the decision-making process is an approach that has been informed by many researchers and writers (Gorton, 1987; Hoy & Miskel, 1991; Maier, 1963; Vroom & Jago, 1988; Vroom & Yetton, 1973; Yukl, 1989). From the work of

**FIGURE 4.2  Approaches to decision making**

1. Autocratic: The leader reaches a decision without any assistance from subordinates. Subordinates have no influence over decisions.
2. Consultation: The leader seeks the opinion of subordinates and asks them for their ideas. After giving consideration to the ideas, opinions, and suggestions of subordinates, the leader makes the decision.
3. Joint Decision Making: The leader meets with subordinates, discusses the problem, and together they develop a workable solution to the problem. The leader serves as a group participant and has no more influence than any other member of the group.
4. Delegation: The leader gives the authority and responsibility for making the decision to the group. Limits are specified and prior approval may or may not be required for decision implementation.

SOURCE: Material compiled from the work of Yukl, 1998.

these individuals, evidence suggests that, under certain conditions, groups outperform individuals. The challenge for school leaders is determining when and under what conditions subordinates should be involved. As was indicated in an earlier section of this chapter, there are some instances when school leaders should make decisions autocratically and some when the leader should invite the participation of subordinates and/or other stakeholders. Some writers have reported that the question of whether a group will do a better job of making a decision than the leader acting independently depends, to a large extent, on the complexity of the issue, the expertise of the participants selected, and whether or not the issue is in the participant's zone of concern (Hersey, Blanchard, and Johnson, 1996; Johnson & Johnson, 1982; Yukl, 1994). Therefore, these three variables will be discussed in the following section.

## The Complexity of the Issue

Vroom and Yetton (1973) offered a normative model that distinguishes between individual and group decision making. The model addresses how the behavior of the leader affects decision quality and acceptance. The originators of the model also suggest when leaders should involve subordinates in the decision-making process and to what extent. The model offers the school leader five decision procedures. Two procedures are autocratic in nature, two speak to consultation in decision making, and one speaks to leaders and subordinates making decisions jointly. The basic assumptions are that the more influence subordinates have, the more they will be motivated to implement a decision, and when decision acceptance is not already high, subordinate participation will increase decision acceptance (Yukl, 1989). This model is considered the best-known model for management of participation in organizational decision making (Hoy & Tarter, 1995). A summary of these decision procedures was presented in Chapter 1.

Vroom and Jago (1988) offered a revision to the model, adding the dimensions of time and subordinate development. Participatory decision making is very time consuming, and the leader must give consideration to the importance of making the decision in a timely manner. If a decision needs to be made with expediency, then selecting a participatory style may be counterproductive. If subordinates have the skills and attributes necessary to participate in the decision process, then, under certain conditions, they should be invited. Such conditions would suggest that an immediate decision is not necessary, and subordinates have the skills and attributes necessary to participate. Then, selecting a participatory style may produce a more acceptable alternative. The revised model adds these criteria as critical factors to be considered in determining the optimal decision procedures to utilize.

The challenge around participation and the inclusion of members in the decision-making process remain a complex issue. Whereas it is touted in research as one of the few approaches leaders can use to increase morale and productivity, its use creates issues in other areas of the organization (Bolman & Deal, 1997). The two major concerns regarding the use of a participatory approach are designing a system in which subordinates can effectively function and the fear from leaders that if subordinates are allowed to participate too frequently they will abuse the privilege (Bolman & Deal, 1997). In spite of these issues, leaders must be concerned with decision quality and decision acceptance, and subordinate participation is a factor in each of these areas.

## The Expertise of the Participants

Group performance is jointly affected by the intervening variables, quality and acceptance (Maier, 1963). Decision quality takes into account the objective aspects of the decision that affect the performance of the group. These objective aspects are considered aside from any effects mediated by decision acceptance. Using the group process depends on the contribution of group members and their ability to communicate effectively, use good judgment, be accurate in their assessment of the concerns and issues, and remain focused. If members of the group do not have the expertise necessary to make a contribution to group discussion, lack interest in the topic, or function in conflict with other members of the group, decision quality is likely to be less than desired (Maier, 1963).

Decision acceptance refers to the degree to which subordinates are committed to implementing a decision in an effective manner (Maier, 1963). In some instances, decisions made by the leader are accepted by subordinates simply because the decisions are beneficial to them or because of the approach used by the leader in reaching the decision. In other instances, subordinates refuse to accept a decision because it was made in an autocratic manner. One approach that is widely accepted in determining if subordinates are to be involved in the decision-making process is two dimensional. First, the leader should determine if subordinates have the expertise to contribute to finding an appropriate solution to the problem being addressed, and second, if the problem lies within the subordinate's zone of concern (Yukl, 1989).

## Participant Expertise and Zone of Concern

A decision is within the subordinate's zone of concern or interest when he/she is affected by the decision and/or expected to be involved in the implementation of the decision. When decisions are outside of the zone of concern or interest of subordinates, they are not likely to be highly motivated to participate in the decision-making process. However, if a decision is within their zone of concern and subordinates are excluded from participating in the process, they are likely to feel deprived and develop a level of dissatisfaction for the administrator. The subordinates included in the decision-making process should not only have a stake in the outcome of the decision, but they should also be able to contribute to the decision outcome and implementation (Bridges, 1967).

If an administrator elects to involve members of a group in the decision-making process, several different techniques can be employed; the Dialectical Inquiry Technique, the Nominal Group Technique, the Delphi Technique, and the Brainstorming Technique are among the most popular. Gorton (1987), Yukl (1989), and Barge (1994) report that these techniques have been found to be very effective in generating ideas from group members to enhance participatory decision making.

# Group Decision Techniques

The Dialectical Inquiry Technique is most appropriate for addressing complex problems when two completely different and contrary approaches are identifiable. Whereas it has proven to be effective, Yukl (1994) reports several accounts where the process failed to enhance group cohesiveness. Barge (1994) characterizes the technique in the following manner:

1. All available information regarding a specific problem or event is collected by the leader and presented to two subgroups. The makeup of each group is as homogenous as possible, but the groups are as different as possible.
2. Each group meets separately, develops an analysis of the problem, identifies a thesis, and provides an argument in support of their analysis and thesis. The argument should include all relevant information, assumptions, and key facts. The analysis and argument should be presented in written form. Groups then meet together to debate the theses and/or their proposal.
3. Using the analysis and argument provided in step 2, the leader searches for arguments and positions that are counter to or negate the theses. The leader also looks for recommendations counter to those developed in step 2. The conditions under which the original analysis would be in error or

open to question should be explored and identified. The analysis and accompanying arguments should be recorded in writing. The antithesis of the original analysis is thus identified.

4. The leader compares the two lists constructed in steps 2 and 3 and engages in a systematic critique of the competing assumptions. The validity of both sets of assumptions is examined. Ultimately, a list of assumptions consistent with both analyses is identified. A synthesis of the two competing positions is developed.
5. On the basis of the remaining assumptions, the leader can develop a set of recommendations.

When using the Nominal Group Technique, six steps are followed. The leader generates ideas in a silent manner by asking group members to write their ideas on slips of paper without engaging in discussion. Several minutes are allotted for the ideas of group members to be written. After the allotted time (5–10 minutes), each member contributes an idea in a round-robin manner. As ideas are suggested, they are written on a blackboard or flip chart. No evaluation or discussion of ideas is permitted during the posting period. The posting process continues until all ideas are presented. Members may pass if they have no additional ideas. After all ideas are posted, the leader reviews the list, inviting discussion on each by asking for questions, statements of clarification, or statements of agreement or disagreement regarding the relevance of the ideas to the problem. After the group has finished, ideas can be combined through a preliminary vote. Additional discussion is held on the combined ideas, and this leads to a final vote (Delbecq, Van de Ven, & Gustafsen, 1986).

The Delphi Technique, developed by researchers at the Rand Corporation in 1969, is a technique that has proven to be very effective when expert advice concerning an issue is needed from a large number of people (Dalkey, 1969). It is a process that generates ideas, allows individuals to react to program proposals, or raises questions concerning a project. Individuals are able to think through complex issues and submit high-quality ideas without the influence of individuals in positions of status. The technique involves the following five steps:

1. The leader defines the problem, decision, or question to which individuals and/or groups are to react.
2. The leader identifies those individuals and/or groups whose opinion, judgments, or expert knowledge would be valuable to obtain in the process of making a decision.
3. The leader asks for responses of identified individuals and/or groups using a written format, often a questionnaire.
4. The results received are summarized and redistributed to the individuals and/or groups, and they are asked to review and indicate any changes in their initial responses.

5. Step 4 is repeated until there is a reasonable consensus on the problem or decision (Gorton, 1987).

Brainstorming is a technique used to encourage group members to contribute to finding solutions to problems by spontaneously suggesting any and all ideas that come to mind (Osborn, 1957). When ideas are suggested, they are written on a blackboard or flip chart. The rules of effective brainstorming do not permit any positive or negative evaluative comments, scowls, groans, sighs, or gestures. All ideas are accepted, and value judgments are deferred. Members of the group are also encouraged to combine or improve on ideas suggested.

There is little doubt that using decision-making groups holds many advantages. Groups tend to generate more ideas and make higher-quality decisions. Working with others often causes members to perform better; they receive support and encouragement and tend to look at alternatives more thoroughly. They acquire a greater understanding of the issues and take ownership of the decisions, realizing they will have to live with the outcomes.

## Barriers and Traps That Inhibit Decision Effectiveness

Although there are a number of advantages to both autocratic and participatory decision making, there are also a number of barriers and traps that interfere with decision effectiveness or cause decisions to be flawed when either is used. Some worthy of note are groupthink, the overuse of groups, and fair process.

Groupthink can become a barrier because sometimes groups become so cohesive that members resist challenging ideas to maintain the integrity of the group. Because members do not want to risk disrupting the stability of the group, information from outside of the group that would possibly enhance decision quality is rejected, and creative thinking is stifled.

The leader must also safeguard against involving too many people in the decision-making process. Some leaders have so many committees operating that they spend the major portion of their time in committee meetings. Involving individuals in decisions that should be made by the leader can be as problematic as not involving individuals when the situation warrants their involvement. This constitutes poor leadership.

Fair process is another issue leaders should give special attention as decisions are reached. In many instances, individuals on the faculty of a school will like the outcome of a decision that has been reached by the principal or others, but will not like the process that was used to produce the decision. The process that produces a decision is a major concern of many individuals. People care about decision outcomes, but they also care about the process that is used to reach those outcomes. They want to have their say, and they want to feel that they had an opportunity to participate in the process, even if their point of view is rejected. When this does not occur, the process can profoundly influence the attitudes of faculty members in a manner that negatively impacts the success of the school (Kim & Mauborgne, 1997). Without fair process, school goals can be difficult to achieve because when the faculty does not trust the process, they are likely to see only the negative side of the issue. Kim and Mauborgne (1997) report three principles of fair process that are worthy of consideration by the school leader. They are:

1. Engagement: Individuals are involved in decisions that affect them. The leader asks for their input and allows them to refute the merits of one another's ideas and assumptions.
2. Explanation: Everyone involved and affected should understand why final decisions are made as they are.
3. Expectation Clarity: Once a decision is made, managers state clearly the new rules of the game (p. 69).

Regardless of an individual's role in the school district or position on the faculty, he/she wants to be treated with respect and appreciated for the expertise brought to the organization. Individuals want their ideas and opinions to be seriously considered, and they want to understand the reasoning behind decisions that are made.

Leaders should also be aware of hidden traps in decision making. Decisions are often flawed because of hidden traps that get in the way of effectiveness. From the work of Hammond, Keeney, and Raiffa (1998a), eight traps that leaders might consider in attempting to safeguard against flawed decision making are:

1. Status quo: We all carry biases, and those biases influence the choices we make. The source of the status-quo trap lies deep within our psyches, in our desire to protect our ego from damage.
2. Sunk-cost: We make choices in a way that justifies past choices, even when the past choices no longer seem valid.
3. Confirming-evidence: We seek out information that supports our existing instinct or point of view while avoiding information that contradicts it.
4. Framing: We can use different frames to assess a problem. The same problem can elicit very different responses when frames use different reference points. A poorly framed problem can undermine even the best-considered decision.
5. Estimating and forecasting: We often fail to get clear feedback regarding the accuracy of our estimates and forecasting.
6. Prudence: When we are faced with high-stakes decisions, we tend to adjust our estimates to be on the safe side.
7. Recallability: We frequently base our predictions about future events on our memory of past events, and we can be overly influenced by dramatic events—those that leave a strong impression on our memory.
8. Overconfidence: We tend to be overconfident about our accuracy relative to our estimates. This can lead to errors in judgment and, in turn, bad decisions (pp. 47–58).

Guarding against groupthink, using groups only when appropriate, insuring a system of fair practice, and safeguarding against hidden traps can assist greatly in improving decision quality and acceptance in schools.

## Summary

The demands on education today are placing pressure on leaders in the field to be effective decision makers and to communicate those decisions in a manner that will improve teaching and learning and promote the success of all students (ISLLC, 1996). In making and communicating decisions in the manner the ISLLC Standards require, leaders will have to take a number of factors under consideration. They will need to understand the values and the culture of the school and community they serve, identify appropriate decision-making models, and act, using a professional code of ethics. Their primary objective will necessarily have to be the involvement of all stakeholders in a manner that will generate decisions that reflect the common good.

## The Scenarios

The scenarios in this chapter approach decision making from three different perspectives: (1) establishing and following policy to provide educational success for all students in a safe environment; (2) acting with integrity, valuing diversity, and bringing ethical principles to the decision-making process to ensure success for all students; and (3) effectively communicating with all stakeholders to ensure that decisions are of quality and will be accepted. The reader will be able to observe three different leaders with three different styles make three different decisions, all of which have some effect on the environment of the school and student learning. Also, the reader can analyze the activities of these scenarios as they relate to ISLLC Standards 5 and 6. Particular attention should be given to the connection between communication and decision making and how each process has the potential of negatively impacting the other.

## SCENARIO 12
### THE REQUESTED CHANGE

#### STANDARD 5

A school administrator is an educational leader who promotes the success of all students by acting with integrity, fairness, and in an ethical manner.

## STANDARD 6

A school administrator is an educational leader who promotes the success of all students by understanding, responding to, and influencing the larger political, social, economic, legal, and cultural context.

*In Scenario 12, a principal is faced with making a decision concerning the instructional program. He is new to the school and is not very clear on the political, social, economic, and cultural context of the community. Nevertheless, the decision he is asked to make will impact students, teachers, and the organizational structure of the school. In responding to the issue and reaching a decision of quality that will be accepted, he will need to be guided by Indicators of ISLLC Standards 5 and 6.*

### ISLLC Standards Indicators Exhibited in Scenario 12

**Knowledge Indicators**

The administrator has knowledge and understanding of:
▲ Information sources, data collection, and data analysis strategies
▲ Effective communication
▲ Effective consensus-building and negotiation skills
▲ Information sources, data collection, and data analysis strategies
▲ Applied learning theories
▲ Curriculum design, implementation, evaluation, and refinement
▲ Principles of effective instruction
▲ Management, evaluation, and assessment strategies
▲ Diversity and its meaning for educational programs
▲ The change process for systems, organizations, and individuals
▲ Emerging issues and trends that potentially impact the school community
▲ The conditions and dynamics of the diverse school community
▲ Various ethical frameworks and perspectives on ethics
▲ The values of the diverse community
▲ Theories and models of organizations and the principles of organizational development
▲ The role of education in developing and renewing a democratic society and economically productive schooling
▲ The political, social, cultural, and economic systems and processes that impact schools
▲ Models and strategies of change and conflict resolution as applied to the larger political, social, cultural, and economic context of schooling
▲ Global issues and forces affecting teaching and learning
▲ The importance of diversity and equity in a democratic society
▲ Legal issues impacting school operations

**Disposition Indicators**

The administrator believes in, values, and is committed to:
▲ Educability of all
▲ Using the influence of one's office constructively and productively in the service of all students and families
▲ Education as a key to social mobility

▲ Using legal systems to protect student rights and improve student opportunities
▲ Developing a caring school community
▲ The right of every student to a free, quality education
▲ Subordinating one's own interest to the good of the school community
▲ Bringing ethical principles to the decision-making process
▲ Collaboration and communication with families
▲ The proposition that diversity enriches the school
▲ Making management decisions to enhance learning and teaching
▲ High-quality standards, expectations, and performances
▲ Involving stakeholders in management processes
▲ Involvement of families and other stakeholders in school decision-making processes
▲ Families as partners in the education of their children
▲ The proposition that families have the best interests of their children in mind
▲ Resources of the family needing to be brought to bear on the education of students
▲ The ideal of the common good
▲ Accepting responsibility
▲ Accepting the consequences for upholding one's principles and actions
▲ Recognizing a variety of ideas, values, and cultures
▲ A willingness to continuously examine one's own assumptions, beliefs, and practices

**Performance Indicators**

The administrator facilitates processes and engages in activities that ensure:
▲ The school community works within the framework of polices, laws, and regulations enacted by local, state, and federal authorities
▲ All individuals are treated with fairness, dignity and respect
▲ Barriers to student learning are identified, clarified, and addressed
▲ There is a culture of high expectations for self, student, and staff performance
▲ Curriculum decisions are based on research, expertise of teachers, and the recommendations of learned societies
▲ A variety of sources of information are used to make decisions
▲ Student learning is assessed using a variety of techniques
▲ Lines of communication are developed with decision makers outside the school community
▲ Multiple sources of information regarding performance are used by staff and students
▲ Knowledge of learning, teaching, and student development is used to inform management decisions
▲ Problems are confronted and resolved in a timely manner
▲ Stakeholders are involved in decisions affecting schools
▲ Potential problems and opportunities are identified
▲ Responsibility is shared to maximize ownership and accountability
▲ Effective conflict resolution skills are used
▲ Effective group-process and consensus-building skills are used
▲ Effective communication skills are used
▲ Relationships with community leaders are identified and nurtured
▲ Information about family and community concerns, expectations, and needs is used regularly
▲ The school and community serve one another as resources
▲ Credence is given to individuals and groups whose values and opinions may conflict
▲ Community stakeholders are treated equitably

▲ Diversity is recognized and valued

▲ A comprehensive program of community relations is established

▲ Opportunities for staff to develop collaboration skills are provided

▲ Communication occurs among the school community concerning trends, issues, and potential changes in the environment in which the school operates

▲ The environment in which schools operate is influenced on behalf of students and their families

▲ There is ongoing dialogue with representatives of diverse community groups

▲ Public policy is shaped to provide quality education for students

▲ Effective problem-framing and problem-solving skills are used

**The administrator**

▲ Examines personal and professional values

▲ Demonstrates a personal and professional code of ethics

▲ Demonstrates values, beliefs, and attitudes that inspire others to higher levels of performance

▲ Serves as a role model

▲ Accepts responsibility for school operations

▲ Examines and considers the prevailing values of the diverse school community

▲ Expects that others in the school community will demonstrate integrity and exercise ethical behavior

▲ Considers the impact of one's administrative practices on others

▲ Treats people fairly, equitably, and with dignity and respect

▲ Demonstrates appreciation for sensitivity to the diversity in the school community

▲ Applies laws and procedures fairly, wisely, and considerately

Mr. Robert Miller was recently (July 1 of the current year) appointed principal of Springview Elementary School. Springview is a school with a student population of 800. The students are from across the city, as Springview has an open enrollment policy.

Everyone appears to be pleased with the racial make-up of the faculty, which is 90 percent Caucasian and 10 percent African American. They are also pleased with the racial composition of the student body, which is 90 percent Caucasian, 8 percent African American, and 2 percent Asian-American. Mr. Miller is only the second principal. Mr. Williams, the former principal, opened the school 10 years ago. Under his authoritarian leadership and firm control, the school became the pride of the Springview School District.

The second week of school, Mr. Miller looked at his calendar to find that he had an appointment with a group of parents from the east section of the city, the area everyone refers to as the "old money part of the city." He was also scheduled to meet with a group of parents from a new area of the city called Lakehills. Lakehills was recently developed, and a large number of minority first-time home owners have moved into the area.

Mr. Miller was wondering why these two groups wanted a meeting. "Perhaps to welcome me to the school," he said as he asked his secretary to show the first group of parents into his office.

Very little was said in the first meeting. Indeed, the parents welcomed Mr. Miller to the school and advised him that he could depend on their support. However, they had one request, which was to establish ability grouping at the school. They gave a number of reasons for wanting this change; however, the major reason expressed was instructional time. It was their contention that the slow children took up a large portion of instructional time, and there was not enough left to challenge the gifted students. The meeting ended with Mr. Miller saying he would consider the request and give them a response in the next several days.

In the second meeting, Mr. Miller was met with quite a different situation, there being no direct request at all. The parents welcomed him to the school and advised him how pleased they were with the education their children were receiving. They also said that they would provide any assistance he needed and hoped there would be no major changes in the instructional program. The meeting ended with all smiling.

## REFLECTIVE THINKING AND SCENARIO ANALYSIS

1. What are the primary issues in this scenario, and what information is Principal Miller likely to need in order to demonstrate appreciation for and sensitivity to the diversity in the school community?
2. What decision-making approaches could Principal Miller use to ensure decision quality while involving families and other community stakeholders in selecting a decision alternative?
3. What action, if any, should Principal Miller take to demonstrate that he is an educational leader who treats people fairly, equitably, and with dignity and respect? Justify your position.
4. What information sources, data collection, and data analysis strategies would you advise Principal Miller to utilize to ensure decision quality and acceptance?
5. What action should Principal Miller take to ensure that the final alternative selected will influence the implementation of a curriculum based on research, expertise of teachers, and the characteristics of a learned society?

## ADDRESSING THE ISSUES

Select the one best answer to the following questions:

1. Based upon your understanding of the circumstances under which various decision-making approaches are used, which of the following approaches would you suggest Mr. Miller employ to ensure decision acceptance and quality?

    a. Seek to find the best alternative to the divergent views of the two groups.

    b. Utilize a structured approach that is focused on specific objectives designed to achieve a desired outcome.

    c. Make several small decisions, assessing the reaction of both parent groups to each, prior to making a major decision regarding the instructional program.

    d. Apply a solution that has worked very effectively with situations of this nature in the past.

**2.** In reaching a decision on the issue, Mr. Miller could demonstrate that he is committed to achieving the greatest good for the total school

 **a.** if he kept the situation from escalating by reaching a decision very quickly and not involving others.

 **b.** if he shared the concern with the faculty and other parents in the district in an effort to collect information that would enable him to reach the best decision possible.

 **c.** by not making a decision on this matter; he might share with the first parent group that he is new to the school and needs time to get adjusted before addressing such a volatile issue.

 **d.** by only working with the first group of parents in reaching an acceptable solution inasmuch as they raised the issue.

**3.** If Mr. Miller wanted to extensively explore the range of views on the key issue in the scenario, which of the following actions might best serve his purpose?

 **a.** Hold a formal meeting, including both parent groups, present critical information on the pros and cons of the issue, allowing time for each group to analyze and debate the merits of their position and provide feedback.

 **b.** Hold a meeting of the two groups, allowing time for group members (without engaging in discussion) to write their ideas on slips of paper, post the ideas, combine them, and then reach a decision from the combined ideas.

 **c.** Create a proposal and present the proposal to each group, allowing time for group members to react to the proposal.

 **d.** Hold a meeting with both groups present and encourage the parents to make suggestions relative to the best solution to the problem.

**4.** Evaluating Mr. Miller's activities from the teaching and learning point of view, which of the following factors should influence the involvement or exclusion of teachers?

 **a.** The issue is in the zone of concern of teachers, and any decision alternative selected in one way or another will affect them.

 **b.** The issue is outside of the zone of concern of teachers, and they would not be receptive to being involved.

 **c.** The issue is one that concerns a powerful group of parents and should be handled by the administration.

 **d.** The issue is one that is highly political and should be handled by the administration.

**5.** Which of the following would be a viable explanation for Mr. Miller wanting to use the Delphi Technique in reaching a final decision?

 **a.** To frame the problem; allow various groups inside and outside the district to give expert opinions; allow individuals supporting both parent groups to raise questions; and then summarize the results.

 **b.** To allow both parent groups to raise questions and provide information.

**c.** To generate a large number of pros and cons regarding the concept of ability grouping.

**d.** To allow each parent group to definitively develop their position on the subject.

## DISCUSSION OF THE SOLUTION

1. Selecting an approach to utilize in identifying a decision alternative regarding a complex issue is a very important part of the decision-making process. To select the decision alternative in this situation, Mr. Miller will need as much information as possible to first generate alternatives and then to select the one that is appropriate to address the issue. Being a new principal, the challenge is even greater because there are a number of factors relative to an issue of this nature that can only be determined after spending considerable time in the school and community in question. Because of the lack of information concerning the groups' motivation, power base (both important factors), and other factors that may exist, the principal is not likely to be able to make a decision based on complete rationality. Thus, he will have to resort to a form of satisficing. His concern necessarily becomes one of acquiring and processing all relevant information to ensure decision quality and acceptance.

The outcome of the decision will have implications for many individuals and groups, as well as for the school's instructional program. In seeking a solution to such a complex problem, Mr. Miller must begin with the end in mind, follow a structured plan, involve the right people, collect extensive information regarding the issues, develop alternatives, test those alternatives, and select the one that is in the best interest of children. The suggested response to question 1 is **(b)**.

2. The principal, being new to the district, will need information concerning: (1) the two community groups, (2) the community at large, (3) the challenges the school has faced that were socially and culturally motivated, (4) how those challenges were addressed in the past, (5) the faculty's and larger community's position on ability grouping, and (6) a host of other educational issues. This information will necessarily be obtained from a variety of sources inside and outside of the school. In addition, the principal will need to have some idea of how the decision alternative selected will affect various individuals and groups, as well as the school's program over the long term.

It is believed by some that the quality and accuracy of information used to make a decision will determine, to a large extent, the effectiveness of that decision. Also, it is postulated that through the use of a shared decision-making approach, the quality of information can be enhanced, thereby resulting in a decision of increased quality (Bolman & Deal, 1997). Considering this factor and given the nature of this situation, using a shared decision-making approach would be in the best interest of the total school program. Entering such a mode would allow Mr. Miller to use the expertise of others, which would enhance decision quality and acceptance. Both factors are of prime importance when addressing an issue of this nature. The suggested response to question 2 is **(b)**.

3. The question of ability grouping is one of great interest to a large number of individuals both inside and outside of the school setting. Much has been written on the subject, and feelings on both sides of the issue run deep. Individuals and/or groups in any given community might have varied opinions on the subject. Therefore, the full

range of views in a given community needs to be explored. The assumptions behind the position "for" and "against" should be evaluated and their importance and feasibility analyzed.

In order for the principal to influence the decision in the direction that is in the best interests of all students and ensure the right of every student to a free, quality education, considerable creativity and expertise will be needed. Individuals on both sides of the issue should have an opportunity to present their points of view. It is important for families and other stakeholders to be involved in the decision-making process (ISLLC, 1996). Therefore, the principal should select and utilize a group decision-making technique that will allow the opinions of both parent groups, as well as other individuals and groups, to be heard. In this way, both sides of the issue will be presented. The Dialectical Inquiry technique described in choice (a) will facilitate this outcome. The suggested response to question 3 is **(a)**.

4. There are several factors an administrator might analyze to determine whether or not to involve teachers in reaching a decision regarding a particular issue. Some of these factors are teacher expertise, teacher interest, whether teachers will be affected by the decision, and the need for teacher involvement in the process of implementing the decision. These factors place the issue in the zone of concern of teachers.

While the decision concerning ability grouping is larger than the classroom, spreading into the community of the school, the ultimate responsibility for its implementation lies with the classroom teacher. Mr. Miller's primary responsibility is schoolwide, while teachers (in addition to new teacher leader roles) devote their time and attention specifically to the teaching and learning process. Quite clearly, teachers have expertise in the area of ability grouping, and the end results of the decision will greatly affect them and the children they teach. Therefore, this is an issue that is in their zone of concern, and Mr. Miller would be well advised to involve them in the decision-making process from the outset. The suggested response to question 4 is **(a)**.

5. All of the group approaches listed could be used in one form or another. However, if the principal is interested in ensuring that communication (concerning trends, issues, and potential changes in the environment in which the school operates) occurs among individuals in the school and community, and then the Delphi Technique (alternative a) is the likely approach to select. The suggested response to question 5 is **(a)**.

## SUMMARY AND CONCLUSION

Mr. Miller, who was recently appointed principal, comes to a well-established school as only the second principal. His goal should be to establish cooperative working relationships and to build on the cohesiveness of the faculty and community. Without a degree of cohesiveness between participants, a social system could not effectively exist (Hanson, 1996).

The concerns of the parents should be explored in an objective manner. If large discrepancies exist between students' abilities and achievement, as perceived by parents, programs should be designed to address those discrepancies. It would be important for parents from both groups to be involved in any planning and program development. Members of both groups would need to be able to understand the others' concerns. Because the quality and acceptance of this decision are very important, a shared decision-making technique would serve the process well. Although time is an issue, the outcome is more essential than time. To attempt to reach a decision on an issue of this magnitude in short order renders the decision maker susceptible to error.

A school is an open social system subject to the influences of forces in its internal and external environments. School leaders must be aware of individuals who have power and how they make use of that power. It is not uncommon for individuals and groups to engage in power struggles, which are often used to gain control over the school's resources and direction (Hanson, 1996). School leaders must be aware of these individuals and groups and the nature of their agendas. Sometimes the agendas of specific groups are overtly debated as expressions of the will of the people. However, the real agenda items are increasingly being hidden from the public view only to surface after the decision has been reached.

The school leader must be committed to using the influence of his/her office constructively and productively in the service of all students and their families (ISLLC, 1996). All decisions should be fair, and the effects of all alternative decisions should be considered. Every student has a right to a free, quality education, and the leader must make decisions to enhance learning and teaching (ISLLC, 1996) in order that the rights of students become a reality. The goal must be the best educational programs possible for all students.

## SCENARIO 13
### RETAINING THE STUDENT RECOGNITION PROGRAM

### STANDARD 5
A school administrator is an educational leader who promotes the success of all students by acting with integrity, fairness, and in an ethical manner.

*In Scenario 13, respect for the work that has been completed in the past challenges a principal who must make a decision regarding work that must be completed in the future, lest the state of student discipline compromise the learning environment of the school. The challenge faced by the principal is one of accepting the responsibility for school operations while demonstrating appreciation for the work of others. He is also challenged to accept the thesis that his faculty can be inspired to perform at a high level.*

### ISLLC Standards Indicators Exhibited in Scenario 13

**Knowledge Indicators**
The administrator has knowledge and understanding of:
▲ Learning goals in a pluralistic society
▲ Information sources, data collection, and data analysis strategies
▲ Effective communication
▲ Effective consensus-building and negotiation skills
▲ Information sources, data collection, and data analysis strategies
▲ Applied learning theories

▲ Curriculum design, implementation, evaluation, and refinement
▲ Principles of effective instruction
▲ Management, evaluation, and assessment strategies
▲ Diversity and its meaning for educational programs
▲ Adult learning and professional development models
▲ The change process for systems, organizations, and individuals
▲ School cultures
▲ Operational procedures at the school and district level
▲ Human resource management and development
▲ Emerging issues and trends that potentially impact the school community
▲ The conditions and dynamics of the diverse school community
▲ Professional code of ethics
▲ Theories and models of organizations and the principles of organizational development
▲ Models and strategies of change and conflict resolution as applied to the larger political, social, cultural, and economic context of schooling
▲ Global issues and forces affecting teaching and learning
▲ The dynamics of policy development and advocacy under our democratic political system
▲ The importance of diversity and equity in a democratic society

**Disposition Indicators**

The administrator believes in, values, and is committed to:
▲ Using the influence of one's office constructively and productively in the service of all students and families
▲ Professional development as an integral part of school improvement
▲ The benefit that diversity brings to the school community
▲ A safe and supportive learning environment
▲ Preparing students to be contributing members of society
▲ Accepting responsibility
▲ Recognizing a variety of ideas, values, and cultures
▲ Developing a caring school community
▲ The right of every student to a free, quality education
▲ Importance of a continuing dialogue with other decision makers affecting education
▲ Bringing ethical principles to the decision-making process
▲ The proposition that diversity enriches the school
▲ Making management decisions to enhance learning and teaching
▲ High-quality standards, expectations, and performances
▲ The ideal of the common good
▲ Accepting responsibility
▲ A willingness to continuously examine one's own assumptions, beliefs, and practices

**Performance Indicators**

The administrator facilitates processes and engages in activities ensuring that:
▲ The school community works within the framework of polices, laws, and regulations enacted by local, state, and federal authorities
▲ Students and staff feel valued and important
▲ The responsibilities and contributions of each individual are acknowledged
▲ All individuals are treated with fairness, dignity, and respect
▲ Barriers to student learning are identified, clarified, and addressed

▲ There is a culture of high expectations for self, student, and staff performance
▲ Student and staff accomplishments are recognized and celebrated
▲ The school is organized and aligned for success
▲ Time is managed to maximize attainment of organizational goals
▲ Potential problems and opportunities are identified
▲ Problems are confronted and resolved in a timely manner
▲ A variety of sources of information are used to make decisions
▲ Lines of communication are developed with decision makers outside the school community
▲ Multiple sources of information regarding performance are used by staff and students
▲ Knowledge of learning, teaching, and student development is used to inform management decisions
▲ Stakeholders are involved in decisions affecting schools
▲ Responsibility is shared to maximize ownership and accountability
▲ Effective problem-framing and problem-solving skills are used
▲ Effective group-process and consensus-building skills are used
▲ Effective communication skills are used
▲ Diversity is recognized and valued
▲ Opportunities for staff to develop collaboration skills are provided
▲ Communication occurs among the school community concerning trends, issues, and potential changes in the environment in which the school operates
▲ The environment in which schools operate is influenced on behalf of students and their families
▲ There is ongoing dialogue with representatives of diverse community groups
▲ Public policy is shaped to provide quality education for students
▲ Operational plans and procedures to achieve the vision and goals of the school are in place
▲ Professional development promotes a focus on student learning consistent with the school vision and goals

**The administrator**
▲ Examines personal and professional values
▲ Demonstrates a personal and professional code of ethics
▲ Demonstrates values, beliefs, and attitudes that inspire others to higher levels of performance
▲ Serves as a role model
▲ Accepts responsibility for school operations
▲ Considers the impact of one's administrative practices on others
▲ Treats people fairly, equitably, and with dignity and respect
▲ Demonstrates appreciation for and sensitivity to the diversity in the school community

Overfield High School is a large 9–12 urban high school with a student population of 3,000. Over the past six years, the school has experienced an increase in discipline problems and a decline in student achievement and attendance. At least two students have been expelled for having weapons on campus.

In an attempt to change this trend, the principal and staff made a commitment to implement a student recognition program. The program has been in operation for four years. During the first two years of the program, there was a decline in discipline problems, attendance increased, and the faculty was pleased with the classroom work of their students. However, the last two years of the program have been quite different. Discipline problems are increasing; attendance has fallen by two percentage points, and Principal Jones has noticed signs of waning faculty enthusiasm for the program. In fact, the original, energetic and enthusiastic core of 15 teachers who conceptualized the program and influenced the faculty and student body to adopt it has now dwindled to a group of 5 overworked individuals. Principal Jones realized that something had to be done or the program would fall apart, and all the original gains would be lost. Therefore, early in the spring, he scheduled a series of meetings to review the program.

During the spring review, teachers voiced concerns that the students were losing their excitement with the rewards associated with the program. The faculty also reported instances where they had heard students complain about boredom—too much time sitting still, the "same old prizes," and too-stiff attendance guidelines. Relative to their involvement, the faculty expressed concerns regarding the behavior of some of the students during assembly programs and the need for a change in the program guidelines. On the positive side, the faculty reported that students expressed enjoyment with the use of field trips, tickets for special events, dances, and food as "prizes." At the conclusion of the review, it was decided that the student recognition program was a good program that simply needed to be revitalized.

Once the faculty recognized which areas of the program they needed to revise, they spent hours in five different meetings, generating and evaluating ideas and identifying possible changes to the program. After the fifth meeting, Principal Jones looked at his exhausted faculty and said to them, "You have done an excellent job. I will take all your suggestions, compile them, and send you a copy of the compilation during June for your review. We will meet in late August to discuss and finalize the program for next school year."

The faculty appeared very energized, and everyone left school feeling a sense of accomplishment and voicing satisfaction with the outlook for the new school year.

## REFLECTIVE THINKING AND SCENARIO ANALYSIS

1. What were some early indicators that the student recognition program needed attention?
2. What were some early decisions that could have been made to reduce the likelihood of the problem escalating to the level that signaled a need for the spring review?
3. If it is true that low faculty morale existed before the spring review, what leadership behavior possibly led to the level of satisfaction expressed by the faculty at the end of the spring review?
4. In the scenario, can you cite passages that would serve as evidence that ethical principles were included in the decision-making process?
5. What effect did the disposition of Principal Jones have on his attempt to address this situation? From the scenario, cite passages to support your response.
6. From the scenario, cite instances that would suggest that subordinate participation increases decision quality and acceptance.

## ADDRESSING THE ISSUES

Select the one best answer to the following questions:

1. Which of the following would you identify as the critical factor influencing the need to hold a review of the student recognition program?

   a. The principal's failure to frame the problem and use effective problem-solving skills.

   b. The principal's failure to identify the critical issues in priority order and accept responsibility for school operations.

   c. Efforts to reach a primary goal at Overfield generated secondary issues, which motivated action by the principal.

   d. The initial action taken by the principal, which generated negative results, creating a need to hold a spring review that involved teachers.

2. Which of the following best explains the reason for the reversal of the success rate of the student recognition program?

   a. Failure of Principal Jones to recognize that the number of original teachers leaving the program indicated a belief that discipline was outside of their zone of concern.

   b. The lack of participation by Principal Jones, which was perceived by the teachers as failure to accept responsibility for school operations.

   c. Lack of commitment from the total faculty because they believed the decision regarding school discipline was made in an autocratic manner.

   d. The absence of a formative and summative evaluation component in the plan, suggesting that additional expertise on the original committee would have been helpful.

3. When assessing the issue from the viewpoint of motivating faculty creativity, the most critical factor to be considered by Principal Jones in the selection of a decision-making approach was:

   a. The implication of using the selected decision-making model, given that two groups of faculty members would have been involved.

   b. The inclusion of stakeholders in the decision-making process, which would ensure decision fairness, quality, and acceptance.

   c. The evaluation component of the selected decision-making model, given that assessment is an important component of any model.

   d. Using existing resources in support of the implementation of the model.

4. In bringing about change in the student recognition program, which of the following actions would likely produce the most effective results?

   a. Hold a conference with the original 15 teachers and share with them what you believe to be the reason they were unsuccessful in implementing the program.

   b. Engage the entire faculty in a partnership for the purpose of finding a solution to the challenges the current program has posed.

c. Select another group of teachers and ask them to provide the leadership for modifying and implementing the revised plan.

d. Consult the faculty for recommendations on who should be in charge of modifying the existing program and implementing the new plan.

5. When one considers the dynamics and the inner workings of the social system at Overfield High School, good judgment dictates that Principal Jones should have

a. made an autocratic decision concerning the program with the expectation that the faculty would implement it.

b. taken the action that he took, become a member of the group, and participated in the development of decision alternatives.

c. consulted with the faculty, solicited their opinions, and used their ideas where possible.

d. assigned the task of revising the plan to the faculty with strong words of encouragement.

## DISCUSSION OF THE SOLUTION

1. The primary goals of the principal and faculty at Overfield were to reduce discipline problems and to increase student achievement and attendance. In an effort to achieve these goals, a student recognition program was implemented. The implementation of the student recognition program was initially successful. However, it did not enable the school to achieve and sustain its primary goals. Further, in the process of attempting to achieve these goals, the school experienced other challenges. These included waning faculty enthusiasm for program implementation, low faculty morale because of an increase in student discipline problems, and students' complaints about the awards component of the program. These complaints became primary, warranting priority attention. The initial goals of reducing discipline problems, increasing attendance, and promoting student achievement became long-term goals. For the principal, faculty morale and the threat that discipline posed to the teaching and learning process became the primary concerns.

At Overfield, the attempt of a select group of faculty members to implement a discipline program generated issues that had to be given priority attention. In providing that attention, the principal took actions that met an ISLLC Standard Indicator. He identified issues, confronted them, and resolved them in a timely manner. The suggested response to question 1 is (c).

2. The student recognition program got off to an excellent start, and progress toward the established goal was being made. However, after the first two years of implementation, there was a drop in the success rate of the program, causing the school to experience problems in other areas. No one was really able to pinpoint the cause of the decline in attendance or the increase in discipline problems. This is likely the case because no formative evaluation was conducted. Also, in the absence of a summative evaluation, the administration and faculty would find it difficult, at best, to determine the effective components of the program.

Had a formative evaluation been conducted during or after the first year, components not working effectively could have been identified, modified, or replaced. To adequately monitor a program, the leader needs to have an understanding of measurement, evaluation, and assessment strategies (ISLLC, 1996). Even the best programs need to be evaluated, generating results that can be used to make modifications and changes in the program. The absence of a program evaluation makes early detection of poorly functioning components difficult and hampers the success of the program.

When a committee is formed to address a school issue, it is beneficial for the leader to support the work of the committee by assisting them in identifying the human and material resources necessary to successfully complete the assigned task (ISLLC, 1996). In the absence of such assistance, there is the possibility that some needed component might be omitted. In this instance, the evaluation component was omitted. The suggested response to question 2 is **(d)**.

3. From the viewpoint of motivating faculty creativity, it was critical for Principal Jones to be concerned with fairness of the revision process, quality of any decision reached, and the acceptance of that decision by the faculty. After all, the faculty was initially committed to the student recognition program (especially the original 15), and at one time it worked well. Before altering the program or changing to a completely different one, it was wise to acquire the faculty's assistance in conducting an analysis of the current program, determining the critical issues, and developing and evaluating possible alternatives. This is an action that is likely to be considered as fair by the faculty, particularly the 15 faculty members who originally conceptualized the program.

In selecting his decision alternative, Principal Jones likely gave consideration to the impact of his behavior on the faculty members assuming responsibility for the initial program. In so doing, he ensured that individuals who had worked to achieve success with the initial program were treated with fairness, dignity, and respect. This is another action that meets an ISLLC Standard. Students and staff need to feel valued and important, and the leader must assume the responsibility of ensuring that the contributions they make are acknowledged (ISLLC, 1996). In so doing, the potential for decision quality and acceptance is enhanced. The suggested response to question 3 is **(b)**.

4. A large number of faculty members were involved in the origination of the student recognition program. These faculty members demonstrated creativity and interest in resolving a challenge faced by the school. Failure of the program cannot be allowed to reflect negatively on the creators. If this occurs, faculty creativity is likely to be stifled, and future attempts by the faculty to solve schoolwide problems are likely to be limited. In addition, without some type of program evaluation, it would be difficult to determine the causes of the lack of success.

Inviting other faculty members to provide the leadership for the program would likely embarrass the initial group of teachers, leading them and their colleagues to believe that they were responsible for the failure of the program. Such an approach is not likely to be well received or motivational.

Principal Jones engaged the faculty in a participatory decision-making approach. Generally, when decision quality is important and subordinates have the expertise to make the decision, a participatory decision-making style leads to more effective decisions than does an autocratic style (Yukl, 1989). The suggested response to question 4 is **(b)**.

5. An administrator should select the appropriate decision-making style to fit the situation. Making an autocratic decision regarding the program would likely have met strong resistance. Discipline is in the zone of concern of the faculty, and in this instance, because of their past involvement, continued involvement is warranted. Obtaining ideas on the merits of the existing program from the faculty would not have been sufficient. In instances of this nature, faculty members will develop respect for the principal when he/she consults and participates with them in generating ideas concerning the solution to a problem. This is important, as the relationship between principals and teachers can enhance the potential for school improvement (Barth, 1990). Considering the dynamics and the inner workings of the social system at Overfield High, the principal took the appropriate action when he became a member of the decision-making group. The suggested response to question 5 is **(b)**.

## SUMMARY AND CONCLUSION

The decision-making process utilized by a school leader should enhance the selection of satisfactory solutions to problems that occur in schools. They should be as rational as possible, and the leader should seek to become skillful in determining when it is appropriate to involve others in the process.

Principal Jones' style followed closely one that is informed by the ISLLC Standards. He was not directive, issuing mandates and stressing rules and regulations; rather, he was collaborative and sought input from stakeholders. His emphasis was not on the performance of the teachers, or placing blame. More specifically, his disposition indicated that he was committed to finding a solution to a problem using a fair and equitable process. When the leader displays this type of disposition, using procedures that provide the faculty an opportunity to have input into decisions that are in their zone of concern, teaching and learning are likely to be enhanced.

## SCENARIO 14
## STEVEN AND HIS KNIFE

### STANDARD 5

A school administrator is an educational leader who promotes the success of all students by acting with integrity, fairness, and in an ethical manner.

*In Scenario 14, the reader will be exposed to the behavior of two leaders, both faced with making decisions that involve school policy. The decisions with which they are confronted relate to the educational success of students functioning in a safe teaching and learning environment. The issues of the scenario are imbedded in communication, ethical practices, and using the influence of one's office constructively and productively in the service of all students and their families. The reader will want to note the possible consequences that can befall a leader who becomes overly sensitive to the needs of students and does not follow procedures.*

## ISLLC Standards Indicators Exhibited in Scenario 14

### Knowledge Indicators

The administrator has knowledge and understanding of:
▲ The purpose of education and the role of leadership in modern society
▲ Professional codes of ethics
▲ Legal issues impacting school operations
▲ The law as related to education and schooling
▲ Principles and issues relating to school safety and security
▲ Student growth and development
▲ Applied motivational theories
▲ Information sources, data collection, and data analysis strategies
▲ Effective communication
▲ Emerging issues and trends that potentially impact the school community
▲ Various ethical frameworks and perspectives on ethics
▲ Global issues and forces affecting teaching and learning

### Disposition Indicators

The administrator believes in, values, and is committed to:
▲ Ensuring that students have the knowledge, skills, and values needed to become successful adults
▲ The ideal of the common good
▲ Using the influence of one's office constructively and productively in the service of all students and families
▲ Student learning as the fundamental purpose of schooling
▲ The variety of ways in which students can learn
▲ A safe and supportive learning environment
▲ Subordinating one's own interests to the good of the school community
▲ Bringing ethical principles to the decision-making process
▲ The right of every student to a free, quality education
▲ Collaboration and communication with families
▲ High-quality standards, expectations, and performances
▲ Involvement of families and other stakeholders in school decision-making processes
▲ Families as partners in the education of their children
▲ The proposition that families have the best interests of their children in mind
▲ Accepting the consequences for upholding one's principles and actions
▲ Recognizing a variety of ideas, values, and cultures
▲ Accepting responsibility
▲ Development of a caring school community

### Performance Indicators

The administrator facilitates and engages in activities ensuring that:
▲ Lines of communication are developed with decision makers outside the school community
▲ The environment in which schools operate is influenced on behalf of students and their families
▲ Effective problem-framing and problem-solving skills are used
▲ A variety of sources of information are used to make decisions

▲ Problems are confronted and resolved in a timely manner
▲ Stakeholders are involved in decisions affecting schools
▲ Potential problems and opportunities are identified
▲ Pupil personnel programs are developed to meet the needs of students and their families
▲ Barriers to student learning are identified, clarified, and addressed
▲ Effective communication skills are used
▲ There is a culture of high expectations for self, student, and staff performance
▲ Community youth family services are integrated with school programs
▲ The school and community serve one another as resources
▲ Public policy is shaped to provide quality education for students

**The administrator**
▲ Demonstrates appreciation for and sensitivity to the diversity in the school community
▲ Serves as a role model
▲ Demonstrates values, beliefs, and attitudes that inspire others to higher levels of performance
▲ Considers the impact of one's administrative practices on others
▲ Examines personal and professional values
▲ Fulfills legal and contractual obligations
▲ Applies laws and procedures fairly, wisely, and considerately
▲ Demonstrates a personal and professional code of ethics
▲ Accepts responsibility for school operations
▲ Treats people fairly, equitably, and with dignity and respect

Steven is a seventh grader at Harrison Middle School. He lives with his grandmother and two younger brothers. His grades are below average, and he is often sent to the principal's office for behavior problems. Steven has missed 20 days of school, and it is only the beginning of the second semester. His grandmother has been called several times because she is listed on school records as Steven's legal guardian. Steven's mother has recently made two trips to the school for conferences with the principal. In each of these conferences, she suggested that school personnel did not provide Steven with the assistance he needed to be successful. She also requested that the principal contact her when there was a problem with Steven.

On Wednesday afternoon during his math class, Steven was showing off a knife to some of his classmates. It caused such a disruption that the teacher, Mrs. Adams, went to the back of the room to find the cause of the commotion. She saw the knife and immediately asked Steven to hand it over to her. He gave her the knife, and they proceeded to the principal's office.

Mrs. Adams explained the incident involving Steven to the principal. She stated that she had confiscated the weapon and immediately brought Steven to the office because she knew the school had a zero tolerance policy regarding weapons on school premises. Mr. Jordan (principal) excused Mrs. Adams and proceeded to talk with Steven about the incident. Steven explained that he was not going to hurt anyone. Rather, he said he had found the knife, thought it was cool, and wanted to show it off to his friends. Mr. Jordan explained to Steven that the school had a zero tolerance policy regarding weapons on school property and asked if he were aware of that policy. Steven said that he was aware and understood that he would be punished. Mr. Jordan, having addressed situations of this nature on several previous occasions, believed that he knew when students were really troublemakers. He looked at Steven, advised him that he had two weeks of detention, and sent him back to class.

During the next two hours, Mr. Jordan tried to contact Steven's mother three times but was unable to do so. Steven's mother was extremely hard to reach, for she worked two jobs and was seldom home. Had he been able to contact her, his plans were to ask her if she were aware that her son was carrying a weapon and had the weapon in school. It was also Mr. Jordan's intention to ask her if she had given him permission to possess the knife. Mr. Jordan was never able to reach Steven's mother.

At the end of the school day, Mr. Jordan held a second conference with Steven. After this conference, he felt that Steven really understood the policy and did not have bad intentions. Mr. Jordan placed the knife in a box on his desk and explained to Steven that if he were ever caught on school property with a weapon again, the zero tolerance policy would be applied, and he would receive severe punishment. Steven nodded in agreement, said that he understood and that he would never bring a weapon to school again.

Just as the conference was concluding, Mr. Jordan's secretary called him to speak with a parent who had been waiting for some time. In a rush to meet with the parent, he did not notice that Steven lifted the knife from the box on his desk.

During his walk home from school, Steven got into a fight with Bob, a classmate. It started out as name calling, but then became physical. During the course of the fight, Steven stabbed Bob with the knife. Bob was not killed but did suffer serious injuries. His family pressed charges, and Steven was taken to the juvenile detention center.

The same afternoon, after receiving the news from a number of sources, Superintendent Walker asked Principal Jordan to meet with him in his office. However, before Mr. Jordan arrived, Superintendent Walker received several calls from the news media, board of education members, and parents. The calls all contained a large outcry for disciplinary action against Mr. Jordan. In between calls, Superintendent Walker reviewed the outstanding record of Principal Jordan and discussed the board's policies on student discipline, attendance, and administrative personnel procedures with the Directors of Student Services and Human Resources. All policies were clear, and even though the board had a zero tolerance policy regarding weapons on school premises, action regarding personnel who failed to implement the policy was at the discretion of the superintendent.

When Mr. Jordan reached the office of the superintendent, he provided Superintendent Walker with a full explanation of what had occurred. The superintendent listened, seemed satisfied, and said to Mr. Jordan, "I will review the matter and meet with you again within the next several days." As Mr. Jordan was about to leave the superintendent's office, three additional calls were received. After completing the third call, Superintendent Walker turned to Mr. Jordan, advised him that he was on suspension with pay and was not to return to Harrison until further notice.

## REFLECTIVE THINKING AND SCENARIO ANALYSIS

1. From the scenario, cite factors that would support the notion that the disposition of Principal Jordan influenced or did not influence the quality of his decision. Specifically identify the ISLLC Standards indicators in the content of the scenario.

2. What are some of the critical decision factors that appear not to have been considered by Principal Jordan?

3. Which of the decision-making models described in this chapter would least likely produce the outcome described in the scenario?

4. Is there ever a time when a principal is justified in exercising flexibility in the implementation of school policy? Provide a rationale for your response.

5. One of the ISLLC indicators states, "Families should function as partners in the education of their children." Subscribing to this indicator, what was the appropriate action for Principal Jordan to take? Justify your response.

6. In what manner did each of the school leaders allow the power of his position to influence the decision he made? What influences impacted the decisions, their quality, and acceptance?

7. Who is likely to be liable in a situation of this nature and why?

## ADDRESSING THE ISSUES

Select the one best answer to the following questions:

1. Evaluating the actions of Mr. Jordan, which of the following would you assess as being the most problematic?

   a. Making a decision without including Steven's family and other stakeholders.

   b. Using judgment that did not reflect a knowledge of effective problem-framing and problem-solving skills.

   c. Allowing his sensitivity to Steven's needs to influence his decision style.

   d. All of the above.

2. Giving consideration to the steps that are followed using various decision-making models, which of the following actions would you suggest for use in a situation of this nature?

   a. Frame the problem, analyze the consequences of various alternatives, and select an alternative following the guidelines of policy.

   b. Make a decision regarding disciplinary actions and hold fast to that decision, regardless of the consequences.

   c. Develop a decision-making strategy and follow the sequential steps.

   d. Make a decision regarding disciplinary actions but only implement the decision after Steven's parents have been contacted.

3. Which of the following factors likely motivated Mr. Jordan's behavior with Steven?

   a. Compassion for Steven and a desire to remove a barrier to student learning.

   b. Visits to the school by Steven's mother and Mr. Jordan's commitment to the involvement of families in the decision-making process.

    c. School policy and its lack of flexibility, which impacted the decision-making process.

    d. None of the above.

4. Reviewing the events that occurred in the conference between Principal Jordan and the superintendent, which of the following had the greatest influence on the superintendent's decision to suspend Principal Jordan?

    a. Prevailing global issues and forces affecting teaching and learning.

    b. Prevailing dynamics of political influence and advocacy under our democratic political system.

    c. Ethical principles brought into the decision-making process by the superintendent.

    d. The superintendent subordinating his interest for the good of the school community.

5. Which of the following actions would you suggest Superintendent Walker take in moving forward?

    a. Take charge of the situation and personally address future occurrences without regard for the political influence of others.

    b. Work cooperatively with other individuals in reaching a joint decision, using the influence of his position to ensure that his original decision is solidified.

    c. Develop a plan of action and work within the framework of policies, laws, and regulations enacted by the board of education.

    d. Assign any necessary follow-up activities to an assistant superintendent.

## DISCUSSION OF THE SOLUTION

1. Many times, school leaders do not use models to make decisions. They feel that they can be effective in making decisions by relying on intuition and experience. Although a principal can be effective using intuition and experience, as was discussed in the introductory section of this chapter, decision effectiveness can be increased through the use of an analytical thought process.

Mr. Jordan did not think through his decision; he made his decision without defining the problem or assessing the seriousness of the situation. He appeared to be very sensitive and took action based on assumptions and the word of a student who was struggling with many challenges. In a situation of this nature, problem analysis can contribute greatly to the identification of an effective solution. A review of Steven's school record would have perhaps suggested several different alternatives. However, drawing on past experience and /or intuition, after a brief session, Mr. Jordan allowed Steven to leave school before contacting his parents. Also, he left the knife in a place where Steven could reclaim it. Now, because of his decision-making procedure, what initially appeared to be a minor routine decision has turned into a major issue. The judgment of Mr. Jordan was problematic; he did not effectively frame the problem, nor did he consider the impact of his decision-making practices on other individuals Steven would encounter. The suggested response to question 1 is **(b)**.

2. Harrison Middle School is subject to the district's zero tolerance policy regarding weapons on campus. This policy should have guided Mr. Jordan's decision.

Policies are in place to protect the rights of all students and to improve their opportunity for success. Failure to make a decision within the framework of the policy compromised the mission of the school and the safety of others and placed Steven in jeopardy.

Because Mr. Jordan was not able to contact Steven's mother and even if he had been able to contact her, an extensive review of Steven's school records, as well as a call to his grandmother (Steven's legal guardian), would have been in the best interest of all concerned. A variety of sources should be used to collect information to make a decision regarding an issue of this magnitude (ISLLC, 1996). Mr. Jordan could have framed the problem, acquired information from stakeholders, analyzed the consequences of not strictly following school policy, and not being able to discuss the situation with Steven's legal guardian or mother. These are only a few of the alternatives that were available to him.

After an in-depth analysis, Mr. Jordan could have developed a tentative action plan, which might have included an out-of-school suspension, a required conference with his mother or grandmother, sessions with the school counselor, sessions with the human services worker, or a number of other services available to school leaders. If such a plan proved to be unsuccessful, he could have attempted another. The leader must be knowledgeable of community family services that are available and use them to support the school program (ISLLC, 1996).

Use of the appropriate decision-making model would have factored the zero tolerance policy into the equation and perhaps influenced the selection of an alternative different from the one selected by Mr. Jordan. It is highly unlikely that the appropriate decision-making model would have generated an outcome that would have provided Steven an opportunity to leave school with the knife. The suggested response to question 2 is **(a)**.

3. Effective decision making is sometimes affected by the disposition of the leader. In this instance, such was the case with Mr. Jordan, who appeared to have compassion for students, or at least Steven. He believed in Steven and made his decision based on the personal belief that Steven would do the right thing. Having this belief, he exercised poor judgment and allowed Steven to leave school before contacting his mother. Quite clearly, he was interested in keeping Steven in school and being as flexible as possible in implementing the zero tolerance policy. He allowed his personal belief system and his personal desires to influence his decision. The section in Chapter 2 that addressed understanding of self is applicable in this instance. It is questionable whether Mr. Jordan realized the influence of his belief system. School leaders must realize that student interest and concern are not a satisfactory substitute for using good judgment, following policy, and being as rational as possible in making decisions. The suggested response to question 3 is **(a)**.

4. The superintendent had reached a decision as to the action that he would initially take regarding Mr. Jordan's behavior. However, the phone calls continued to come, and they influenced an action different from the one the superintendent initially intended to take. As the number of individuals involved increased, political pressure came into play, and the influence of individuals outside of the normal decision-making process became a factor. Everyone making a phone call likely had an agenda or a

desired goal they wanted to reach for various reasons. The desires of the superintendent gave way to the goals of the individuals, who apparently had sufficient power to influence his behavior. The political system became the overriding force. In situations of this nature, attention must be given to one's personal and professional code of ethics, an ISLLC Standards indicator. This is not to suggest that the suspension was an incorrect decision; that is not the point of this discussion. The concern is that the leader bring ethical principles to the decision-making process and use the influence of his/her position in the service of all faculty, staff, and students and their families (ISLLC, 1996). The suggested response to question 4 is **(b)**.

5. The original problem has escalated, and what once was a discipline problem to be addressed at the local school level by the principal has become a major problem that lies within the zone of concern of a number of individuals. Now as a result of decision quality, or better stated the lack of it, the conditions and dynamics of the diverse school community will have to be given consideration.

In suspending Mr. Jordan, the superintendent made a decision; now he must take the lead and accept the consequences for his actions. In moving forward, the superintendent will need a plan of action to inform his decisions. Considerable information will be needed from multiple sources. Necessarily, he will have to recognize and respect the legitimate authority of others. Certainly, he will want to consult district policy, legal representation, and members of the school board. Formulating his discussion with these individuals and groups, he can examine and consider the prevailing values of the community, identify a solution, and, to the extent possible, avoid making errors and/or selecting an inappropriate alternative. The suggested response to question 5 is **(c)**.

## SUMMARY AND CONCLUSION

Electing to make decisions based on intuition and experience is a practice that many school leaders are forced into because of time pressures and other constraints. However, when decisions are made in this manner, they should be made within the framework of school policies and with some certainty that the desired outcome will be achieved. When this does not occur, the practice used can result in concerns and problems of a magnitude greater than the original challenge.

Mr. Jordan made the decision regarding Steven and his knife based on experience and intuition, depriving himself of the benefits that are derived from framing the problem, analyzing the difficulties, and developing possible alternatives. In fact, it seems as if he did not even consider other alternatives or explore the consequences of the alternative selected. Whenever possible, school leaders should make use of time and available resources in the decision-making process (Barge, 1994). Mr. Jordan had sufficient time to explore several alternatives, but chose not to do so. Also, he failed to use resources such as the school counselors. Involving others in the decision-making process would have possibly generated conversation regarding Steven's behavior problems, poor attendance, and academic difficulties. A discussion of these factors would likely have generated several different alternatives.

Things are seldom what they seem. Problems may seem similar and minor in nature; however, more often than not, they are unique, so much so that a different solution than the one applied to a previous problem (which seems similar) is applicable. Because he failed to identify fully and critically examine the assumptions inherent in his solution to Steven's problem, Mr. Jordan invited the involvement of a number of other individuals who will want to examine the issue and express an opinion.

## CHAPTER SUMMARY

All decisions in schools have some influence on the performance of both faculty and staff. Therefore, it is important for the school leader to realize the magnitude of the problem and to be as rational as possible in selecting a decision alternative. The basic decision-making model includes the following steps: (1) identification of the problem, (2) analysis of the problem, (3) identifying alternative solutions, (4) assessing the alternatives, (5) selecting an alternative, (6) implementing the selected alternative, and (7) evaluating the process.

In the process of making decisions, the leader can elect a normative or descriptive approach. Also he/she may elect to make decisions independently or involve others. The determination should be based on several factors, among which are time, the situation, the issue, and the expertise needed. As challenging as decision making is, the leader can minimize its negative impact by eliminating barriers and traps that inhibit effectiveness.

Working independently, the leader can improve the decision-making process by recognizing his/her own biases and those of others and being fair and displaying ethical principles in the process. Using group decision-making techniques and safeguarding against groupthink and the overuse of groups, he/she can enhance participatory decision making. In either instance, the leader must know that the quality of the decision reached and the manner in which it is implemented will not only have an impact on the faculty, staff, and students, but will also have an impact on the perceived effectiveness of the leader.

## MOVING INTO PRACTICE

Review the scenarios in Chapter 4. Using the pros and cons of the various situations, identify several approaches that you would use to address the following school-related issues in an actual school situation. Project yourself into the role of the principal and/or superintendent and take care to formulate a rationale for your selected behavior.

▶ Revisit the Floating Communiqué discussed in Chapter 1. Using one of the decision-making models, develop an appropriate response to the communiqué.

▶ It is early September at Frost, and you have all the students assigned to classes. A parent group enters the school, insisting that many special students have been inappropriately placed. In fact, they make claims that the inclusion laws have not been followed. They demand to see the master schedule and to work cooperatively with you in rescheduling the children. They threaten to carry the issue to the superintendent if you do not comply with their request. What action do you take, and upon what do you base your decision?

▶ Develop a list of decision alternatives that could be used by Mr. Miller at Springview Elementary.

▶ Develop a statement that could be presented to the media explaining the rationale behind Mr. Jordan's suspension.

▶ Make a list of five situations in which a leader should involve others.

▶ Draft a statement that would inform the school and community of the enactment of a zero tolerance policy banning weapons on campus.

▶ Design a shared decision-making model that involves students, faculty, staff, parents, and community members in meaningful decision making. Take care to establish the relationship that must exist between role groups as they function as members of the team.

## ACQUIRING AN UNDERSTANDING OF SELF

▶ What is your basic belief regarding student discipline and the characteristics of a well-disciplined school?

▶ What have you previously allowed to influence the manner in which you discipline students?

▶ What decision-making style works best for you?

▶ What safeguards do you have in place to ensure that you are making the best possible decisions?

▶ What is your position regarding fair process, and what steps do you take to ensure that your position on issues is fair, equitable, and gives consideration to the rights of others?

## SUGGESTED READINGS

Bridges, E. A. (1967). A model for shared decision-making in the school principalship. *Educational Administrative Quarterly, 3,* 49–61.

Golanda, C. (1995). Decision-making practices of principals: Implications for practitioners and preparation programs. *People and Education, 3,* 351.

Hammond, J. S., Keeney, R. L., & Raiffa, H. (1998). *Smart choices: A practical guide to decision-making.* Boston: Harvard Business School Publication.

Hill, G. W. (1982). Group versus individual performance: Are N + 1 heads better than one? *Psychological Bulletin, 91,* 517–539.

Kim, C., & Mauborgne, R. (July-August 1997). Fair process: Managing in the knowledge economy. *Harvard Review 75*(4), 65–75.

# 5

## MANAGING CONFLICT IN TODAY'S SCHOOLS

### THE ISLLC STANDARDS

#### STANDARD 3

A school administrator is an educational leader who promotes the success of all students by insuring management of the organization, operations, and resources for a safe, efficient, and effective learning environment.

#### STANDARD 5

A school administrator is an educational leader who promotes the success of all students by acting with integrity, fairness, and in an ethical manner.

#### STANDARD 6

A school administrator is an educational leader who promotes the success of all students by understanding, responding to, and influencing the larger political, social, economic, legal, and cultural context.

## Factors Influencing Conflict in Today's Schools

Conflict is a major occurrence in today's schools. Many of the factors influencing that conflict have surfaced as a result of massive change. Supporters of the current educational reform movement are advocating massive changes in the way schools are structured; the curriculum format; the role of faculty, staff, and administrators; and in the way schools are administered (Conley, 1997). These suggested changes, in one way or another, emphasize empowerment, participation, and collaboration. All of these concepts suggest that individuals and groups in the school and its community can work in harmony. However, under the best of conditions, when decisions and changes of the magnitude suggested occur, conflict is likely to emerge. Therefore, if leaders are to meet the standards set by ISLLC (1996), their behavior will have to reflect a knowledge of principles of organizational development that minimize conflict.

The purpose of this chapter is to present in summary format a definition of conflict, the types of conflict that frequently occur in schools, the sources of those conflicts, and strategies commonly used to manage them. Because the literature refers to most conflict occurring in today's schools as organizational conflict (Barge, 1994; Fullan, 1999; Goodlad, 1984; Greenberg, 1996a; Katz & Lawler, 1993; Sashkin & Morris, 1984), the scenarios of the chapter are focused on the disposition, decision-making behavior, and communication skills of the leader and his/her interaction with individuals and groups. It is intended that as a result of working through the scenarios, the reader will develop a greater appreciation for the influence of leader behavior on conflict in schools and gain insight into how effective management, collaboration, and the use of ethical principles can reduce the negative dysfunctional aspects of that conflict. Reflected in these scenarios are indicators of ISLLC Standards 3, 5, and 6.

## Definition of Conflict

Putnam and Poole (1987) define conflict as "the interaction of interdependent people who perceive opposition of goals, aims, and views, and who see the other party as potentially interfering with the realization of these goals" (p. 352). Conflict is a social phenomenon that is heavily ingrained in human relations, expressed and sustained through communication, and occurs when individuals and or groups become dependent on one another to meet identified needs (Barge, 1994). Because of the interdependent nature of individuals and groups, conflict in organizations is inevitable, endemic, and often legitimate. It is a normal part of social relations and can be either functional (positive) or dysfunctional (negative).

Given that a school is an open social system consisting of individuals and groups who often have opposing interests but are dependent on each other to achieve individual as well as organizational goals, it is understandable that conflict is an inevitable and all-pervasive element in today's schools.

## The Nature of Conflict in Schools

There is general agreement that conflict occurring in schools is latent (ever present) and exists because of divergent (or apparently divergent) views and incompatibility of those views (Owens, 1995; Sashkin & Morris, 1984). Conflict is considered to be both functional and dysfunctional. When it is functional, the organization benefits; there is a win-win attitude, and harmony exists. Functional conflict facilitates the accomplishment of goals by members of the organization and/or generates new insights into old problems (Putnam & Poole, 1987). When conflict is dysfunctional, there is a win-lose attitude, and hostility is produced (Owens, 1995). Dysfunctional conflict can negatively affect members of the organization to the extent that their activities are disrupted. Therefore, if schools are to effectively achieve established goals, it is incumbent on the leader to develop an understanding of the nature of conflict in schools and to acquire skills sufficient to manage it in a functional manner.

## Conflict Occurring in Schools

Conflict often occurs over situations in which individuals and/or groups experience some degree of difficulty in obtaining an action alternative (March & Simon, 1958). In schools, it can occur within an individual, between individuals, or among faculty members of a particular grade level. Conflict can also be experienced between groups within the larger faculty, between the school leadership and the central office leadership, or between the faculty of one school and the faculty of another school. Regardless of where the conflict lies or its source, the individuals affected may feel a sense of deprivation and respond in a reactive or proactive manner that may negatively impact student success. Because of the impact on school effectiveness, each of the above-mentioned instances in which conflict can occur will be examined.

### The Context and Content of Conflict

The type of conflict that occurs in schools can be differentiated in two ways, context (the type of conflict that might occur) and content (the issues over which the conflict occurs). Then there are the feelings and responses of the individuals (deprivation, reactive, and proactive) involved in the conflict (Gross, 1958). To ensure that the organization's resources are managed in a way that promotes a learning environment that is safe, efficient, and effective, leaders should seek to understand each of these areas and its implications for behavior in schools (ISLLC, 1996).

Conflict occurs in three contexts:

1. *Interpersonal*—conflict that exists between individuals within a group or organization;
2. *Intergroup*—conflict between two groups within a larger social system; and
3. *Interorganizational*—conflict that exists between two organizations (Barge, 1994, p. 163).

Interorganizational conflict is a somewhat infrequently occurring phenomenon, but interpersonal and intergroup conflict can be observed to some extent in all organizations, as this type of conflict is seen as a natural part of social relationships (Wexley & Yukl, 1984). In each of the above-mentioned areas, conflict might emerge because of the following reasons:

1. *Competition for scarce resources:* Often in school situations, decisions have to be made regarding who will receive space in a given building, who will receive the new computers, or who will be assigned the last bell as his/her planning hour. Such issues are competitive in nature, and conflict is produced.
2. *A desire for autonomy:* There are instances in schools in which teachers, administrators, and parents are so committed to a program or activity (allocating booster club funds, directing the senior play, facilitating curriculum planning) that they lay claim to it and want total autonomy over its operation. If there is interference with the activity, conflict occurs. In such an instance, the conflict is over a desire for autonomy.
3. *Divergence in goals:* If individuals in the primary unit of a school have different views over which approach to use in the teaching of reading—whole language or phonetics—and cannot agree on which of the approaches to use, divergent goal conflict occurs (Pondy, 1967).

Two other contexts in which conflict might occur are intrapersonal conflict and intragroup conflict (Barge, 1994). Intrapersonal conflict refers to conflict that is occurring within an individual. In such instances, the individual is at odds with himself/herself because of uncertainty about the action to take regarding a particular issue. Imagine that the principal of Clark High School has spent two years working with the faculty and community establishing a set of long-range goals for the school. The goals have been developed, and sufficient progress has been made toward their attainment. However, because of his success at Clark, at the end of his second year, the superintendent offers him a position in the central office. If he accepts the position, he would have developmental responsibilities for the district's curriculum with a reasonable increase in pay and responsibility. Making the decision to stay and finish the job at Clark and keeping a commitment to that school and its constituency or taking the new assignment and fulfilling a career dream is one that is likely to require much thought. The challenge of making such a decision could produce considerable intrapersonal conflict.

During the course of the tenure of a school leader, there will be many instances when he/she will be faced with situations of a similar nature. These situations may concern school programs, personnel, and issues in the community. Because such a decision involves morals, values, or personal goals, and the outcome is of an impending nature, the leader may experience intrapersonal conflict.

Intragroup conflict occurs when there are divergent opinions within a group on a particular issue (Barge, 1994). If some members of the senior faculty support the seniors' desire to hold the after-prom party at a local night-club, as opposed to other faculty who prefer the school gym, intragroup conflict has occurred.

Conflict content refers to the issues involved in the conflict, of which there are two types—substantive and affective (Barge, 1994). The issues, ideas, and positions taken on a particular problem may result in substantive conflict. Conflict deriving from the emotional aspects of the problem (the interpersonal relationships among members of the organization) is considered affective conflict (Barge, 1994). For example, teachers engaging in a discussion concerning the merits of a curriculum program for the school may have different ideas and positions regarding the appropriate grade level the curriculum is designed to serve and the amount of instructional time that should be allotted for its use. These differences of opinions provoke what is classified as substantive conflict. When disagreements occur among members of a school faculty over power, status, role development, or personality issues, affective conflict occurs. Emotions are involved as individuals strive to achieve their own preferred outcome, which, if achieved, will deny another his/her desired outcome, thus producing hostility. Such is the case when individuals engage in a struggle for control of a group or express concern about the attitude that an individual brings to the group.

The content of an issue can provoke both substantive and affective conflict, producing barriers to student learning. Therefore, the leader should seek to become knowledgeable about the diversity that exists in the school so that operational procedures can be designed and managed to ensure that opportunities for successful student learning are maximized (ISLLC, 1996).

As a result of conflict that occurs between individuals and groups in schools, individuals may respond in a reactive or proactive manner (Greenberg, 1996). If they respond to a particular conflict, displaying behavior in an attempt to escape or avoid a perceived unfair state or occurrence, the behavior is considered reactive. An example of reactive behavior would be a principal's distribution of new computers to select members of the faculty. If a principal acquires new computers and distributes them to select members of the faculty with the expectation that other faculty members would continue to use old and somewhat out-of-date computers, the individuals expected to use the old computers may tend to feel that they have been treated unfairly. In a general sense, they may feel that unfair and inequitable treatment exists among all school personnel. As a result of these feelings, they may display certain negative emotions, which will motivate them to initiate action to eliminate the experienced inequity.

The conflict just described is not between the two groups of individuals, but rather with the state of affairs in the school. Berger, Zelditch, Anderson, and Cohen (1972) advise that individuals in organizations make comparisons with a generalized order, rather than with other individuals. Such comparisons relate to status and value, and, as a result, individuals can develop a feeling of inequity to which they respond. When this occurs, faculty effectiveness can be compromised, negatively affecting the academic achievement of students. In order to address such a situation, ISLLC Standard 5 holds that school leaders should bring ethical principles to the decision-making process and treat all individuals fairly, equitably, and with dignity and respect.

Further informing leader behavior regarding the feelings of followers, Martin (1981), in addressing the "theory of relative deprivation," asserted that certain reward distribution patterns could encourage individuals to make certain social comparisons. When social comparisons are made, they can lead to followers feeling a sense of deprivation and resentment, causing a variety of reactions, ranging from depression to the outbreak of violent riots (Martin, 1981). To eliminate such feelings, the effective school leader strives to identify and implement procedures that ensure fair and equitable treatment of all individuals, another indicator of ISLLC Standard 5.

In other instances, individuals and/or groups in schools display behavior in an effort to promote justice and create fair treatment and equitable distribution of resources when they do not exist. In such instances, this type of behavior is considered proactive (Greenberg, 1996b). Individuals observing inequity in the treatment of school personnel relative to the reward system and/or the distribution of resources sometimes proactively strive to create an equitable distribution system. Such action is taken because these individuals feel a positive change in the distribution system is ultimately in the best interest of all parties (Leventhal, 1976).

Freedman and Montanari (1980), addressing the equity norm, offer a possible solution to such occurrences in schools. They theorized that when it is perceived that resources are being distributed in a manner that is not equitable, as was the case in the previously mentioned computer distribution plan, leader behavior can improve the situation. For example, if the leader values maintaining social harmony among the faculty, he/she would advocate the equity norm. In so doing, an attempt would be made to apply strategies that would facilitate the equal division of computers among the faculty, regardless of their possible differential contributions.

Individuals and groups in schools, as well as those served by the school, tend to seek and appreciate just and fair treatment. Thus, the effective school leader seeks to acquire a working knowledge of approaches to use in providing such treatment. Before taking action, he/she considers the impact of his/her administrative practices on others and attempts to maintain harmony between individuals and among group members. This type of leader behavior is supported by the indicator of ISLLC Standard 5 that suggests that the effective school leader treats individuals fairly, equitably, and with dignity and respect.

## Role Conflict

Another type of conflict that frequently occurs in schools is role conflict. School leaders and their subordinates face conflicts and pressures, not only because of change, but also because of the roles and expectations that people hold for them. Individuals and groups inside and outside the organization also have expectations for the organization in terms of goals the organization is expected to achieve and in roles various individuals and groups are expected to play in achieving those goals. Often, it is by these expectations and the extent to which goals are met that the effectiveness of the organization is measured (Hoy & Miskel, 1991). When the goals of the organization are not achieved to the extent expected and the roles of individuals and groups do not meet expectations, conflict occurs. A factor in these instances is the behavior definition of the leader.

## Role Expectations for the School Leader

The behavior definition of school leaders is comprised of two sets of role expectations, one formal and the other informal. The formal role is defined by the school district in the form of a job description and is governed by school policies, whereas individuals and groups who hold expectations for the leader define his/her informal role. These individuals and groups reside inside the school and within the greater school community. Together, the formal and informal expectations comprise a behavior definition that characterizes how different individuals and groups affiliated with the organization believe the leader should perform in a given situation (Getzels, 1958).

School leaders must be knowledgeable of these expectations, as they represent a powerful source of influence on their behavior and serve as informal evaluation standards that are applied to their performance. The work of the Interstate School Leaders Licensure Consortium, through the establishment of the six standards, has assisted in identifying the formal role of school leaders; however, only through feedback from the individuals served at a particular school is it likely that the leader's informal role will be identified.

## The Leader's Expectations for Self

In addition to the formal and informal expectations of others, leaders must understand and address the expectations that they hold for themselves. Consistent with the need for leaders to have an understanding of self as presented in Chapter 2, they need an understanding of the expectations that they hold for themselves. Self-expectations are influenced by the manner in which leaders perceive they should behave and may be more important than the expectations of others in the determination of the decision they make in a given situation (Greenberg, 1996b). This behavior is derived from the leader's personal needs.

In Scenario 15 of this chapter, Mr. Smith entered a faculty meeting with a preplanned agenda and behaved in a manner that he perceived was appropriate for him as principal. However, some members of the faculty held a different expectation for him; therefore, conflict occurred. After the faculty meeting, in an effort to reduce the conflict that had occurred, he began to ponder his behavior and the behavior of members of the faculty. As a result of his reflections, he gave importance to the expectations of members of the faculty, subordinating his position. Had he persisted in implementing his planned agenda, his perception of his role would have been given primary importance, despite the expectation of members of his faculty. In situations of this nature, it is not uncommon for leaders to subordinate their own interests for the good of the school and community. In fact, being willing to do so is necessary if the leader is committed to meeting one of the indicators (subordinating one's own interest to the good of the school community) of ISLLC Standard 5.

The personal needs of the leader and the expectations of members of the organization and the larger culture are major factors that influence role behavior (Getzels, 1958). The interactions between the leader's need disposition, the role expectations of other individuals in the organization, and the larger culture influence his/her behavior (Getzels, 1958). Given Getzels's (1958) model, it seems reasonable to believe that the greater the compatibility between the leader's need disposition and the expectations of individuals affiliated with the organization, the greater the compatibility. Therefore, a leader's knowledge of the expectations of others for his/her behavior should prove to be helpful in managing the school.

## Direction, Clarity, and Intensity of Expectations

Expectations can vary in direction, clarity, and intensity. Direction refers to the extent to which a leader and subordinates are in agreement on a decision (Gorton, 1987). Because of the direction of a decision, the leader and subordinate may be either in complete agreement or in absolute opposition. The point to be given consideration is the perception of the individuals as to the right of the leader to behave in the selected manner (Gorton, 1987). In making judgments regarding such situations, the leader might give consideration to the nature of the situation and make a determination relative to the perceived direction in which it falls.

Clarity refers to the adequacy of communicating expectations (Gorton, 1987). It is helpful when leaders have an understanding of the expectations individuals and groups hold for their role. Expectations that are not clearly communicated produce role ambiguity, making it difficult for the school leader to really determine the expectations others hold for his/her behavior. When the leader misperceives the expectations of others, disagreement occurs, producing role conflict. There are also instances when individuals from reference groups feel the leader must act in a particular manner, or perhaps should act in a particular manner. The magnitude of the feelings of these groups is known as the intensity of the conflict (Gorton, 1987). Leaders should find it beneficial to diagnose a conflict for direction, clarity, and intensity.

School leaders will also find it in their best interest to recognize the importance of being knowledgeable of the expectations of others regarding their role. Developing an understanding of these expectations can enhance the leader's ability to anticipate and assess the reactions of others relative to their behavior regarding specific decisions (Campbell, 1968). It is not likely that school leaders will be able to develop an understanding of all individuals in the school community. They must, therefore, be advised by an indicator of ISLLC Standard 6, which suggests that they bring ethical principles to the decision-making process and seek to have an understanding of individuals who can impair or enhance their effectiveness.

## Conflict Management

As was previously stated in an earlier section of this chapter, conflict exists to some degree in all schools, for it is a natural part of social relationships. When the school leader makes decisions that are satisfying to some and not to others, conflict is likely to occur. Conflict may also occur without the leader being involved, as school issues or situations resulting in conflict may concern parents, students, or programs in the school. Regardless of the nature of the conflict, the school leader is likely to be engaged in its management.

According to Wexley and Yukl (1984), the challenge for the leader is not to eliminate all conflict, but rather to minimize its disruptive impact and make it a positive force in the school. This can be accomplished best through the use of a series of conflict management strategies.

### Strategies for Managing Conflict

Conflict management is the process of resolving and minimizing the disagreements resulting from perceived or real differences. A conflict has been managed when its cognitive barriers have been changed to agreement (Greenhalgh, 1986). The parties involved reach a level of commitment that enables the barriers of the conflict to be removed and allows for a dissipation of the forces that cause the initial stress (Hanson, 1996). Approaches to conflict management can range from a win-win orientation (both parties achieving some or all of their desired goals) to a win-lose orientation (only one party clearly achieving the desired goal). Much of the theoretical literature strongly suggests the contingency approach—diagnosing a conflict to identify the optimal way of managing it under the given conditions (Owens, 1995). Using the contingency approach, the leader will not be able to identify the one best way of managing all conflict, but he/she can identify the approach that will acquire optimal results under the prevailing conditions. Then, the primary concern for the school leader is to determine if a conflict really exists; if it does, the conflict should be diagnosed, various management strategies should be reviewed, and the strategy that will lead to an effective solution to the conflict should be selected. The following section provides a rationale for following these steps.

First, it should be determined if a conflict really exists—if the goals of the individuals or groups are incompatible. In many instances, having the parties engage in a general discussion can result in a satisfactory solution. However, in instances where the goals are truly incompatible, the leader should seek to determine how the parties have conceptualized the situation and how they really feel about the issues involved. When individuals are involved in a confrontational situation, the way they view the situation will determine to a large extent the way they will respond regarding finding a solution (Owens, 1995). These uncertainties can be removed by diagnosing the conflict. Through such diagnosis, the specific pattern of behavior of the individuals involved can be identified.

## Diagnosing the Conflict

According to Thomas (1976), when engaged in a conflict, an individual may display cooperative behavior, indicating the degree to which he/she is interested in reaching a satisfactory solution to the concerns of others. In other instances, the individual may display assertive, uncooperative behavior, which displays the extent to which he/she is desirous of satisfying individual interests. There are also instances in which one of the parties engaged in conflict will display complete apathy toward a situation, ignore it, and eventually completely withdraw. Then, on other occasions, that individual might feel a high sense of cooperation and will be accommodating, displaying a willingness to attend to the concerns of the other party while sacrificing his/her own concerns.

In other instances, an individual might be very competitive and fight to satisfy his/her own concerns at the expense of the other party. If the parties are willing to collaborate and engage in mutual problem solving to satisfy their concerns, still another option is available for use by the leader. If the parties are moderately assertive and moderately cooperative, they may be willing to engage in a sharing orientation that often leads to compromise.

Making a determination as to the extent and magnitude of the feelings of the individuals and/or groups involved in the conflict will allow the leader to fully conceptualize the conflict and apply a strategy that is likely to resolve the disagreement. Various sources were consulted (Barge, 1994; Gorton, 1987; Hanson, 1996; Owens, 1995; Rahim, 1986; Thomas, 1976) to identify styles that could be used to successfully manage conflict after it had been diagnosed. Although different terminology was often used, these sources offered the following five approaches as those best suited for leaders to use in managing conflict, contingent on the desired outcome:

1. *Avoidance:* The leader has a desire to maintain a rational climate and copes with the conflict by avoiding it completely. The issues are so minimally important that investing the time and resources necessary to resolve the conflict appears unwise. The desire for a peaceful coexistence and the avoidance of a hostile aftermath are given priority. There are both advantages and disadvantages to using this approach. Although the conflict and the possible hostility that could result are avoided in the near term, the potential for conflict remains and could resurface at any given time.

2. *Smoothing:* The leader has a desire to maintain positive interpersonal relationships. In order to maintain these positive relationships, disagreements and differences of opinions on substantive issues are minimized.

3. *Bargaining:* Moderate levels of concern for both task and relationship are displayed. The parties must voluntarily agree to enter a problem-solving approach. A solution to the conflict is reached as a result of both parties making concessions. Neither party is a winner, but neither party is a loser. Sometimes a third party may be called in to serve as a mediator and be given the responsibility of providing assurance that everyone is treated fairly, and an equitable compromise is reached.

4. *Power struggle:* There is little concern for interpersonal relationships between the parties involved. The major focus is on task accomplishment. Power and force are used to break down the opposition and win, regardless of the consequences to the other party.

5. *Problem solving:* Problem solving is a collaborative approach to managing conflict. Both parties collaborate in an attempt to achieve the best solution to the conflict. The primary concern is accomplishing the task in a manner that is rational and allows a positive climate to be maintained.

## Summary

In today's school, the leader works with individuals and groups who have varied ideas, beliefs, opinions, and positions. In attempting to influence them to cooperate in moving the organization toward established goals, the leader must realize that individuals who have divergent views often cannot agree on a single approach. In addition, some individuals or groups in the school seek autonomy and, for one reason or another, attempt to control activities or resources belonging to another individual or unit. In such instances, the second individual or unit will attempt to fend off such interference; this type of behavior results in conflict.

The effective leader should seek the conflict management approach that best fits the situation, giving consideration to the nature of the conflict, its intensity, the people involved, and the seriousness of issues. Consideration should also be given to the authority, resources, and knowledge of the people involved. There is no one best approach to conflict management. However, it is commonly agreed among many conflict management theorists that the problem-solving approach is the most effective (Lunenburg & Ornstein, 1996). If individuals and groups perceive their goals as being the same as the goals of the school or, although different, see their own goals being satisfied as a direct result of working for the goals of the school, conflict is likely to be minimized (Hanson, 1996).

## The Scenarios

The basic premise of the scenarios in this chapter is that the negative effects of conflict in schools can be minimized. However, in order for that to occur, the leader will need knowledge and understanding of principles of organizational development, as these principles will need to guide the leader's behavior in managing the school. In addition, these procedures and principles have to be established and implemented to facilitate the distribution of resources. Also, stakeholders need to perceive the process as being fair, equitable, and in support of the attainment of the shared mission and goals of the school. Finally, members of the faculty and staff and other stakeholders need to be invited to participate in the governance of the school and should be treated fairly with dignity and respect and their contributions to school excellence recognized and appreciated.

The above-mentioned characteristics are some of those being advocated by contemporary writers and researchers (Barth, 1990; Fullan, 1999; Gardner, 1990; Senge, 1990; Sergiovanni & Starratt, 1998) who proffer how today's schools should be led. They are also reflective of ISLLC Standards 3, 5, and 6. Because of the interface between decision making, problem solving, and conflict management and the notion that conflict in schools often occurs as a result of decisions that are made in an attempt to solve problems, the scenarios center around leader decisions that could result in conflict.

## SCENARIO 15
## THE DISCIPLINE PLAN

### STANDARD 3

A school administrator is an educational leader who promotes the success of all students by ensuring management of the organization, operations, and resources for a safe, efficient, and effective learning environment.

*Scenario 15 addresses conflict that emerges as a result of Principal Smith's decision regarding a discipline plan for the school. The intent of this scenario is to demonstrate how leader behavior can positively or negatively affect the learning environment of the school. In analyzing the scenario, the reader might seek to determine the best approach to use in initiating a new discipline program while building a strategy to minimize conflict among faculty, parents, and students.*

## ISLLC Standards Indicators Exhibited in Scenario 15

**Knowledge Indicators**

The administrator has knowledge and understanding of:

▲ Effective communication
▲ Effective consensus-building and negotiation skills
▲ Applied motivational theories
▲ Adult learning and professional development models
▲ The change process for systems, organizations, and individuals
▲ School cultures
▲ Theories and models of organization and the principles of organizational development
▲ Organizational procedures at the school and district level
▲ Human resource management and development
▲ Emerging issues and trends that potentially impact the school community
▲ The values of the diverse school community
▲ Models and strategies of change and conflict resolution as applied to the larger political, social, cultural, and economic context of schooling
▲ Global issues and forces affecting teaching and learning
▲ The importance of diversity and equity in a democratic society

**Disposition Indicators**

The administrator believes in, values, and is committed to:

▲ Continuous school improvement
▲ The inclusion of all members of the school community
▲ A willingness to continuously examine one's own assumptions, beliefs, and practices
▲ Professional development as an integral part of school improvement
▲ The benefit that diversity brings to the school community
▲ A safe and supportive learning environment
▲ Making management decisions to enhance learning and teaching
▲ Taking risks
▲ Trusting people and their judgment
▲ Accepting responsibility
▲ High-quality standards, expectations, and performances
▲ Involving stakeholders in management practices
▲ A safe environment
▲ Involvement of families and other stakeholders in school decision-making processes
▲ The proposition that diversity enriches the school
▲ The idea of the common good
▲ Bringing ethical principles to the decision-making process

▲ Subordinating one's own principles to the good of the school community
▲ Accepting the consequences for upholding one's principles and actions
▲ Development of a caring school community
▲ Using the influence of one's office constructively and productively in the service of all students and their families

### Performance Indicators

The administrator facilitates processes and engages in activities ensuring that:
▲ The vision is developed with and among stakeholders
▲ All individuals are treated with fairness, dignity, and respect
▲ Students and staff feel valued and important
▲ Barriers to student learning are identified and addressed
▲ Diversity is considered in developing learning experiences
▲ The school is organized and aligned for success
▲ The school culture and climate are assessed on a regular basis
▲ A variety of sources of information is used to make decisions
▲ Pupil personnel programs are developed to meet the needs of students and their families
▲ There is a culture of high expectations for self, student, and staff performance
▲ Operational procedures are designed and managed to maximize opportunities for successful learning
▲ Problems are confronted and resolved in a timely manner
▲ Financial, human, and material resources are aligned to the goals of schools
▲ Stakeholders are involved in decisions affecting schools
▲ Responsibility is shared to maximize ownership and accountability
▲ Effective conflict resolution skills are used
▲ Effective group-process and consensus-building skills are used
▲ Effective communication skills are used
▲ Human resources functions support the attainment of school goals
▲ Credence is given to individuals and groups whose values and opinions may conflict
▲ Diversity is recognized and valued
▲ Opportunities for staff to develop collaboration skills are provided

### The administrator

▲ Examines personal and professional values
▲ Demonstrates values, beliefs, and attitudes that inspire others to higher levels of performance
▲ Serves as a role model
▲ Accepts responsibility for school operations
▲ Considers the impact of one's administrative practices on others
▲ Uses the influence of the office to enhance the educational program rather than for personal gain
▲ Treats people fairly, equitably, and with dignity and respect

The parents of Barnsbury Elementary School left the office of the superintendent smiling because the superintendent had informed them that a new principal had been assigned to their school with specific instructions to give discipline top priority. For several years, discipline had been a problem at Barnsbury Elementary; however, over the last two years, this situation had really escalated. Parents and students became concerned about student safety. The PTO had scheduled this meeting with the superintendent to demand action.

The previous principal had operated with very few discipline rules and regulations. In fact, the student handbook on discipline had not been updated during his five-year tenure. Discipline consequences were out of line with the offenses, and students were aware of this fact. Parents believed the principal was not fulfilling his role.

The PTO members had voiced this concern on several occasions, but their complaints fell on deaf ears because many senior faculty members had control of their classes and were content with the status quo. The major discipline incidents occurred before school, during lunch, and after school, and it was the unofficial position of the faculty that discipline during these periods was the responsibility of the administration. Even though teachers new to the school wanted a change in policy, it had been resisted by many senior faculty members because a change in discipline policies might mean teacher duty at these times. The superintendent informed the PTO that he had given the new principal a free hand to improve discipline at the school. Thus, they were pleased with the news of Principal Smith's appointment.

Principal Smith, having been appointed in late June, worked all summer organizing a new list of expected school behavior regulations and a discipline plan for the school. He read books, talked with other principals in the district, and studied several discipline programs offered by various companies before putting together what he felt was the best overall method to maintain a well-disciplined school. Having discussed discipline with the superintendent and other principals, he felt, as principal, it was his responsibility to develop a workable plan for the faculty.

When Mr. Smith presented his completed behavior and discipline plan to the faculty at their first meeting, he was instantly bombarded with resistance from several faculty members. According to Mrs. Jones, "This discipline plan is too rigid. It doesn't allow me the flexibility to address the differences in the ages of students or extenuating circumstances that often occur. I want to have flexibility; I don't want my hands tied when it comes to disciplining my students. I want to be in control."

Mrs. Moore complained, "I've been teaching for almost 20 years now, and I certainly feel I can control my students. I've never had any complaints before, and I don't expect any this year."

"Although a schoolwide discipline plan might be helpful to all of us, I feel teachers should have input. I resent having a plan forced on me. I think I've earned the right to have a voice in the way I manage discipline in my classroom. However, I do agree that we need a workable plan in place before school begins," stated Mrs. Hall.

"Well, that may be true! However, you must agree things are out of control with all the fights and children out in the halls all times of the day; it really is difficult to teach," voiced Mrs. Green.

Other faculty members also had negative comments. "The plan is too lenient for many of our students. Things were bad enough last year, and we need to lay down the law."

Mrs. Williams stated, "If it's going to work, it should definitely allow some flexibility for the teachers. You probably won't get much cooperation without giving teachers some flexibility."

Mr. Frank offered, "I just don't think it's right for someone to tell us how to manage our own classrooms. It might have been okay if we had been asked our opinion first, but I don't think you asked anyone."

"We really need a change. I believe we should form committees and study the situation, then implement a plan that is acceptable to all faculty members. I don't think we should conduct an extensive study for the purpose of improving discipline," offered Mrs. Williams.

Mr. Smith was perplexed after the various comments from his faculty.

## REFLECTIVE THINKING AND SCENARIO ANALYSIS

1. After reviewing Mr. Smith's behavior, which of the ISLLC disposition indicators was he ineffective in meeting? Give a rationale for your response with consideration to factors that are relevant to a principal implementing a new program plan at a school with characteristics similar to those at Barnsbury.
2. What are the different types of conflict occurring in the scenario?
3. Judging from the comments of various faculty members, how would you assess the intensity of the conflict between the principal and the faculty?
4. What conflict management strategies would you use at Barnsbury to reduce the negative effect of the conflict? Justify your response.
5. What is likely to be the result if Mr. Smith uses position power to ensure the implementation of his plan? Cite evidence for your response.

## ADDRESSING THE ISSUES

Select the one best answer to the following questions:

1. Which of the following would you identify as the root cause of the conflict occurring at Barnsbury Elementary?

   a. Divergent views of teachers regarding the discipline plan.

   b. Difference of opinion over the role expectation of the principal.

   c. A desire of the principal to have complete control over the faculty.

   d. All of the above.

2. If you were Mr. Smith and had to diagnose the conflict at Barnsbury Elementary, which of the following would you accept as a reasonable conclusion regarding the manner in which the faculty has conceptualized the situation?

   a. The faculty is exhibiting proactive behavior, and a problem-solving approach is warranted.

   b. The faculty is exhibiting cooperative behavior, and an avoidance approach would be effective. *p. 179*

   c. The faculty is exhibiting proactive behavior that can be addressed through a bargaining approach.

   d. The faculty is displaying complete apathy; therefore, if Mr. Smith withdraws his plan, the problem will be resolved.

**3.** Which of the following is the least advisable approach for Mr. Smith to use in managing the conflict?

   **a.** Turn the plan over to a committee selected by the faculty and allow them to suggest modifications to the plan.

   **b.** Thank the faculty for their comments and rethink the plan.

   **c.** Offer to modify the plan and invite suggestions from the faculty.

   **d.** Use the influence of his office to insist that the plan be implemented in its current form.

**4.** Based on the collective comments of the teachers, it is in the best interest of Principal Smith to give consideration to which element of the conflict?

   **a.** intensity

   **b.** direction

   **c.** clarity

   **d.** a and b

**5.** After designing a discipline plan and meeting with the faculty regarding the implementation of that plan, Mr. Smith finds himself in the midst of a conflict. In getting the faculty to implement this plan or any new discipline plan, which of the following should he effectively communicate to the faculty?

   **a.** He should identify barriers to student learning and ask the faculty to assist him in determining what needs to be accomplished in the school relative to discipline.

   **b.** He should express the idea of the common good and how the faculty will benefit from the implementation of a new plan.

   **c.** He should seek to build consensus by describing to the faculty the importance of the role they will play in making the new plan a success.

   **d.** All of the above.

## DISCUSSION OF THE SOLUTION

1. In an attempt to improve discipline at Barnsbury Elementary, Mr. Smith, the newly assigned principal, designed a discipline plan for implementation during the first year of his principalship. However, when he presented the plan to the faculty, the plan met with great resistance. The faculty expressed different views relative to various components of the plan, and some members questioned the approach used by the principal to design the new plan. This incompatibility caused conflict between the faculty and the principal and between various faculty members.

The discipline plan is being revised because of a needed change (level of student behavior) in the school environment. The change proposed was in the discipline rules and regulations. Rules and regulations often serve to prevent or manage conflict by clarifying such issues as how to proceed, when, and who has what responsibility (Owens, 1991). But when individuals disagree with the substance of the rules and regulations and/or the manner in which they are carried out, the individuals or the rules can become dysfunctional and cause or exacerbate conflict.

Some members of the faculty viewed the discipline plan as being in their zone of concern. When the principal did not involve them in its modification, he did not meet their expectation of his role. There existed both role conflict, as well as conflict caused by the exclusion of teachers from a process that they perceived to be one in which they should have been involved. There were divergent views between the teachers, as well; however, the root cause of the conflict was the principal taking unilateral action in developing a plan that was in the zone of concern of teachers. The manner in which a plan is developed or modified can either generate conflict or facilitate problem solving. There must be a degree of compatibility between the leader's need disposition and the expectations others hold for his/her role. In the name of consensus building, it may be necessary for Mr. Smith to subordinate his interest in the plan and begin the design of a new plan using a collaborative approach. The suggested response to question 1 is **(b)**.

2. Given the situation that exists at Barnsbury Elementary School, Mr. Smith would be well advised to take a win-win orientation to the resolution of the conflict using a problem-solving approach. This approach is likely to be successful if he collaborates with the faculty and involves them in the decision-making process. The faculty is exhibiting proactive behavior as they view the principal as being unjust in his action in that he developed and/or modified a discipline plan that lies in the zone of concern of teachers. The vision for a safe and supportive learning environment should be developed with stakeholders' involvement (Barth, 1990). Given that this did not occur and considering that he is a new administrator, the faculty is likely to believe that this type of behavior will be repeated. Therefore, the problem cannot be resolved by the principal simply withdrawing his plan.

If school discipline is an issue, it must be addressed. By collaborating with the entire faculty and listening to the different perceptions and expectations, a plan could be designed with input from everyone. The faculty would have an opportunity to work together to define the problems and to achieve a workable solution. Working collaboratively, the faculty could develop a sense of ownership for the plan and a commitment to make it work. In addition, through such a process, they could gain new problem-solving skills, which could be transferred to other areas of the school.

When a problem-solving approach is used, competitiveness is removed and no one loses; there are no hard feelings or bitterness that might result from less than ideal ways of handling the situation. It is important for the leader to have a knowledge of the change process for systems, organizations, and individuals and to use that knowledge to ensure that barriers to student learning are identified and addressed (ISLLC, 1996). Forcing a faculty to accept a discipline plan that they had no input in developing is likely to create an unnecessary barrier that will interfere with teaching and learning. The suggested response to question 2 is **(a)**.

3. The faculty has already expressed disagreement with Principal Smith regarding the plan. If he competes with them (insisting that the faculty implement the plan in its current format), a power struggle will develop, and someone will win and someone will lose. Eventually, the students will lose, as the teachers, under forced conditions, would not be fully committed to implementation of the plan. Engaging in a power struggle with the faculty would produce a winner and a loser. It is advisable that this approach be

avoided whenever possible (Lunenburg & Ornstein, 1996). An educational leader promotes the success of all students, uses the influence of his/her office constructively and productively, and does not champion issues that provoke conflict. The suggested response to question 3 is (d).

4. Quite clearly, based on the comments made by various faculty members, they held certain expectations for the principal, and those expectations were not met. In fact, there was considerable disagreement on the plan the principal had developed (causing a variance in role direction). In addition, the intensity of the concerns of teachers has reached the point that if he does not alter the plan, they are likely to attempt to avoid implementing it, using whatever sanctions are available to them. At this point, the principal must be concerned with direction and intensity. Mr. Smith would better serve the school program by seeking to determine the level at which the conflict is rooted, what outcome will foster a smooth opening of school, and how he can achieve that outcome. The suggested response to question 4 is (d).

5. The teachers at Barnsbury Elementary are resisting a change in the school's discipline plan. That resistance stems from a number of factors, and teachers are not likely to be motivated to effect the change until those factors have been addressed. Sergiovanni (1992) offers that, in such situations, before individuals are motivated to change, they must receive answers to several questions. These questions, espoused by the expectancy theory, relate to what needs to be accomplished, the benefits to be derived from the accomplishments, a clear idea of the extent of individual involvement, and the likelihood that individuals involved will achieve success.

The teachers at Barnsbury who are resisting a change in the discipline plan have adjusted to the current state of affairs; however, they could possibly be motivated to support the change. Mr. Smith could provide that motivation by effectively communicating their role in the implementation process, the benefits to be derived from the new plan, the material resources that are available to them, and the success they are almost certain to personally experience.

Faculty involvement in the change process when the change is in their zone of concern is of utmost importance, as the faculty is interested in the benefits the change holds for them (Fullan, 1993). The suggested response to question 5 is (d).

## SUMMARY AND CONCLUSION

Mr. Smith has provoked conflict between himself and members of his faculty and among the faculty, primarily by his leadership style. Whereas any change in the existing discipline plan is likely to initiate some conflict, a more inclusive style of leadership would have minimized the disruption. Given that the action has been taken and the conflict exists, it must be managed. A contingency management approach appears to be appropriate. The contingency approach suggests that there is no one best way of resolving the conflict; rather, the situation must dictate the action to be taken (Owens, 1995). Given the attitude expressed by the members of the faculty, it is best that Principal Smith avoid a power struggle, work collaboratively with the faculty, and attempt to be as accommodating as possible.

# SCENARIO 16
## I AM YOUR NEW PRINCIPAL

### STANDARD 5

A school administrator is an educational leader who promotes the success of all students by acting with integrity, fairness, and in an ethical manner.

*In Chapter 2, the major focus was the identification of characteristics of a school environment that promotes the success of all students. In Scenario 16, a principal new to a school uses a transitional approach that is counterproductive to acquiring those characteristics. Identifying an approach to use in making a transition into a new assignment in a manner that creates an effective learning environment should be beneficial to any leader. This scenario offers the reader an opportunity to witness the approach one principal used and to assess its implications and some possible outcomes.*

### ISLLC Standards Indicators Exhibited in Scenario 16

**Knowledge Indicators**
The administrator has knowledge and understanding of:
▲ Effective communication
▲ Effective consensus-building and negotiation skills
▲ Applied motivational theories
▲ Adult learning and professional development models
▲ The change process for systems, organizations, and individuals
▲ School cultures
▲ Theories and models of organization and the principles of organizational development
▲ Organizational procedures at the school and district level
▲ Human resource management and development
▲ Legal issues impacting school operations
▲ Emerging issues and trends that potentially impact the school community
▲ The purpose of education and the role of leadership in modern society
▲ Various ethical frameworks and perspectives on ethics
▲ The values of the diverse school community
▲ Professional code of ethics
▲ Models and strategies of change and conflict resolution as applied to the larger political, social, cultural, and economic context of schooling
▲ Global issues and forces affecting teaching and learning
▲ The importance of diversity and equity in a democratic society

**Disposition Indicators**
The administrator believes in, values, and is committed to:
▲ Continuous school improvement
▲ The inclusion of all members of the school community
▲ A willingness to continuously examine one's own assumptions, beliefs, and practices

▲ Professional development as an integral part of school improvement
▲ The benefit that diversity brings to the school community
▲ A safe and supportive learning environment
▲ Making management decisions to enhance learning and teaching
▲ Taking risks
▲ Trusting people and their judgment
▲ Accepting responsibility
▲ High-quality standards, expectations, and performances
▲ Involving stakeholders in management practices
▲ Involvement of families and other stakeholders in school decision-making processes
▲ The proposition that diversity enriches the school
▲ The idea of the common good
▲ Bringing ethical principles to the decision-making process
▲ Subordinating one's own principles to the good of the school community
▲ Accepting the consequences for upholding one's principles and actions
▲ Development of a caring school community
▲ Using the influence of one's office constructively and productively in the service of all students and their families
▲ Recognizing a variety of values and cultures

### Performance Indicators

The administrator facilitates processes and engages in activities ensuring that:
▲ The vision is developed with and among stakeholders
▲ All individuals are treated with fairness, dignity, and respect
▲ Students and staff feel valued and important
▲ The responsibility and contributions of each individual are acknowledged
▲ Barriers to student learning are identified and addressed
▲ Diversity is considered in developing learning experiences
▲ The school is organized and aligned for success
▲ The school culture and climate are assessed on a regular basis
▲ A variety of sources of information is used to make decisions
▲ Pupil personnel programs are developed to meet the needs of students and their families
▲ There is a culture of high expectations for self, students, and staff performance
▲ Student and staff accomplishments are recognized and celebrated
▲ Operational procedures are designed and managed to maximize opportunities for successful learning
▲ Problems are confronted and resolved in a timely manner
▲ Financial, human, and material resources are aligned to the goals of schools
▲ Stakeholders are involved in decisions affecting schools
▲ Responsibility is shared to maximize ownership and accountability
▲ Effective conflict-resolution skills are used
▲ Effective group-process and consensus-building skills are used
▲ Effective communication skills are used
▲ Human resources functions support the attainment of school goals
▲ Confidentiality and privacy of school records are maintained
▲ Credence is given to individuals and groups whose values and opinions may conflict

▲ Diversity is recognized and valued

**The administrator**
▲ Examines personal and professional values
▲ Demonstrates values, beliefs, and attitudes that inspire others to higher levels of performance
▲ Serves as a role model
▲ Accepts responsibility for school operations
▲ Considers the impact of one's administrative practices on others
▲ Treats people fairly, equitably, and with dignity and respect
▲ Protects the rights and confidentiality of students and staff
▲ Recognizes and respects the legitimate authority of others
▲ Fulfills legal and contractual obligations
▲ Applies laws and procedures fairly, wisely, and considerately

Lakeside Elementary School is a large inner-city school with the highest suspension rate in the district. Over 90 percent of the faculty has been in the building for 15 years or more. The current principal, Mr. Downey, is retiring after serving the district for 40 years, the last 6 at Lakeside Elementary as principal.

In a reorganization of the district's administrators, Principal Early was assigned to Lakeside Elementary School. The assignment was made in June to become effective in July. Principal Early, a veteran administrator with over 20 years experience, knew Mr. Downey and had discussed various issues with him at district meetings over the years. Therefore, in the interest of a smooth transition, Mr. Downey invited her to the final staff meeting of the school year at Lakeside Elementary.

Principal Early attended the meeting wearing a suit and very high-heeled shoes. She walked toward the front of the group and began passing out papers to the faculty. On the paper was printed the Board of Education's policy regarding faculty appearance and dress, which she proceeded to read to the group. She explained her philosophy on dressing "professionally" and informed the faculty that some of them dressed inappropriately, and this would have to change.

She then passed out lists of expectations; one list contained what she expected from the faculty, and one contained what the faculty could expect from her. She informed the faculty that she had read the personnel files of all faculty members and knew all the "troublemakers" in the building. She also stated that she would be watching test scores, and if faculty members were not effective in their current placements, they would be transferred to another school. She further emphasized that teachers who had been in the same classroom for many years would be moved because they did not own their rooms.

After admonishing the faculty several times about current practices within the building and informing the faculty that it was not too late to apply for a transfer, she asked the faculty for questions, waited 15 seconds, and when there were none, she walked out of the room leaving a stunned and speechless group of teachers.

When the new school year began, Principal Early filled seven of nine open faculty positions with individuals from her former school. These included positions that were not posted for the entire faculty, a practice inconsistent with district policy. The new faculty members were given special treatment and were permitted privileges that continuing faculty members were not allowed. In one of her first faculty meetings as the new building administrator, Principal Early informed the "continuing faculty" that the "incoming faculty" members did not feel welcome in the building, and that it was their fault. At the end of the first quarter, Principal Early wondered why there was conflict between the two groups and why the year had not gotten off to a smooth start.

## REFLECTIVE THINKING AND SCENARIO ANALYSIS

1. In your judgment, what was the substance of the initial conflict at Lakeside?
2. In the scenario, can you cite instances where members of the faculty would be justified in feeling a sense of deprivation?
3. In the scenario, what information, implied or stated, could you use to justify the disposition of Principal Early?
4. Reflecting on the indicators of the ISLLC Standards, what justification might be offered to support Principal Early's decision to fill the vacant positions with teachers from her former school?
5. Cite three of Principal Early's actions that directly contributed to the conflict that existed at Lakeside after the beginning of the school year. Justify your selection with indicators from the ISLLC Standards.
6. What influence, if any, might the past stability of the faculty and the climate of the school have on the nature of the current conflict?

## ADDRESSING THE ISSUES

Select the one best answer to the following questions:

1. Which of the following factors provides the best explanation for the initial conflict that emerged between Principal Early and the established faculty at Lakeside?

   a. Opposition of goals, aims, and values.

   b. Lack of role clarification.

   c. Disruption of the equilibrium of the organization.

   d. All of the above.

2. The type of conflict that emerged in the initial meeting between Principal Early and members of the "continuing faculty" was provoked:

   a. because the ideas presented by Principal Early did not include faculty input.

   b. by the disposition of Principal Early and the content of her presentation.

   c. because Principal Early set high standards for the school.

   d. none of the above.

3. Which of the following would be an accurate assessment of the cause of the conflict that occurred between the two groups of teachers on the faculty at Lakeside?

   a. Competition for scarce resources.

   b. Divergence in goals.

   c. A desire for autonomy.

   d. Equity norms.

4. Which of the following actions taken by Principal Early most likely motivated the behavior of the "continuing faculty"?

   **a.** Relating to the faculty the fact that she had read their personnel files, violating her professional code of ethics.

   **b.** Informing the faculty that some of them would be moved to different classrooms.

   **c.** Using practices that did not suggest fair and equitable treatment for all faculty members.

   **d.** Passing out the Board of Education's policy on faculty appearance and dress, thus violating their rights as teachers.

5. At the beginning of the second quarter, if Principal Early made a commitment to uniting the two groups of teachers, opening the lines of communication between her office and the total faculty, and involving all teachers in the decision-making process, what should be her first course of action?

   **a.** Change her leadership style.

   **b.** Make a commitment to the faculty that all decisions would be fair and equitable.

   **c.** Diagnose the conflict.

   **d.** All of the above.

## DISCUSSION OF THE SOLUTION

1. The initial conflict created at Lakeside Elementary with the arrival of Principal Early occurred for a number of reasons. First, the equilibrium of a well-established faculty (with very little turnover) was disrupted by a change in principals. The uncertainty of the personality of the new principal and the idea of having to meet a new set of expectations are frequently stress-producing for a school faculty (Gorton, 1987). In addition, when Principal Early made her comments in the initial meeting, it became clear to the faculty that her norms, beliefs, and expectations were different from those that had previously existed. If individuals in a school have different views over what should occur and the role that the principal should play, conflict is likely to exist (Barge, 1994). A third conflict-producing factor emerged when Principal Early established expectations for the faculty before making a determination of the faculty's expectations for her role. Failure of leaders to assess current conditions and develop an understanding of the expectations that followers have for them will inhibit their ability to establish directions with any degree of certainty of how those directions will be received by the faculty (Gorton, 1987).

Conflict occurred at Lakeside because of opposition of goals, aims, and values, lack of role clarification, and a disruption of the equilibrium of the organization. Principal Early would have been well advised to have entered the initial meeting for the purpose of developing mutual respect between herself and her new faculty. She could have advocated high-quality standards, expectations, and performance, but in a manner that invited shared responsibility and accountability. Her behavior could have demonstrated values, beliefs, and an attitude that would have inspired her new faculty to collaborate in setting standards and achieving the desired level of performance. The suggested response to question 1 is **(d)**.

2. In her initial meeting, Principal Early created interpersonal conflict with the faculty at Lakeside. Her presentation was directive and boss-centered, setting a tone for a power struggle to emerge. Her statement concerning the personnel files gave the impression

that she was looking for "troublemakers" so she could "deal with them." Announcing that she would be looking at test scores implied that teachers were solely responsible for test scores, and threatening to move teachers to different rooms exacerbated an unsettled situation created because of the retirement of Mr. Downey. She introduced fear into the workplace as opposed to removing fear. Principal Early's disposition in the initial meeting, coupled with the content of her presentation, created the notion of a "we-they" climate, thus initiating conflict between her and the faculty. Emotions got involved, and hostility was produced. The suggested response to question 2 is **(b)**.

3. When Principal Early elected to bring members of her former faculty to Lakeside, they became members of the Lakeside faculty organization and should have been identified as such. Principal Early should have taken definitive steps to unite the two groups. The leader should use the influence of his/her office to develop faculty cohesiveness. A major problem was created when the faculty became identified as consisting of two groups. The distinct identification led to intraorganizational conflict (conflict between two groups within the faculty). Allowing special privileges to the incoming group further built resentment and angered members of the faculty who were not receiving them. The "continuing faculty" members perceived the action to be unfair and sought to promote justice. They believed that the equity norm had been violated. When an individual or group perceives an action to be unfair, they will often react in a proactive manner in an attempt to achieve fair treatment (Greenberg, 1996b). The suggested response to question 3 is **(d)**.

4. When the new school year began, Principal Early recruited members from the faculty of her former school to fill vacant positions that existed at Lakeside. Focused recruitment is an acceptable practice, and it is understandable that a principal faced with the challenges posed at Lakeside would want several individuals on staff with whom rapport had already been established. However, the acquisition of these individuals must occur within the realm of policy. This was not the case at Lakeside.

The matter was further complicated when the "continuing faculty" members perceived the incoming faculty members to be getting special treatment. Martin (1981) asserts that certain reward distribution patterns will encourage individuals to make certain social comparisons. The "continuing faculty" made such comparisons, and as a result, they developed feelings of deprivation and resentment. The perceived treatment of the incoming faculty members fueled the conflict. The suggested answer to question 4 is **(c)**.

5. Principal Early entered Lakeside using a leadership style based in classical theory. She was directive and structured and used her position power to set the tone for her first year as principal of Lakeside. She took a very strong position prior to obtaining an understanding of the individuals on the faculty or allowing them to participate in any restructuring efforts that were to occur. She did not factor into her actions the power of informal groups in the organization. We have seen in Chapters 1 and 2 how such behavior is counterproductive. Now, if Principal Early wants to change the faculty's perception, she might be well advised to consider a leadership style that is less directive, more people centered, considerate, and one that reflects an understanding of and a respect for the behavior of individuals and informal groups in organizations. Such a leadership style would be based in human relations theory. The behavior of Principal Johnson in Scenario 2 could serve as an example.

According to indicators of the ISLLC Standards, production in organizations tends to improve when human factors, such as morale, a feeling of belonging, participative decision making, and effective communication, are factored into leader behavior (ISLLC, 1996). In order for this to occur in an effective manner at Lakeside, Principal Early must first diagnose the conflict.

She must seek to determine how the parties have conceptualized the situation and then select an appropriate approach for change. The suggested response to question 5 is **(c)**.

## SUMMARY AND CONCLUSION

Lakeside Elementary School is a large inner-city school with the highest suspension rate in the district. This factor alone suggests a school that is in need of strong, effective leadership. Any principal who assumed the leadership for the school would need to analyze the situation, develop a shared vision for change, and rally the faculty around the implementation of that vision.

Someone apparently assessed the situation and made the determination that Principal Early is a leader with those capabilities, unless a major selection error occurred. One would have to assume that she was reasonably successful in her prior position and commanded the respect and support of her faculty. After all, she was assigned to Lakeside, and a number of teachers from her previous faculty chose to join her.

Nevertheless, she is off to a less than effective start. The wagons have been circled and are likely to remain that way until her style of leadership is changed to one that manages trust, demonstrates respect, and facilitates the inclusion of the entire faculty in the decision-making process. Most leaders like to enjoy the comfort of having individuals on their team who have proven they are trustworthy and have the expertise to complete assigned tasks. However, acquiring a supportive faculty cannot be done at the expense of organizational effectiveness or in violation of policy. The vacant positions at Lakeside should have been posted, applicants accepted, and screening done through the selection process. To do otherwise placed the incoming faculty members in a tenuous position and made a difficult situation worse.

Principal Early's goals appear to be aligned with the needs of the school. However, her disposition and process of achieving them leaves much to be desired. The authoritarian style she used is limited in its effectiveness. In schools, adult relationships are competitive. When you approach people with an element of criticism, you disempower them, and reduce their ability to make a contribution, as well as their potential for growth (Barth, 1990). Little assistance is likely to be forthcoming from a faculty when adversarial relations exist between adults, and their actions may not be of much assistance in bringing about meaningful sustained results. If the faculty is to assist Principal Early in reducing suspensions and improving academic achievement, she must respect their major interests and utilize their constructive expertise.

## SCENARIO 17
## THE ASSIGNMENT OF AN ASSISTANT SUPERINTENDENT OF INSTRUCTION

### STANDARD 6

A school administrator is an educational leader who promotes the success of all students by understanding, responding to, and influencing the larger political, social, economic, legal, and cultural context.

*Scenario 17 presents a clear picture of the relationship between decision making and conflict. A leader made a poor decision, and, as a result, conflict emerged. Then, the strategy selected to be used in managing the conflict was inappropriate; this caused an escalation of the problem and the conflict. In addition, several of the indicators of the ISLLC Standards were violated.*

## ISLLC Standards Indicators Exhibited in Scenario 17

### Knowledge Indicators
The administrator has knowledge and understanding of:
▲ Effective communication
▲ Effective consensus-building and negotiation skills
▲ Applied motivational theories
▲ Adult learning and professional development models
▲ The change process for systems, organizations, and individuals
▲ School cultures
▲ Theories and models of organization and the principles of organizational development
▲ Organizational procedures at the school and district level
▲ Human resources management and development
▲ Legal issues impacting school operations
▲ The purpose of education and the role of leadership in modern society
▲ Various ethical frameworks and perspectives on ethics
▲ The values of the diverse school community
▲ Professional code of ethics
▲ Models and strategies of change and conflict resolution as applied to the larger political, social, cultural, and economic context of schooling
▲ The dynamics of policy development and advocacy under our democratic political system
▲ The political, social, cultural, and economic systems and processes that impact schools
▲ Principles of representative governance that undergird the system of American schools
▲ The importance of diversity and equity in a democratic society

### Disposition Indicators
The administrator believes in, values, and is committed to:
▲ Continuous school improvement
▲ The inclusion of all members of the school community
▲ A willingness to continuously examine one's own assumptions, beliefs, and practices
▲ The benefit that diversity brings to the school community
▲ A safe and supportive learning environment
▲ Making management decisions to enhance learning and teaching
▲ Taking risks
▲ Trusting people and their judgment
▲ Accepting responsibility
▲ High-quality standards, expectations, and performances
▲ Involving stakeholders in management practices

▲ A safe environment
▲ Involvement of families and other stakeholders in school decision-making processes
▲ The proposition that diversity enriches the school
▲ The idea of the common good
▲ Bringing ethical principles to the decision-making process
▲ Subordinating one's own principles to the good of the school community
▲ Accepting the consequences for upholding one's principles and actions
▲ Development of a caring school community
▲ Using the influence of one's office constructively and productively in the service of all students and their families
▲ Recognizing a variety of values and cultures

**Performance Indicators**
The administrator facilitates processes and engages in activities ensuring that:
▲ The vision is developed with and among stakeholders
▲ Barriers to student learning are identified and addressed
▲ Diversity is considered in developing learning experiences
▲ The school is organized and aligned for success
▲ The school culture and climate are assessed on a regular basis
▲ A variety of sources of information is used to make decisions
▲ There is a culture of high expectation for self, students, and staff performance
▲ Operational procedures are designed and managed to maximize opportunities for successful learning
▲ Problems are confronted and resolved in a timely manner
▲ Stakeholders are involved in decisions affecting schools
▲ Responsibility is shared to maximize ownership and accountability
▲ Effective conflict resolution skills are used
▲ Effective group-process and consensus-building skills are used
▲ Effective communication skills are used
▲ Human resources functions support the attainment of school goals
▲ Credence is given to individuals and groups whose values and opinions may conflict

**The administrator**
▲ Recognizes and values diversity
▲ Provides opportunities for staff to develop collaboration skills
▲ Examines personal and professional values
▲ Demonstrates values, beliefs, and attitudes that inspire others to higher levels of performance
▲ Influences the environment in which the school operates on behalf of students and their families
▲ Communicates among the school community concerning trends, issues, and potential changes in the environment in which the school operates
▲ Serves as a role model
▲ Accepts responsibility for school operations
▲ Considers the impact of one's administrative practices on others
▲ Uses the influence of the office to enhance the educational program rather than for personal gain
▲ Treats people fairly, equitably, and with dignity and respect

▲ Recognizes and respects the legitimate authority of others
▲ Fulfills legal and contractual obligations
▲ Applies laws and procedures fairly, wisely, and considerately

Superintendent Morgan of the Bellwood School District (a district that had undergone considerable controversy as a result of a city-county school district merger) sat in his office, realizing that the new school year was only a month away. Considering the parent and student complaints from the previous year, there was simply no way to enter the new school year without changes in the assignment of principals. Given that the Director of Human Resources had just advised him of a letter of retirement from Walter Robins, Assistant Superintendent of Instruction, and a resignation of the Assistant Principal at Clark Middle School, he believed this to be an excellent opportunity for some districtwide changes to improve the district's effectiveness. After all, he thought "Wilma Henderson, principal at Williamsburg High, is an excellent person to assume the role of Assistant Superintendent of Instruction. The achievement scores of students in her school are the best in the district and above the state average. She is very knowledgeable relative to curriculum issues, attends state and national meetings, and appears to command the respect of administrators and teachers. Filling this position with Wilma would mean the best of all worlds. It would add an excellent person to the central office team and, at the same time, create an opportunity to reassign principals and enhance the climate in the school district."

After calling the Director of Human Resources and acquiring the personnel files of all current principals and assistant principals, Superintendent Morgan began his deliberations. He looked at various strengths and weaknesses and compared successes to projects attempted. He reviewed parent, student, and teacher complaints of the previous year, looked at student achievement scores, discipline problems occurring in the various schools, and even the attendance records of administrators, teachers, and students. After completing the review, he compiled a list of personnel changes to be made by the Director of Human Resources. He did not seek board approval, as the law in the state where he was employed empowered the superintendent to make personnel changes, under certain conditions, without Board approval. The following changes were made:

Wilma Henderson from Principal of Williamsburg High to Assistant Superintendent of Instruction in the Central Office

Allen Harris from Principal of Walker High to Principal of Williamsburg High

Anthony Reed from Principal of Northside High to Principal of Walker High

Linda Hart from Principal of Central City High to Assistant Principal of Clark Middle

Evelyn Morris from Assistant Principal of Clark Middle to Principal of Northside High

Charles Adams from Assistant Principal of Clark to Principal of Clark Middle

A posting for an assistant principal at Clark Middle

Three days after Superintendent Morgan announced the changes to the school district personnel and the general public, he began to receive a number of complaints. On the fourth day, in a meeting with the Director of Human Resources, he discussed the following complaints, some of which had been presented to him and others that were appearing in the local newspaper.

One of the Board of Education members was complaining that the position of Assistant Superintendent was not posted. Bill Johnson, Assistant Principal of Williamsburg High (who happens to be African-American), complained that once again he had been passed over for promotion. Charles Walker, a teacher in the district and a longtime seeker of an administrative position, expressed concerns that the positions should have been posted. Linda Hart (also African-American) was believed to have had at least two meetings with Bill Johnson as he was attempting to get her to join him in filing a class action suit.

Over the next several days, the local newspaper, which is not very supportive of the school district, printed articles concerning fairness, the superintendent's annual evaluation, infighting, and unethical personnel practices. One headline read "Superintendent's Evaluation Drops in Twenty-two of Twenty-three Areas." Another read "Superintendent Loses Favor with Some Board Members over Fairness Issue." In one article a board member stated, " The superintendent makes his own rules." In responding to the superintendent's evaluation, the article quoted one board member as saying, "The only area in which the superintendent's evaluation increased was sense of humor and the ability to laugh at personnel mistakes." Another article quoted still another board member as having said, "The superintendent should resign as he is unethical in his behavior."

In his soft jolly mannerism, Superintendent Morgan comments, "I will not speak to these charges. The law gives me the right to make personnel changes, and I followed the law. As far as posting, the assistant superintendent's position was posted, and that is sufficient."

The debate over the issue continued at the board level and in the community for weeks. As time passed, the conflict became more intense, pressure mounted, and the superintendent resigned.

## REFLECTIVE THINKING AND SCENARIO ANALYSIS

1. What effect did the political, social, and cultural aspects of the climate in the Bellwood School District have on the nature of the conflict that emerged?
2. If it is true that policy permitted the superintendent to take the personnel action described, what other actions might have been necessary to avoid the conflict that emerged?
3. What are some of the critical factors that must be considered in managing the type of conflict that has emerged in the Bellwood School District?
4. What are some of the actions a superintendent might take when board members publicly make critical statements about his/her effectiveness? Base your response on the ISLLC Standard indicators.
5. To what extent did the knowledge, disposition, and performance of the superintendent contribute to the conflict?

## ADDRESSING THE ISSUES

Select the one best answer to the following questions:

1. Having analyzed the conflict that occurred in the Bellwood School District, which of the following would you identify as the critical factor causing the conflict?

    **a.** Competition for scarce resources in a troubled district.

    **b.** A desire for autonomy on behalf of the board of education and superintendent.

    **c.** A divergence in goals between the board of education and superintendent.

    **d.** All of the above.

2. Having diagnosed the conflict, in your judgment, which of the following approaches is least likely to be effective in minimizing the dysfunctional effects of the conflict?

    **a.** The superintendent should admit an error and keep a positive climate in the district by working collaboratively with the board of education to achieve the best solution.

    **b.** The superintendent should hold firm to his position; he is acting within policy, and after all, personnel actions are his responsibility. He cannot afford to allow the board to interfere in personnel matters.

    **c.** Both the board and the superintendent have rights and responsibilities; the superintendent should meet with the board and talk through the matter in a give-and-take manner, even if he loses face.

    **d.** There is really no need for additional action; the decision has been made, and the superintendent should just wait and see what happens.

3. Which of the following strategies should Superintendent Morgan use to avoid the possibility of board members developing a feeling of relative deprivation and resentment?

    **a.** Refrain from making any comments that seem to hold a negative connotation and simply state the purpose of his decision and ask for clarification as to how the board would like future personnel actions to be handled.

    **b.** Take no action and just hold his position.

    **c.** Retract the personnel actions and start again, keeping the same objective in mind.

    **d.** None of the above.

4. The comments that people are making in the newspaper can best be characterized as:

    **a.** The substance of the conflict and must be taken by the superintendent as critical factors that have an influence on his stability in the district.

    **b.** Proactive comments of individuals who believe the superintendent acted in an unfair and unjust manner.

    **c.** Comments individuals are making in an effort to create equity in the system.

    **d.** All of the above.

**5.** When Superintendent Morgan said, "I will not speak to these charges ..." he exemplified:

    **a.** a person who is concerned with self-expectation and is not sensitive to the intensity of the situation.

    **b.** an individual who is reluctant to create interpersonal conflict.

    **c.** an individual who stands on principle and holds expectations for himself as superintendent of the district.

    **d.** none of the above.

## DISCUSSION OF THE SOLUTION

1. Superintendent Morgan established a goal of improving the delivery of instructional services to students. His process of achieving that goal included the appointment of an assistant superintendent of instruction and making various changes in the assignment of principals. He reviewed personnel files and selected individuals who he felt had the skills and experience necessary to meet his established goals. However, after the changes became public knowledge, some members of the board of education, individuals in the community, and personnel in the district expressed a different viewpoint regarding the goals of the superintendent and the approach he was taking to reach them. The goals of these individuals were not compatible with the goals of the superintendent.

When individuals and or groups in a school district have different goals from the superintendent, conflicts emerge. That was the case in Bellwood; conflict emerged, and the source of that conflict was goal divergence. The suggested response to question 1 is **(c)**.

2. In managing the conflict, Superintendent Morgan took the position that policy should prevail. However, this position was not acceptable to the opposing parties. When two parties assume opposing points of view and use the power of their position to prevail in their way of thinking, they are engaging in a power struggle (Sashkin & Morris, 1984). Such was the case in the Bellwood School District when Superintendent Morgan held firm to the notion that policy gave him the authority to make his desired changes, in spite of the intensity of the opposing point of view. Effective communication no longer existed, which reduced the possibility of the conflict being resolved in a win-win manner. It is very important for the leader to have a continuing dialogue with other decision makers regarding issues affecting education (ISLLC, 1996).

Both the board and the superintendent have rights and responsibilities, and each is aware, or should be aware, of the position and power of the other. Therefore, the approach taken by Superintendent Morgan (power struggling) is likely to be the least effective approach in a situation of this nature. When two parties engage in a power struggle as a method of resolving conflict, one will emerge as a winner and the other as a loser. There is little concern for interpersonal relationships, as the major focus is on task completion and prevailing in one's position. Gorton (1987) writes that this is a very disruptive method that should be avoided if at all possible. It should be noted that when such an approach is used, the losing party does not totally dismiss the conflict but retreats, regroups, and returns when he/she perceives the timing is better to address the opposition (Barge, 1994).

When issues between a board of education and the superintendent of schools are addressed via open power struggles, the end results are often very disruptive to the district. Such struggles often result in the departure of the superintendent and sometimes board members. Some action must be taken and if collaboration is an option, it should be taken. The suggested response to question 2 is **(b).**

3. Moving toward tranquillity requires great effort and often a specific plan of action. The superintendent should attempt to engender a positive climate by refraining from making any comments that appear to hold a negative connotation. He should clarify his position and seek clarification from all board members regarding personnel matters. According to Covey (1989), an effective leader seeks first to understand and then to be understood.

In addition, the superintendent should be flexible in his mannerism, displaying a willingness to continuously examine his assumptions, beliefs, and practices (ISLLC, 1996). Following policy alone is not sufficient for effective leadership. The climate of the times, norms of the district, and the individuals involved are all factors that influence action and must be given consideration. Public policy is shaped to provide quality education for students (ISLLC, 1996). Given that his original intent was to enhance the climate of the district, he should not allow his behavior to be counterproductive to that intent. The suggested response to question 3 is **(a).**

4. The comments being made in the newspaper clearly characterized the substance of the conflict existing in Bellwood. These statements conveyed the opposing viewpoints that various individuals in the school district and in the larger community held regarding the issue. The individuals voicing comments perceived the superintendent's actions to be unfair. Greenberg and Baron (1997), in explaining their proactive dimension of conflict, speak to the behavior an individual might display when he/she perceives the action of others as being unjust and unfair. In such instances, the individual or group members make statements and take action in an effort to promote justice and create fair treatment.

When reviewing the comments made by Bellwood board members in the newspaper, one would quickly conclude that they were expressing dissatisfaction because of perceived unfair treatment and a pervasive element of injustice. People often take these actions in an attempt to create equity in the system (Greenberg & Baron, 1997). The leader should be knowledgeable of the political, social, cultural, and economic systems and processes that impact schools, and he/she should use these systems to promote the success of the school district (ISLLC, 1996). The suggested response to question 4 is **(c).**

5. Quite clearly, the superintendent understood his role and had explicit expectations for his behavior as superintendent of the Bellwood School District. Self-expectations are influenced by the manner in which a leader perceives that he or she should behave (Gorton, 1987). However, some board members had developed a very strong negative feeling regarding the legitimacy of the superintendent's perception, and they were very intense in their feelings. Intensity may be defined in this situation as the extent to which individuals or groups believed that certain actions should or should not have been taken, and that certain behavior should or should not have been displayed.

Superintendent Morgan felt strongly that he should perform his duties within the realm of policy, and once that had occurred, no other action was necessary. He was very intense in his feelings and did not act as if he were sensitive to the intensity of the feelings of some board members. Both self-expectations and intensity are factors reflected in the statement, "I will not speak to these charges...." Such a statement challenged the compatibility between the superintendent's need disposition and the intensity of the expectations some board members held for his role. Clearly this is not a statement that is made by a leader who recognizes and respects the legitimate authority of others or one who is committed to the ideal of the common good (ISLLC, 1996). The suggested response to question 5 is **(a)**.

## SUMMARY AND CONCLUSION

Superintendent Morgan had a perception of the role he should play as superintendent. Board members and other individuals in the school system also had expectations for their superintendent (his informal role). The difference in these expectations provoked conflict. The situation was exacerbated when the conflict was not effectively diagnosed and the appropriate resolution strategy applied.

A superintendent has to be sensitive to the environment of the school, and issues have to be resolved within the context of the prevailing climate. In today's educational climate, many superintendents are using shared decision making, collaboration, and other participatory governance models to address issues that have districtwide ramifications (Etheridge & Green, 1998). Rather than being adversarial, confrontational, and steadfast in their way of thinking, school leaders are turning to more cooperative and nonconfrontational approaches. Instead of using policies to defend their position, they are involving people in shaping their positions.

## CHAPTER SUMMARY

Conflict is "the interaction of interdependent people who perceive opposition of goals, aims, and views, and who see the other party as potentially interfering with the realization of these goals" (Putnam & Poole, 1987, p. 352). It occurs in varying degrees in all organizations, as it is a normal part of social relations (Greenberg & Baron, 1997). It often occurs in today's schools as a result of change and the need for people to work in harmony.

Conflict of the type that occurs in schools can be differentiated in two ways—context and content. The leader should seek to understand each of these areas and its implications for behavior in schools. Another type of conflict that frequently occurs in schools is role conflict. There are formal organizational roles and informal organizational roles, and the two must coexist. When they do not, conflict is likely to emerge.

If conflict occurs in schools, it must be assessed for direction, clarity, and intensity, then effectively managed. Therefore, leaders need a knowledge of the principles of organizational development. For, if not managed effectively, over time conflict will erode the creative professional environment of a school and render a faculty unable to see opportunities and collaborate with one another (Hanson, 1996). Considering the effects of such an occurrence, the leader must be knowledgeable of strategies and skillful in processes for the effective management of conflict. Some identified approaches are avoidance, smoothing, bargaining, power struggle, and problem solving. The challenge for the leader is matching the appropriate approach with the situation.

There is no one right way to lead a school district or to eliminate all conflict. Nevertheless, when thought and consideration are given the variables that impact a situation, optimal ways of managing conflict can be identified. One can reach the optimum by communicating effectively, making decisions with the involvement of appropriate individuals, and selecting appropriate strategies.

## MOVING INTO PRACTICE

Review the scenarios in Chapter 5. Using the pros and cons of the various situations, identify several approaches that you would use to address the following issues in an actual school situation. Project yourself in the role of the principal and take care to formulate a rationale for your selected behavior.

- If you were principal of a middle school and half of your faculty wanted to have reading in the content areas for all students and the other half wanted self-contained remedial classes for only those students who needed assistance with their reading development, how would you resolve the conflict?
- In a high school where you serve as principal, several teachers want to move to a form of block scheduling. The majority of the faculty is convinced that block scheduling is a fad and that the benefits gained would not be worth the time invested in the change. After a negative vote of the faculty regarding the implementation of the concept, you learn that the original group of teachers has gone into the community and generated parental support for the concept. Parents have asked for a meeting with you to discuss block scheduling. You are aware that some parents are referring to you as the traditional administrator who is keeping their school in the dark ages. How would you resolve this conflict?
- Develop a conflict management strategy that you believe would be effective in managing the conflict that occurred in the Bellwood School District.

## ACQUIRING AN UNDERSTANDING OF SELF

- Cite at least three of Principal Early's statements that would have made you uncomfortable had you been a member of the faculty at Lakeside.

▶ What is your style of managing conflict? When you resolve a conflict, what evidence do you secure to determine if your approach to conflict resolution is effective?

▶ Make a list of five educational activities that you feel are morally wrong, but that you have recently observed in a school situation.

▶ When you managed your last conflict, what strengths did you use? What would you do differently if you had to manage the same conflict again?

## SUGGESTED READINGS

Burton, J., & Dukes, F. (1990). *Conflict practices in management: Settlement and resolution.* New York: St. Martin's Press.

Katz, N., & Lawler, J. W. (1993). *Conflict resolution: Building bridges.* Thousand Oaks, CA: Corwin Press, Inc.

Kreidler, W. T. (1993). *Creative conflict resolution.* New York: Scott Foresman and Company.

# 6

# FACILITATING CHANGE IN SCHOOLS

## Leadership and Change

When an individual assumes a leadership role in a school or school district, it is often expected that he/she will bring to that organization knowledge, expertise, and ideas that can be transformed into a shared vision for the enhancement of the school's programs and activities. Meeting these expectations often requires some degree of change. To be effective, the leader must have knowledge and understanding of the change process for systems, organizations, and individuals (ISLLC, 1996). On a deeper level, it is essential for leaders of today's schools to be effective students of change.

This chapter explores the process of change. The focus is on a school's capacity for change and the forces that positively and negatively influence the change process. The concept of change is examined, change theories are reviewed, and a discussion is held on processes school leaders might use in bringing about change. The chapter ends with the presentation of two scenarios where change is occurring. The first scenario addresses the change process a newly appointed principal uses to increase student achievement in his assigned school. The second scenario entitled "The Strategic Planning Process" (a continuation of activities in the Arrowhead Consolidated School District) exposes the reader to a process of establishing a shared vision and fostering a climate conducive to student learning and professional development. Through these scenarios, the reader will be able to relate the concepts described in the introductory section to practical school situations and reflect on the implications they hold for school leaders who participate in the change process.

Given that schools are open social systems and forces in their internal and external environments influence the interactions between and among their parts, change is likely to impact the entire organization. For that reason, to some extent, all ISLLC Standards are addressed in this chapter. However, the primary focus is on the four that are listed at the beginning of the chapter. It should be noted that such comprehensive reflections of the standards in the change process further emphasize the impact of change in schools.

## The Concept of Change

When the leader attempts to alter the behavior, structure, program, purpose, or output of some unit of the school or school district, he/she is attempting to make a change. Change is a process, not an event; it can be planned or unplanned and can be influenced by forces inside and outside of the school. The process can be viewed in three steps (see Figure 6.1). The first step consists of establishing the vision and/or goals; in essence, a determination is made of the standard of excellence the school staff desires to reach. The second step involves determining the state of existing programs, or current reality. Finally, a determination of what is needed in order to reach the desired goals is made. This step, often called a discrepancy analysis, assesses the difference between current reality and the stated goal (Schmidt & Finnigan, 1992). Imbedded in the process is the need to assess human potential (skills and attributes of faculty and staff) and draw conclusions about how to remove the discrepancy (decision making about programming) that existed between current reality and the desired goals (Schmidt & Finnigan, 1992).

**FIGURE 6.1    Three steps in the change process as identified by Schmidt and Finnigan (1992).**

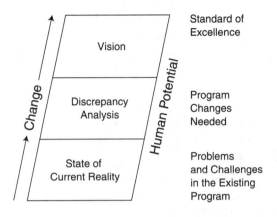

For various reasons in schools, individuals have a difficult time accepting and adjusting to change. Therefore, in order for change to be effective and sustained, while minimizing disruption, the leader must be skilled in implementing the change process, and the strategies employed must be carefully selected. In addition, prior to engaging in the change process, the leader should determine the magnitude of the change and the degree of difficulty involved in eliminating the discrepancy (Fullan, 1993). There are various theories and suggested practices that enlighten the approach leaders can take when attempting change, and in the following section, some of the most noted ones are reviewed.

## Theories and Practices Informing Change

Change occurring in schools can be classified as either continuous, or first-order, change or discontinuous, or second-order change (Meyer, Brooks, & Goes, 1990). Meyer and his associates report that continuous, or first-order change, occurs without a disruption to the system; the system remains stable (equilibrium is maintained) although some small modifications are made. With first-order change, the leader improves the efficiency and effectiveness of the school without extensively altering the manner in which teachers and students routinely behave, and upheaval and conflict are often avoided. With discontinuous, or second-order change, the equilibrium of the system is disrupted as the fundamental properties of the system are changed. The existing order is broken. New goals are established, the structure and programs change, and individuals have to perform differently. This type of change has proven to be very challenging in schools and is a major producer of resistance and conflict (Conley, 1997).

We witnessed second-order change in Chapter 1 when Principal Sterling (newly appointed principal of Frost Elementary School) attempted change, and again in Chapter 5 when Principal Early (newly transferred principal at Lakeside Elementary) outlined to the faculty her expectations and intentions for change. In both instances, the leaders experienced resistance and conflict. The resistance and conflict occurred because in each instance, the leader was asking the faculty to make major alterations in the school structure, accept new programs, and perform differently.

First-order change also occurred in Chapter 1 as Principal Johnson took action to change the school's science program. She changed the science program, but did not substantially alter the way the faculty performed their roles. The science program was simply taken through a renewal process (change occurred to allow the faculty to teach in a more effective manner a subject they were already teaching). Principal Johnson introduced the idea and gradually took steps toward its implementation. Her practice followed the incremental decision-making model presented in Chapter 5. As Lindblom (1959) describes, she makes a series of decisions, and based upon the outcome of each, other decisions may be made.

Determining the order of the change is very important as it allows the leader to determine the extent to which the faculty and staff are ready for the change and what preparation is necessary before the change is undertaken. In essence, the leader determines the school's capacity for change.

## The Capacity for Change

When one is asked to make program changes, particularly if they run counter to one's beliefs, the changes are not likely to occur without disruption or conflict. This is minimized when the school has the capacity for the desired change (readiness of the school for the change process). Schmidt and Finnigan (1992) advise that in determining the school's capacity for change, leaders should consider:

1. the level of dissatisfaction the stakeholders are experiencing with current conditions,
2. the short- and long-term costs,
3. the extent to which individuals understand the vision to be achieved by the change,
4. the consequences of the change, and
5. the degree of difficulty in making the change.

Consideration should also be given to factors that influence the faculty's attitude toward the components of the change, new information, if any, that will have to be learned, identities that will be lost, and new beliefs that will be formed. Also, the amount of extra time and attention that will be required to implement the new program must be considered. People generally support change efforts if they believe current conditions need improving. However, they must also believe that achieving the vision will improve current conditions; that the desired change is realistic, has been clearly outlined, and can be achieved; and that the cost is not too high (Schmidt & Finnigan, 1992).

In addition to the issues addressed in the previous section, there are a number of other factors that the leader should consider in establishing a school's capacity for change. A list of these factors appears in Figure 6.2. Among items on the list, the leader should perhaps be most concerned with the fear of failure that may exist among the faculty. Fear of failure is one of the major sources of resistance to change (Ryan & Oestreich, 1991). As a result of that fear, teachers might be prone to say, "I would have tried that approach; however, I was afraid it would not be considered the right approach; or we have always done it this way; or our former principal wanted us to do it this way" (Ryan & Oestreich, 1991).

For the leader to make change that is effective and sustained, producing the least amount of conflict, the school must have a capacity for change. In the absence of that capacity, the leader must build it. Some theories and strategies that inform the process of building capacity for change are presented in the following section.

## Force Field Analysis

Kurt Lewin's (1951) Force Field Analysis theory of change is very applicable to school situations and can be used to assess the school's readiness for change, reduce conflicts, and enhance change effectiveness. Lewin theorized that the environment in which change occurs contains a force field. The field consists of two forces, which he categorized as driving and restraining. Driving forces move one toward the desired change, and restraining forces resist the desired

---

**FIGURE 6.2   Actions that build a capacity for change**

1. Establishing effective lines of communication between the school leader and the community
2. Securing community support for the change concept
3. Acquiring expertise in the new program concept
4. Driving fear out of the school
5. Working out collective bargaining regulations that facilitate change
6. Acquiring necessary approvals from the State Department of Education
7. Identifying sources of the necessary resources
8. Utilizing effective change strategies

SOURCE: This list was developed from various references reviewed in developing this chapter.

change, inhibiting its attainment. In Lewin's theory, people are viewed as constantly seeking equilibrium between the power status of the two forces, which allows the status quo to be maintained in a frozen state of existence. Change causes a disruption in the balance of these forces. When one set of forces is substantially altered, reflecting a change in the power status of the other, the state of equilibrium is "unfrozen," and there is a break in the status quo, which prevails until a new state of equilibrium is established. When the change is completed, "freezing" occurs on a new level, thus establishing a new state of equilibrium between the two sets of forces. The change becomes the norm and remains such until the next change.

It is the power of these forces and their interaction relative to a particular change that determine the degree of difficulty a leader will experience in making that change. Lewin (1951) advises that if the driving forces far outweigh the restraining forces in power and frequency, the school leader might push the change forward, overpowering the resisting forces. However, if the reverse is true, and the restraining forces are much stronger than the driving forces, the school leader would be well advised to give serious consideration to abandoning the change. Lewin further advises that in making a change, it is far better to convert restraining forces to driving forces than simply increasing driving forces or overpowering restraining forces.

Given that change in schools is likely to meet with less resistance and there is likely to be less conflict in the school when restraining forces are converted to driving forces, the leader should consider this factor in pursuing change. For example, if the principal would like to change the first-grade reading program from a strong phonics-based approach to an exclusive whole language approach, and teachers are convinced that reading is best taught using a phonetic approach, they may resist the change and become a strong restraining force.

Changing to a new approach would mean the teachers would have to adjust to a new way of teaching. Thus, they are likely to become a restraining force and remain such until they can see the benefit to be derived from the new method. Changing the program, in spite of the concerns of the first-grade teachers, could negatively impact the entire instructional program. However, if they could be persuaded (in a positive manner) to accept the new program approach prior to the change, not only would a restraining force be removed, but also a driving force would be added, as the teachers would likely become supporters of the change.

Assessing the force field provides the leader with an idea of the degree of difficulty that might be experienced in the change process. In that way, he/she can determine the likelihood of success. Only after it has been determined that change is promising, or the leader agrees to take the risk of making change that is not promising, should he/she proceed.

## Change Strategies

Chin and Benne (1969) offered a topology of change strategies that can also guide the leader through the change process: empirical-rational, normative–re-educative, and power-coercive. Using the empirical-rational strategy, the leader does not have to be coercive; he/she simply assembles and presents the necessary information regarding the desired change. Once the information is presented, the group selects the action suggested by the data. This strategy is based on the Theory Y assumption, which offers that people are rational and will select the best course of action when that action is justified with objective data.

If the group addressing the change is open to a consensus approach, the leader may elect to use the normative–re-educative strategy. Group activities are initiated to bring about changes in the norms of the group through changes in attitudes, values, skills, and relationships. This strategy facilitates the desired changes being made by the group, without the leader applying strong pressure. This concept was used in Chapter 4, Scenario 13, when the principal worked cooperatively with the faculty to revise the student recognition program.

The power-coercive strategy is used when the leader has a solid power base. This power may result from the leader's position, expertise, ability to punish or reward individuals, or a number of other sources. The key factor in using this strategy is the influence of the power of the leader over those with less power. Such was the case in Scenario 11, when the superintendent took action, much to the displeasure of Mr. Sims.

In bringing about change, the leader may choose either of these strategies or some combination of the three. The determining factors are likely to be the culture of the school, the leader's knowledge of the culture, and his/her respect for it as a powerful force in the change process (Cusick, 1973).

## Change Agentry

Another theory relative to change and the capacity of the organization to make change is Fullan's (1993) Change Agentry Theory. As a part of this theory, Fullan advances four core capacities required by the change agent to build change capacity in an organization: personal vision building, inquiry, mastery, and collaboration. He suggests that these core capacities must be compatible with institutional counterparts, which are shared vision building, organizational structure, norms and practices of inquiry, focus on organizational development and know-how, and collaborative work cultures (p. 12). He further theorizes that the change approach is dual, working simultaneously on the individual and institutional development, and the leader must be self-conscious about the nature of the change and the change process. The following section contains a brief explanation of the four capacities offered by Fullan (1993):

*Shared vision:* The power for the change is provided through personal purpose. Every individual in the organization has a vision, and that personal vision causes each individual to raise questions about his/her role in the change process and to take a stand for a preferred future. A shared vision is developed, and when the vision of the change is shared, change comes as a result of everyone fostering the change. This collective sense of purpose fosters power for deeper change.

*Inquiry:* Through the process of inquiry, an individual internalizes norms, habits, and techniques for continuous learning. The individual continuously checks, views, and assesses the initial mental map to make sure it fits.

*Mastery:* When individuals demonstrate an understanding and acceptance of new ideas and skills through their behavior, continuously clarifying what is important and learning how to see current reality more clearly, mastery has occurred.

*Collaboration:* In order to collaborate, an individual needs to involve both attitude and ability. "Collaboration involves the attitude and capacity to form productive mentoring and peer relationships, team building and the like. It consists of the ability to work in organizations that form cross-institutional partnerships such as school districts, university and school-community and business agency alliances, as well as global relationships with individuals and organizations from other cultures." (Fullan, 1993, p. 17). With collaboration, skills, and relationships, individuals can learn and continue to learn what is necessary to improve the organization.

The net result of using these core capacities is a positive step toward establishing a learning community within the school. Once a learning community has been established, if maintained, the likelihood of the school's achieving the vision that the change seeks is tremendously enhanced.

The aforementioned theories and practices are just four of the many that inform the process of change in schools. However, if they are utilized in an effective manner, they should greatly assist the leader in initiating, implementing, and sustaining change.

# The Process of Change in Schools

The primary purpose for change in schools is to improve the instructional program and, in so doing, improve student achievement. When educational change is offered in schools, most individuals will agree that instructional improvement is needed; however, there is still likely to be resistance. The resistance, more often than not, centers on the programs that will be changed, the process used to make the change, or the modified program or new program.

Resistance in these areas can be reduced, if not eliminated, provided the school has the capacity previously discussed. That capacity is likely to exist if the process respects stakeholders and involves them in decision making. Also, the programs being implemented must represent high-quality standards, expectations, and performances for all students (ISLLC, 1996). Having previously discussed change capacity, we now turn to stakeholder involvement and the performance of all students.

## Stakeholder Participation

Change in schools, in one way or another, affects teachers, as it often alters teaching practices in some manner. A change may be made in materials or structure (curriculum change); practices, behaviors, or skills (changes in teaching methods); or beliefs, rationales, or philosophies (orientation). Regardless of the area of change, teachers are affected, and their equilibrium will be disrupted. For example, if a teacher has been assigned to teach in a particular program; has become well versed in teaching that program; and has adequate plans, materials, supplies, and support, a request to change to a completely different program might meet with considerable resistance. This resistance may involve a feeling of inadequacy on behalf of teachers relative to: (1) their ability to teach the new program, (2) acquiring adequate materials for implementation of the new program, (3) relocating for program implementation, or (4) a combination of these concerns.

Resistance might also exist because teachers have a negative attitude about the new program, lack information about the positive aspects of the new program (particularly if new skills are required), or simply feel a concern over leaving one set of colleagues to work with another. Although the school leader might be able to identify a new program or mandate change in the use of materials and structure of an existing program, he/she is not likely to be able to mandate changes in the skills and/or beliefs of teachers and other personnel (Fullan, 1992). Therefore, to reduce some of the resistance to the change, increase the quality of decision making, and enhance successful implementation of the new program or activity, stakeholders should be invited to participate in the change process.

## Leader Behavior in the Change Process

In the change process, school leaders might use one of two strategies, directive or participatory decision making; both were discussed in Chapter 4. When a directive strategy is used, instructions, purpose, and parameters are given to individuals to execute and implement the change. An example of a leader using a directive strategy would be a principal of a high school who enters a faculty meeting and announces a change from the traditional scheduling format to block scheduling, then, proceeds to pass out information that provides new course assignments, new time schedules, and new instructional locations. Fullan (1993) reports research that suggests the institutionalization of such change is very difficult. He further reports that school improvements that are significant and lasting can seldom be prescribed, mandated, or directed by agencies or individuals. In such a change, there may be several risk factors, for teachers may feel a sense of inadequacy or lack of preparation or they may fear the unknown or perceive a loss of power or control.

Participatory change is likely to have a better reception. With the onset of the reform movement, much has been written about using a participatory strategy and the advantages it offers for bringing about school change in an effective manner (Barth, 1990; Conley, 1997; Ryan and Oestreich, 1991; Short & Greer, 1997). The works of these individuals have produced such program concepts and practices as site-based management, shared decision making, participatory governance, and others that advocate stakeholders collaborating with leaders in deciding how schools are administered. Also, these program concepts are in line with the school of thought presented by writers and researchers who offer that the learning environment of the school needs to be redefined.

When a participatory strategy is used, change is made in a manner that allows all individuals or persons desirous of the opportunity to assist in the change process; they feel valued, take ownership for implementation of the change, and are willing to assume responsibility for outcomes (Barth, 1990). Such was the case in Chapter 1, when Principal Johnson introduced the idea for a change in the science program at Walton Elementary School. The entire faculty was involved, and the change process was moving in a positive direction. In addition, the ISLLC Standards (1996) strongly support this approach. When a participatory approach is used and school improvement committees have a voluntary membership comprised of representatives from all stakeholder groups, change is more effective (Fullan, 1993).

## Addressing the Needs of All Students

As was initially stated, the purpose of school change more often than not is to improve the teaching and learning process. In addition, the major focus of ISLLC Standard 2 is teaching and learning. Thus the question regarding change becomes: How do school leaders determine the area in which to make instructional change? Several indicators of ISLLC Standard 2 address this question with a very definitive response. One indicator suggests that curriculum decisions be based on research using a variety of informational sources. Another advocates that any decisions made about the management of the school be informed by knowledge of teaching, learning, and student development. Given the emphasis of ISLLC Standard 2, the next section addresses making decisions regarding teaching and learning through the use of data.

## Data-Driven Instructional Change

Change involving teaching and learning should be data driven and contain certain elements, if it is expected to make a positive impact on student learning. Etheridge and Green (1998), having interviewed individuals in six school districts making instructional change to promote student learning, found the following steps were used and generated very positive results:

1. *A review and analysis of assessment reports*—Assessment reports were used to analyze student outcomes for several consecutive years. Reports from such measures as the Scholastic Achievement Test, Comprehensive Test of Basic Skills, American College Test, and TerraNova were used to acquire an understanding of the strengths and weaknesses in the instructional program. Scholarship reports, student interviews, teacher-made tests, criterion-referenced tests, and other measures were also used for this purpose. Data from the assessment tools were disaggregated to obtain information concerning the academic progress of students by race, gender, grade level, and subject area. Students experiencing success and difficulty and the specific questions frequently missed and/or answered were identified.

2. *Assessment of current conditions*—Using data from the assessment analyses, a content analysis was conducted to determine the current status of the curriculum. Teachers engaged in conversations raising questions about where the problematic concepts were taught, the amount of instructional time being devoted to the teaching of the concepts, the material used, and other curriculum content issues. Teachers also reasoned regarding the inability of students to apply concepts that were taught. Responses to these questions and other information acquired were used to inform the development of a school improvement plan.

3. *Review of content material*—At this point, the instructional review process became very focused. An analysis of all instructional material was conducted to determine if the content material was aligned with concepts posing difficulty for students. The depth and other aspects of the program materials were also assessed to determine if the materials were effectively achieving what they were designed to achieve (program evaluation). In addition, instructional approaches were also reviewed to determine if teaching styles matched learning styles and other aspects of learner needs. More importantly, this analysis was conducted to determine if there was a cause/effect relationship associated with the instructional material, teaching approaches, and the student's inability to master and apply the concepts identified by the assessment tools as being problematic.

4. *Broad-based review and discussion*—During this phase, parents, students, outside consultants, and other individuals were invited to participate in a series of group meetings and individual reaction sessions. These sessions were conducted to allow the decision-making team to capture and assess

the perceptions, opinions, ideas, and suggestions of the invited individuals regarding student performance, school processes, student work activities, and home-related matters. At this point, all the players were engaged in conversations in an attempt to identify where the problems existed. Was it time on task, the amount of instructional time, teaching or learning styles, instructional materials, or instructional methods? Is there enough substance in the materials to address the problem areas? Once these conversations were held, decisions were made regarding what needed to be changed. The involvement of students was very important, as students specifically offered suggestions about their learning styles, teaching styles, and other factors they felt were affecting their success.

5. *Formulation of curriculum groups*—Once data were acquired regarding program areas needing change, broad-based committees were formed to review the data and make suggestions about the type of program changes that would likely increase student acquisition of the needed concepts. The committees were very comprehensive, consisting of teachers of the focused grade level(s), those above and below the focused grade level(s), and parents and other individuals who may have had expertise in the area(s) being discussed.

6. *The plan for instructional improvement*—The committees then designed a comprehensive plan for instructional improvement, often using one of the group decision-making techniques identified in Chapter 4. The plan necessarily was very comprehensive, including goals, objectives, human and material resources, a professional development plan, assessment tools, a time frame, and other components essential to effective implementation of the desired instructional change.

These six steps provide a definitive process to use in making change to improve instruction and enhance student achievement. In addition to these steps, the plan for change should include an evaluation component. Using an effective evaluation design, the leader can monitor the status of the change and determine its effectiveness.

## Evaluating Change

The two forms of evaluation often associated with educational change are formative and summative. Formative evaluations acquire information about the program before it is fully implemented or during the refinement stage. This type of evaluation is conducted to ensure that there are no flaws in the program design and that the program is appropriate for the area of change. In some instances, the program changes are implemented as a pilot. In doing so, modifications can be made to the program in its early stages or prior to its full implementation.

A summative evaluation should occur after a specified period of time, often after four to five years. This evaluation can be used to determine improvements and/or progress that have been made relative to established goals. Assessing progress in achieving established outcome expectations allows a determination concerning the effectiveness of the new program. If the established expectations are being reached, it can be inferred that the program change is making a significant difference. If such is not the case, the change has not been fully effective, and a more in-depth assessment process is warranted to determine the program components that are not contributing to goal attainment.

## Summary

In today's schools, leaders who are effecting change with a minimum amount of conflict and disruption are using a participatory style of leadership and are skilled in securing the expertise and services of teachers, parents, and members of the community in support of the desired change (ISLLC, 1996). All stakeholders should be invited to participate in school governance; instructional decisions should be data driven and made as close to the teaching and learning process as possible (ISLLC, 1996).

However, such actions require a change in the traditional roles of superintendents, central administrators, principals, and teachers (Ethridge & Green, 1998). The traditional top-down directive style of leadership must give way to the new form of participatory leadership, which requires collaboration (Fullan 1999). This new thrust is being fostered through the implementation of national reform initiatives, such as the New American School Designs, Equity 2000, school site-based teams, school-based councils, and other school organizations that offer a forum for shared decision making (Conley, 1997).

Recent studies have generated several suggestions regarding the process leaders might utilize to accomplish these outcomes. In summarizing the research, Greenfield (1995) offers that the leader must be willing to give the change permanent, rather than innovative status, and during the implementation process, teachers must be provided emotional, technical, and fiscal support. Teachers must also be allowed to learn through practice, receive feedback, reflect, and review. Real change is possible if the right forces are present and operative. Essentially, it revolves around a committed, authentic, and strong leader who has developed hope around a shared vision and is able to motivate wide-scale planning of and participation in the change effort. A sense of community exists, and the fear of taking risks has been removed. In addition, a solid database is in place; the district offers a well-planned professional development program; and adequate time is allotted for the change.

## The Scenarios

In Scenario 18, Brady Jones, newly appointed principal of Eastern Hills Elementary School, has the responsibility of raising student achievement test scores. In Scenario 19, Mr. Clark coordinates the development of a strategic plan for the Arrowhead School District. In both scenarios, change is attempted involving a number of individuals. The reader might find it beneficial to compare the steps followed by each of the change agents in the scenarios with those presented in the introductory material, as well as to identify the ISLLC Standard indicators met or not met by both agents.

## SCENARIO 18
### JUST GET THOSE TEST SCORES UP

#### STANDARD 4

A school administrator is an educational leader who promotes the success of all students by collaborating with families and community members, responding to diverse community interests and needs, and mobilizing community resources.

*In Scenario 18, Principal Jones is charged with raising test scores in a school where the faculty members are complacent and do not fully accept or understand current reality. His disposition, understanding of information sources, and data collection and analysis strategies, as well as his ability to identify operational plans and procedures to achieve an established goal, are key factors in the change process. In addressing this scenario, a large number of ISLLC Standards indicators must be considered.*

### ISLLC Standards Indicators Exhibited in Scenario 18

**Knowledge Indicators**

The administrator has knowledge and understanding of:

▲ Learning goals in a pluralistic society
▲ The principles of developing and implementing strategic plans
▲ Information sources, data collection, and data analysis strategies
▲ Effective communication
▲ Effective consensus-building and negotiation skills
▲ Student growth and development
▲ Applied learning theories
▲ Applied motivational theories
▲ Curriculum design, implementation, evaluation, and refinement
▲ Principles of effective instruction
▲ Measurement, evaluation, and assessment strategies
▲ Diversity and its meaning for educational programs
▲ The change process for systems, organizations, and individuals
▲ The conditions and dynamics of the diverse school community
▲ The purpose of education and the role of leadership in modern society
▲ The importance of diversity and equity in a democratic society

## Disposition Indicators

The administrator believes in, values, and is committed to:

▲ The educability of all
▲ A school vision of high standards of learning
▲ Continuous school improvement
▲ The inclusion of all members of the school community
▲ Ensuring that students have the knowledge, skills, and values needed to become successful adults
▲ A willingness to continuously examine one's own assumptions, beliefs, and practices
▲ Doing the work required for high levels of personal and organization performance
▲ Student learning as the fundamental purpose of schooling
▲ The proposition that all students can learn
▲ Lifelong learning for self and others
▲ Professional development as an integral part of school improvement
▲ The benefit that diversity brings to the school
▲ A safe and supportive learning environment
▲ Preparing students to be contributing members of society
▲ Making management decisions to enhance learning and teaching
▲ Accepting responsibility
▲ High-quality standards, expectations, and performances
▲ Schools operating as an integral part of the community
▲ Collaboration and communication with families
▲ Involvement of families and other stakeholders in school decision-making processes
▲ The proposition that diversity enriches the school
▲ Families as partners in the education of their children
▲ The proposition that families have the best interests of their children in mind
▲ The idea of the common good
▲ The right of every student to a free, quality education
▲ Development of a caring school community
▲ Education as a key to opportunity and social mobility
▲ Recognizing a variety of ideas, values, and cultures

## Performance Indicators

The administrator facilitates processes and engages in activities ensuring that:

▲ The vision and mission of the school are effectively communicated to staff, parents, students, and community members
▲ The core belief of the school vision is modeled for all stakeholders
▲ The vision is developed with and among stakeholders
▲ The school community is involved in school improvement efforts
▲ The vision shapes the educational programs, plan, and actions
▲ An implementation plan is developed in which objectives and strategies to achieve the vision and goals are clearly articulated
▲ Assessment data related to student learning are used to develop the school vision and goals
▲ Relevant demographic data pertaining to students and their families are used in developing the school mission and goals

▲ Barriers to achieving the vision are identified, clarified, and addressed
▲ Needed resources are sought and obtained to support the implementation of the school mission and goals
▲ Existing resources are used in support of the school vision and goals
▲ The vision, mission, and implementation plans are regularly monitored, evaluated, and revised
▲ Barriers to student learning are identified, clarified, and addressed
▲ Diversity is considered in developing learning experiences
▲ Lifelong learning is encouraged and modeled
▲ There is a culture of high expectations for self, student, and staff performance
▲ The school is organized for student success
▲ Curriculum decisions are based on research, expertise of teachers, and the recommendations of learned societies
▲ A variety of sources of information is used to make decisions
▲ Student learning is assessed using a variety of techniques
▲ Multiple sources of information regarding performance are used by staff and students
▲ A variety of supervisory and evaluation models is employed
▲ Pupil personnel programs are developed to meet the needs of students and their families
▲ Knowledge of learning, teaching, and student development is used to inform management decisions
▲ Operational procedures are designed and managed to maximize opportunities for successful learning
▲ Emerging trends are recognized, studied, and applied as appropriate
▲ Operational plans and procedures to achieve the vision and goals of the school are in place
▲ Problems are confronted and resolved in a timely manner
▲ The school acts entrepreneurially to support continuous improvement
▲ Stakeholders are involved in decisions affecting schools
▲ Responsibility is shared to maximize ownership and accountability
▲ Effective group-process and consensus-building skills are used
▲ Effective communication skills are used
▲ Diversity is recognized and valued

**The administrator**
▲ Demonstrates values, beliefs, and attitudes that inspire others to higher levels of performance
▲ Demonstrates appreciation for and sensitivity to the diversity in the school community

Brady Jones, newly appointed principal of Eastern Hills Elementary School, left the superintendent's office somewhat perplexed but energized. The superintendent had shared with him that he was selected principal of Eastern Hills because he had placed a strong focus on instruction during his interview. The superintendent had further stated that he was very pleased that Mr. Jones had taken the assignment and intended to give him a free hand. "Just get those test scores up! Parents in the community have high hopes for their children now that you are principal," the superintendent had stated. "The last two principals were not instructionally oriented and spent most of their time on discipline and working with about 250 students (bussed into the school) who are in a special gifted and talented program; however, I am confident that you will address the needs of all students."

Principal Jones thought, "Only two weeks into my principalship, and the superintendent is expecting the implementation of a new instructional program to reduce the numbers of students who are unsuccessful on the state proficiency test. Well," he said, "I have taken this job, and now I have to go to work."

Principal Jones went to his office and indeed he went to work. He called several teachers but found that most were on summer holiday or unavailable. However, he was able to contact six who said they had some free time and would be able to participate in an instructional planning session.

The six teachers were from various grade levels and disciplines, and Principal Jones considered this to be a plus. Over the next week for about two hours a day, working with the six teachers, he reviewed student records, proficiency test scores, state standards, discipline reports, attendance records, and curriculum guides. At the end of the week, Principal Jones thanked the teachers and informed them he would see them in September. The teachers left, feeling that Eastern Hills Elementary School was in for a major change.

Reviewing the data compiled over the past week, as well as the evaluation reports of the teachers, Principal Jones noted the following:

Eastern Hills Elementary School was a large inner-city school of about 1000 students. The school had a grade organizational structure of Pre-K–6. The fourth graders and the sixth graders take the state proficiency test (which is the Comprehensive Test of Basic Skills), and for the last five years, the scores at Eastern Hills have been the lowest in the district and close to the bottom in the state. For instruction, students are grouped and assigned to classes based on ability testing. They are then regrouped inside the classroom for instruction in reading, mathematics, science, and social studies.

The average teacher's tenure at the school is 15 years. However, there will be one new teacher who has recently moved into the district, and she was teacher of the year in her last assignment. Two other teachers have just been assigned to the school to fill positions that occurred because of retirements. The school is allotted 40 teaching positions from the state for every 1,000 students in grades 1–6 and a kindergarten teacher and an aid for every class of 25 kindergarten students. The local district funds one teaching position out of the local budget. His personnel report revealed the assignment of 37 teachers to the building, with 3 teaching positions vacant.

## THE STUDENT BODY

STUDENT ENROLLMENT 1,038

| | Grade K | Grade 1 | Grade 2 | Grade 3 | Grade 4 | Grade 5 | Grade 6 | Total |
|---|---|---|---|---|---|---|---|---|
| Males | 10 | 78 | 83 | 91 | 92 | 60 | 65 | 479 |
| Females | 15 | 94 | 96 | 98 | 93 | 88 | 75 | 559 |
| Total | 25 | 172 | 179 | 189 | 185 | 148 | 140 | 1038 |
| African-Americans | 3 | 48 | 55 | 63 | 58 | 21 | 12 | 260 |
| Caucasians | 21 | 118 | 118 | 118 | 120 | 120 | 120 | 735 |
| Hispanics | 1 | 6 | 6 | 8 | 7 | 7 | 8 | 43 |
| Total | 25 | 172 | 179 | 189 | 185 | 148 | 140 | 1038 |

## THE FACULTY

There are 37 teachers (including 33 Caucasians, 3 African-Americans, and 1 Hispanic); average number of years in the profession is 26. The average number of years at Eastern Hills Elementary School is 15. Subject area changes did not occur over the last three years; room assignment changes over the last three years were four. There are four teachers with less than three years of service, and there were no teacher transfers over the past three years. The teacher evaluations are excellent, and over the past 10 years, the state teacher of the year had been selected from the faculty four times. In addition, all teachers on the faculty are members of the local union, and the union president's wife teaches sixth-grade mathematics.

## THE ORIENTATION MEETING

At the fall orientation meeting of the faculty, Principal Jones introduced the concept of "site-based management" to the faculty. He told the faculty that the concept was still in the planning stage, but he wanted the faculty to have some idea of what he believed should be the new thrust for Eastern Hills Elementary School and how the new concept could be utilized to improve instruction for all students. He said he had worked with several teachers over the summer and had identified three instructional goals for the school, but he did not want to present them until the faculty had been given time to review the site-based management concept and comment on its implementation. However, he said, "State proficiency scores are one of three major concerns that appear to need attention."

He also informed the faculty that parents, students, and members of the community would need to be involved in all instructional planning. Principal Jones then asked the faculty to meet in grade-level groups for 30 minutes to discuss his remarks and generate questions and concerns. The grade-level meetings were convened, and several teachers generated questions. When the faculty reconvened, Principal Jones asked for questions and comments. The following were offered:

Mrs. Walker of the math department, "I don't believe we can change the way we teach math; many of our students simply cannot learn the reasoning problems."

Principal Jones responded, "OK."

Mr. Clark, a teacher of social studies, "I am ready for a change, but some of the new concepts are foreign to me. Will we have adequate professional development activities?"

Principal Jones replied, "The superintendent has advised that in the current budget there are no funds for additional staff development. However, he will provide staff time to draft federal grant proposals."

Mrs. Polls stated, "I understand that teachers who met with you this summer did not get paid. Is that not a violation of the union contract?"

Principal Jones replied, "That is a concern that I will have to review."

Mrs. Green commented, "I like what I have heard about site-based management; however, I don't quite understand how we can participate in all the meetings and teach the children all day."

Principal Jones responded, "With adequate release time, we can address that issue."

Mrs. Polls reflected, "Yes, we have been promised release time before, but it never came."

Mr. Frank questioned, "Are you aware of the attitudes of the children who attend this school, the daily discipline problems, the poor attendance rate, and the lack of parental involvement? We are currently doing all we can do, and I trust this is not another one of those educational reform efforts everyone is talking about."

Principal Jones responded, "Those are interesting comments, Mr. Frank, and I hope we can resist taking on some of the fads of which you speak."

Ms. Harris offered, "Principal Jones, there are three of us who have recently completed instructional seminars at the university, and in those seminars, we were introduced to several approaches that I believe would enhance instruction here at Eastern Hills. If you plan to form an instructional planning committee, the three of us would very much like to serve."

Principal Jones, "Thank you Ms. Harris! After those comments, I believe this is an excellent time to pass out these committee lists and allow individuals to sign up for the committee of choice. I will review the list and speak with each of you individually, but now, let's have lunch."

When Principal Jones reviewed his phone messages at the end of the day, he noticed he had a phone call from the union president, requesting a meeting.

### THE COMPREHENSIVE TEST OF BASIC SKILLS SCORES

#### Total Reading in Percentiles

| Grades | 1994 | 1995 | 1996 | 1997 |
|--------|------|------|------|------|
| 2 | 41 | 44 | 40 | 40 |
| 3 | 60 | 43 | 46 | 44 |
| 4 | 48 | 57 | 42 | 41 |
| 5 | 61 | 42 | 52 | 35 |
| 6 | 44 | 54 | 39 | 42 |

#### Total Language in Percentiles

| Grades | 1994 | 1995 | 1996 | 1997 |
|--------|------|------|------|------|
| 2 | 40 | 45 | 50 | 56 |
| 3 | 47 | 47 | 38 | 47 |
| 4 | 55 | 69 | 51 | 54 |
| 5 | 56 | 60 | 59 | 41 |
| 6 | 46 | 59 | 54 | 52 |

#### Total Math in Percentiles

| Grades | 1994 | 1995 | 1996 | 1997 |
|--------|------|------|------|------|
| 2 | 34 | 34 | 39 | 32 |
| 3 | 62 | 50 | 49 | 50 |
| 4 | 42 | 55 | 43 | 38 |
| 5 | 54 | 54 | 60 | 44 |
| 6 | 48 | 75 | 56 | 59 |

## REFLECTIVE THINKING AND SCENARIO ANALYSIS

1. When Principal Jones assumed the principalship and approached the faculty for the first time at Eastern Hills Elementary, how would you characterize the school's change capacity?

2. How would you assess the approach used by Principal Jones when he introduced the concept of change to the faculty at Eastern Hills? Identify instances in the scenario that denote the manner in which the vision is being developed.

**3.** What models and strategies of change and conflict resolution would you utilize if you were principal in a similar situation?

**4.** What instances can you cite in the scenario that would serve as evidence that Principal Jones has knowledge and understanding of information sources, data collection, and analysis strategies?

**5.** What opportunities could Principal Jones provide for the faculty to develop collaborative skills?

**6.** What emerging issues and trends do you observe in the enrollment and test data?

**7.** What approach would you use to determine the type of instructional change strategies that would be best for the students of Eastern Hills? Identify where you would begin and define your position.

## ADDRESSING THE ISSUES

Select the one best answer to the following questions:

**1.** Which of the following statements regarding Eastern Hills is most likely to be accurate?

   **a.** The school, in its current state, has a capacity to change.

   **b.** The school, in its current state, does not have a capacity to change.

   **c.** The school, in its current state, does not have a capacity to change, but one could be developed with very little effort.

   **d.** The school, in its current state, does not have the capacity to change without the emergence of conflict, and it will take considerable effort to create one.

**2.** In bringing about instructional change at Eastern Hills, which of the following is likely to be the source of greatest resistance?

   **a.** Getting the faculty to share a common vision.

   **b.** Getting the faculty to understand the problems with the current program.

   **c.** Getting the faculty to implement a new program concept.

   **d.** Getting the faculty to engage in site-based management.

**3.** Which of the following trends appears in the test data?

   **a.** A regression of all third-grade students each year in the area of mathematics.

   **b.** A regression of fifth- and sixth-grade students in the area of language.

   **c.** A steady increase in math scores across all grade levels.

   **d.** No regression of fourth-grade students in the area of reading.

**4.** In selecting individuals to fill the three vacant positions that exist in the school, which of the following characteristics should the successful candidate possess in order to best meet the needs of the school?

   **a.** Skills in site-based management.

   **b.** Skills in teaching reading/language arts, group dynamics, and instructional program planning.

   **c.** Skills in gifted education.

   **d.** Skills in remedial education.

**5.** If the new principal made a decision to discontinue ability grouping, which of the following is likely to be the major restraining force?

**a.** Teacher resistance.

**b.** Parental opposition.

**c.** Functional level of students.

**d.** Ability to acquire the necessary instructional resources.

## DISCUSSION OF THE SOLUTION

1. The new principal is coming into a school with a well-established organizational culture. The average teacher's tenure is 15 years. This would indicate a definite, "This is the way we do things around here" attitude. A change would require members of the faculty to alter past practices. One major challenge would be getting the faculty to adopt new teaching approaches and to overcome the tendency to want to return to previous practices. This type of resistance to change is cultural system resistance and is based on the premise that there is security in past practice (Tichy & Ulrich, 1984, p. 479).

A second source of resistance is characterized by the power of informal groups. There are at least two groups on the faculty (one group teaching gifted and talented students and another teaching in the traditional program), and it is highly possible that there are others. The group teaching gifted and talented students has acquired power as a result of having a common focus and will likely resist relinquishing that power. The new principal will have to safeguard against being viewed as an individual who is disrupting the security of past practice. When a faculty has ownership for the current state of existence, it is difficult for them to accept changing an instructional program that they have helped to create (Tichy & Ulrich, 1984, p. 479). Finally, only three teachers will be new to the school. If change is proposed, a large number of teachers, out of necessity, will need to participate in professional development programs to acquire skills in new programs and instructional practices. Their technical skills will need to be enhanced.

Although change appears to be needed at Eastern Hills, to successfully bring about that change, the new principal will have to address many challenges including those listed above. Change will not come quickly, but will require time, an adequate assessment of student needs, and the alignment of human and material resources. In the change process, the principal will need to be considerate of the values and skills of individuals currently affiliated with the school, the motivation of those individuals, and have patience sufficient to allow change to occur. The school, in its current state, does not have the capacity to change without considerable conflict emerging. However, with effort, and using the appropriate strategies, a capacity for change could be built. The suggested response to question 1 is **(d)**.

2. It is obvious from the comments made at the orientation session that some faculty members do not appreciate a need to change the existing instructional program. They appear to be safe and secure, or at least content with current conditions. Until the faculty accepts the notion that the current instructional program is not meeting the needs of all students, change will be difficult (Senge, 1990). A faculty that does not understand and accept the existing problems is not likely to be able to focus on what needs to be accomplished, develop an appreciation of the benefits to be derived from a change, and reach a comfort level with the change (Sergiovanni, 1991). This is least

likely to occur by placing blame on any individual or on teachers who teach at a particular grade level. Rather, relevant data pertaining to students and their families will have to be compiled and used in developing a mission and goals for the school. The responsibility for school improvement must be shared to maximize ownership and accountability (ISLLC, 1996), and this is most likely to occur when the faculty understands and accepts the problems that currently exist. The suggested response to question 2 is **(b)**.

3. An analysis of the data across the grade levels in reading, language, and math indicates that percentile scores are at or slightly below the national average. From the data, only the second and third grades can be assessed from 1994 to 1997. During those years, in the area of language, the scores of these students increased in grades three and four. However, there was a decline in the scores of both groups in grades five and six. This decline occurred between 1995 and 1996. A further drop is observed for these students in 1997. The trend that appears to be forming is in the area of language. The language scores for many students tend to increase in grades three and four and decrease in grades five and six. The suggested response to question 3 is **(b)**.

4. An analysis of the test results reveals regression in student reading scores at the fourth-grade level continuing through grade six. They also reveal a regression of student language scores in grades five and six. There is a need to improve instruction in both of these areas. However, simply employing teachers in these areas will not be sufficient. Other actions will be necessary, and these actions will involve engaging the entire faculty in the development and/or alteration of programs and instructional strategies. It will mean developing a shared vision for change that will require skills in the areas of group dynamics and instructional planning (ISLLC, 1996). Therefore, the leader will need to unite the faculty and develop a collaborative working relationship among them. The greater the assistance from individuals trained in group dynamics and instructional planning, the more likely the faculty will develop a collaborative relationship and facilitate successful change. Giving consideration to this factor, the principal would greatly benefit the school by employing teachers who are skilled in teaching reading and language arts and could couple those skills with providing teacher leadership for instructional improvement. The suggested response to question 4 is **(b)**.

5. Change at Eastern Hills will cause a disruption for several individuals and is likely to upset the power relationships at the school. If ability grouping is discontinued, the change will raise concerns among faculty members who subscribe to homogeneous grouping. These individuals are likely to become restraining forces in the change process. Providing for a wide range of individual differences in the classroom may prove to be challenging to teachers who have grown accustomed to teaching ability grouped classes. In addition, there are parents who support the concept of homogeneous grouping and believe their children benefit most when they are grouped in such a manner. If change is offered, some parents are also likely to become a restraining force.

The superintendent has openly stated that the new principal has a free hand, and thus, he is likely to provide the necessary material resources to implement any proposed change that is within reason. Then needed professional development programs can be funded. Therefore, teachers given the opportunity to participate in the change process and provided adequate professional development are likely to accept the change, even though they may accept it reluctantly. From this line of thinking, the faculty is likely to reluctantly accept an alternative to ability grouping. On the other hand, parents who are allowing their children to be bussed to this school may be somewhat more difficult to convince to accept a change in this area. Feeling that they are deriving tremendous benefits from the existing program, they are likely to become a strong restraining force and will need to be provided considerable evidence that the new program will not cause their children to suffer. This evidence should be provided before the change is attempted. The suggested response to question 5 is **(b)**.

## Summary and Conclusion

The new principal of Eastern Hills Elementary has accepted a very challenging assignment. However, with effective planning and involvement of the right individuals, he should be able to move the school forward. When change occurs in schools, all role groups should be involved. There are a number of role groups who will have a strong interest in any change taking place at Eastern Hills and will want to participate in the process. Therefore, a school improvement team should be created, and the team should consist of representatives from all concerned role groups—teachers, parents, students, central office personnel, and, perhaps, state instructional department personnel. Once the school improvement team is organized, it should be commissioned to develop a plan for school improvement. The plan should consist of the following items:

1. A needs assessment.
2. A shared vision.
3. A shared mission.
4. Schoolwide goals and expectations for all students.
5. A list of programs that need to be modified or replaced.
6. A list of new instructional programs that address the needs of all students.
7. A list of needed professional development program activities.
8. An implementation plan that includes assessment tools that will generate pupil and program data that can be used to make revisions to the instructional program.

When the initial planning process is completed, team members should become partners in the implementation of the plan and in making decisions about the administration of the school. With the establishment of a team, decision quality and acceptance are likely to be enhanced, for collaborating with others on change strengthens the partnership and enhances the likelihood of the school achieving its desired goal (Fullan, 1993).

## SCENARIO 19
## The Strategic Planning Process

### Standard 1

A school administrator is an educational leader who promotes the success of all students by facilitating the development, articulation, implementation, and stewardship of a vision of learning that is shared and supported by the school community.

*In Scenario 19, the reader will be able to follow the process a superintendent uses in developing a strategic plan. Management decisions are made to enhance learning and teaching, and the vision of the school district is communicated to all stakeholders. The reader will want to note the leadership behavior of both Superintendent Wallace and Director Clark as they both meet several ISLLC Standards indicators.*

## ISLLC Standards Indicators Exhibited in Scenario 19

### Knowledge Indicators
The administrator has knowledge and understanding of:
▲ Learning goals in a pluralistic society
▲ The principles of developing and implementing strategic plans
▲ Information sources, data collection, and data-analysis strategies
▲ Effective communication
▲ Effective consensus-building and negotiation skills
▲ Student growth and development
▲ Applied learning theories
▲ Applied motivational theories
▲ Curriculum design, implementation, evaluation, and refinement
▲ Principles of effective instruction
▲ Measurement, evaluation, and assessment strategies
▲ Diversity and its meaning for educational programs
▲ The change process for systems, organizations, and individuals
▲ The conditions and dynamics of the diverse school community
▲ The purpose of education and the role of leadership in modern society
▲ The values of the diverse school community
▲ The importance of diversity and equity in a democratic society

### Disposition Indicators
The administrator believes in, values, and is committed to:
▲ The educability of all
▲ A school vision of high standards of learning
▲ Continuous school improvement
▲ The inclusion of all members of the school community
▲ Ensuring that students have the knowledge, skills, and values needed to become successful adults
▲ A willingness to continuously examine one's own assumptions, beliefs, and practices
▲ Doing the work required for high levels of personal and organizational performance
▲ Student learning as the fundamental purpose of schooling
▲ The proposition that all students can learn
▲ Lifelong learning for self and others
▲ Professional development as an integral part of school improvement
▲ The benefit that diversity brings to the school
▲ A safe and supportive learning environment
▲ Preparing students to be contributing members of society
▲ Making management decisions to enhance learning and teaching
▲ Accepting responsibility
▲ Trusting people and their judgment

▲ High-quality standards, expectations, and performances
▲ School operating as an integral part of the community
▲ Collaboration and communication with families.
▲ Involvement of families and other stakeholders in school decision-making processes
▲ The proposition that diversity enriches the school
▲ Families as partners in the education of their children
▲ The proposition that families have the best interests of their children in mind
▲ The idea of the common good
▲ The right of every student to a free, quality education
▲ Development of a caring school community
▲ Education as a key to opportunity and social mobility
▲ Recognizing a variety of ideas, values, and cultures

**Performance Indicators**

The administrator facilitates processes and engages in activities ensuring that:

▲ The vision and mission of the school are effectively communicated to staff, parents, students, and community members
▲ The core beliefs of the school vision are modeled for all stakeholders
▲ The vision is developed with and among stakeholders
▲ The school community is involved in school improvement efforts
▲ The vision shapes the educational programs, plan, and actions
▲ An implementation plan is developed in which objectives and strategies to achieve the vision and goals are clearly articulated
▲ Assessment data related to student learning are used to develop the school vision and goals
▲ Relevant demographic data pertaining to students and their families are used in developing the school mission and goals
▲ Existing resources are used in support of the school vision and goals
▲ The vision, mission, and implementation plans are regularly monitored, evaluated, and revised
▲ Barriers to student learning are identified, clarified, and addressed
▲ Barriers to achieving the vision are identified, clarified, and addressed
▲ Diversity is considered in developing learning experiences
▲ Lifelong learning is encouraged and modeled
▲ There is a culture of high expectations for self, student, and staff performance
▲ The school is organized for student success
▲ Curriculum decisions are based on research, expertise of teachers, and the recommendations of learned societies
▲ Student learning is assessed using a variety of techniques
▲ Multiple sources of information regarding performance are used by staff
▲ Pupil personnel programs are developed to meet the needs of students and their families
▲ Knowledge of learning, teaching, and student development is used to inform management decisions
▲ Operational procedures are designed and managed to maximize opportunities for successful learning
▲ Emerging trends are recognized, studied, and applied as appropriate
▲ Operational plans and procedures to achieve the vision and goals of the school are in place

▲ Problems are confronted and resolved in a timely manner
▲ The school acts entrepreneurially to support continuous improvement
▲ Stakeholders are involved in decisions affecting schools
▲ Responsibility is shared to maximize ownership and accountability
▲ Effective group-process and consensus-building skills are used
▲ Effective communication skills are used
▲ Diversity is recognized and valued

**The administrator**
▲ Demonstrates values, beliefs, and attitudes that inspire others to higher levels of performance
▲ Demonstrates appreciation for and sensitivity to the diversity in the school community

In the fall of 1998, with Mr. Clark coordinating the process and the superintendent serving as a member of the committee, the district began developing a strategic plan that would propel the district into the 21st century. Care was taken to place individuals who represented the diversity of the district on the committee. Thirty-nine individuals, half district personnel (teachers, administrators, students) and half community people (business affiliates, religious leaders, parents, and city government), formed the strategic planning committee. First, they met for several days in very intense sessions to identify operational procedures. An outside consultant was invited to provide training in the art of collaboration. Rules were established, and everyone agreed to follow the rules, respecting the right of individuals to disagree and foster a difference of opinion. After the collaboration training was concluded and operational procedures were in place, Superintendent Wallace offered comments to the committee regarding her view of district needs, passed out material on state and national standards and assessment measures, and spoke to current trends in educational reform. She concluded her remarks by acknowledging Director Clark's leadership skills and voicing support for him in the position of coordinator.

Operating on the assumption that everyone's views were important and had a meaningful role to play, the planning committee used a modified Delphi technique to generate information from all segments of the school community for inclusion in the strategic plan. From the process, which took several months, a mission statement that incorporated the core values of the district was developed. The committee distributed the statement and sought and received district- and communitywide acceptance before continuing with the strategic planning process. The mission statement read as follows: "It is the mission of the Arrowhead Consolidated School District to teach all students to the fullest extent, instilling in them a passion for learning and a readiness to pursue their personal careers in a manner that will enhance our democratic society." This mission emerged from the values that the committee identified from a values clarification study conducted throughout the district. The following core values emerged from the study:

1. Families are the foundation of the community, and parents and community members should participate in the educational process.
2. All individuals are accountable and responsible for their choices and actions.
3. All individuals have values.
4. All individuals have the capacity for continuous growth and development.

5. Honesty and integrity are central to building and maintaining trust and relationships.
6. Diversity is a strength that enriches a community.
7. People working together toward a common goal are more likely to accomplish that goal.
8. Schools should prepare students to be contributing members of society.

To achieve this mission, the planning committee identified five goals to be achieved by the year 2005:

1. Improve the readiness level of all students.
2. Improve educational outcomes at every school.
3. Improve staff effectiveness by providing professional development programs that are tailored to the needs of teachers in individual schools.
4. Strengthen parent and community participation in the educational process.
5. Design an open assessment process to measure student progress and make curriculum decisions.

After getting districtwide acceptance of the mission statement, the list of districtwide goals was agreed upon and under the leadership of building principals, local site-based councils were established for each building. The councils consisted of administrators, teachers, staff, students, parents, and other representatives of each local school community. The councils then worked within each school to establish local school goals that were aligned with the district goals. The attainment of the local goals was facilitated by the establishment of school committees in the areas of curriculum, resource allocation, and professional development.

After the planning process was completed to foster effective communication, the superintendent provided periodic written updates to every board member. In addition, she met weekly in face-to-face meetings with the board president and had monthly meetings with every board member. In almost every instance, staff made presentations with Mr. Clark taking the lead. Full disclosure was practiced with the board and the community.

## REFLECTIVE THINKING AND SCENARIO ANALYSIS

1. What activities in the planning process adhered to the knowledge indicators of ISLLC Standard 1?
2. Can you cite statements in the scenario that would provide evidence that Superintendent Wallace believes in the inclusion of all members of the school community in developing plans for the district?
3. Now that local councils exist at each building, reflecting on the performance indicators of ISLLC Standard 2, what are the implications for the authority, roles, and responsibility of the central staff? Is there reason to believe that ownership and accountability for student success will be maximized?
4. How would you rate the amount of collaboration that occurred between and among administrators, teachers, and community stakeholders? Did the planning process give credence to individuals and groups whose values conflicted? What approach would you use to ensure stakeholder involvement in a strategic planning process?
5. Identify theoretical information from the introductory section of this chapter and Chapter 2 and relate that information to passages in the scenario in a manner that will verify that appropriate procedural steps were followed in establishing the strategic plan.

## ADDRESSING THE ISSUES

Select the one best answer to the following questions:

1. According to the suggestions of the contemporary reform movement, which of the following is likely to be most effective?

   a. Superintendent Wallace's belief in a participatory style of leading schools.

   b. Superintendent Wallace's concern with the composition of the planning committee.

   c. Implementation of a participatory planning model, which reflects new roles for all stakeholders committed to the process.

   d. Development of a strategic plan to bring about change.

2. From the point of view of teaching and learning advocated by ISLLC Standard 2, which of the following actions taken by the superintendent was most appropriate?

   a. Coordinating the planning process with Mr. Clark.

   b. Development of a comprehensive planning process.

   c. Expansion of the role of classroom teachers.

   d. Involvement of parents in the process.

3. With regard to each school's improvement plan, which of the following actions is likely to contribute most to instructional improvement?

   a. Frequent meetings of the comprehensive planning committee.

   b. Frequent assessment of pupils and programs.

   c. Frequent reports to the community on the district's progress.

   d. Frequent revisions to the plan.

4. Which of the following is a weakness in the planning process?

   a. A districtwide commitment.

   b. A focus on the values of the community

   c. A plan for school-based implementation.

   d. A plan for professional development.

## DISCUSSION OF THE SOLUTION

1. Successful models of school reform suggest collaboration, open communication, trust, and shared accountability (Conley, 1997). From all indications, Superintendent Wallace subscribed to collaboration and used a participatory style of leadership. Her attitude indicated a respect for diversity, and she was concerned with the composition of the committee. Her approach was well designed; using a participatory leadership style and establishing a committee with a diverse composition are very important characteristics of an effective strategic planning process. However, the implementation model is also critical; one might have an outstanding plan, but without an implementation model supported by participants who have a commitment to its success, the plan is likely to be extremely difficult to implement, and therefore of little value. Conley (1997) reports that two strong components of successful restructuring efforts are a

change in the roles of principals and teachers and a commitment from all stakeholders. Acceptance of new roles and a commitment to program implementation by all stakeholders is key to change effectiveness. The suggested response to question 1 is **(c)**.

2. Developing a plan for instructional improvement within itself will not necessarily have a positive effect on the teaching and learning process. Also, whereas the involvement of parents is an important factor and is likely to yield great results in terms of improving instruction in schools, they are not directly delivering instruction to children. On the other hand, involving teachers in a manner that allows them to utilize their expertise in resolving problems that affect student learning can have a very positive effect on students. Teachers know their students, are aware of a variety of ways to teach them, and can identify and remove barriers to learning (ISLLC, 1996). The primary leadership for bringing about improvements in a school district should come from the educational level where the change is to take effect (Barth, 1990). Therefore, of the alternatives listed in question 2, the greatest benefit to be gained relative to teaching and learning is to involve teachers in a new empowered role. The suggested response to question 2 is **(c)**.

3. Effective school improvement plans are data driven (Sergiovanni, 1991). School leaders should have various means of determining if programs are working and if the diverse needs of students are being met. To that end, frequent assessments should be made of pupils and programs to acquire data that can be used to make changes for instructional improvement (ISLLC, 1996). Without sufficient data to drive decisions, change is not likely to be focused and can become educated guesses at best. The suggested response to question 3 is **(b)**.

4. The plan started with a focus on the values of the community and acquired a strong commitment from all stakeholders. A component for local school implementation was also outlined. What appeared to be missing is a plan to facilitate professional development. Professional development is key to change effectiveness. Many programs are designed in an excellent manner. However, without an effective professional development component, successful goal attainment may never become a reality because teachers may not have skills sufficient to implement the new concept. The planning process must include a professional development component. The suggested response to question 4 is **(d)**.

## SUMMARY AND CONCLUSION

The successful development of a strategic plan in Arrowhead resulted from hard work. Also, people in the internal and external environment realized that in order for students to achieve, everyone in the district had to rally around a single focus. Throughout the process, the leadership respected individuality and diversity, addressing the unique needs of each section of the community. Superintendent Wallace chose to place Director Clark in a highly visible role in the district, one with major responsibility. Then she supported him in that role. The community, as well as Director Clark, could see that the superintendent respected his expertise and trusted him to do the right thing. Although she demonstrated many indicators of ISLLC Standards, quite clearly she demonstrated that she was committed to trusting people and their judgment and involving stakeholders in management processes, two indicators of Standard 3.

## CHAPTER SUMMARY

Individuals who make changes in today's schools need knowledge, understanding, and commitment. They need knowledge of change processes for systems, organizations, and individuals, an understanding of organizational stakeholders, and a commitment to addressing the needs of all constituent groups (ISLLC, 1996).

Change is a process, not an event; it can be planned or unplanned and can be influenced by forces inside and outside of the organization. The change process can be viewed in three steps: (1) establishing a vision, (2) determining the state of existing programs, and (3) determining what is needed to reach the desired vision (Schmidt & Finnigan, 1992). As these steps are taken, the leader or change agent needs to be sensitive to human potential in the organization and the general capacity of the organization to address change because either of these factors can negatively impact the change process.

A number of theories and processes inform change in schools. Three worthy of note are Kurt Lewin's Force Field Analysis, Chin and Benne's empirical-rational, normative–re-educative, and power-coercive strategies, and Fullan's Change Agentry Theory. Any of these theories or strategies can assist the leader through the change process. However, prior to engaging in the change process, it is advisable for the leader to determine if the change to be made is a first-order or second-order change and the extent to which the organization has the capacity to make that change. If the change capacity does not exist, the emergence of conflict is almost a certainty.

In addition to assessing the capacity of the organization to engage in change, the leader will need to determine if the change is best made using an autocratic or participative process. Knowing which process to use can influence the degree of success and the extent to which the change is likely to be accepted. In a learning organization, one individual does not administer a school district; rather, a combination of individuals work cooperatively, each bringing their skills to the table and debating the merits of their position in a collegial manner. If the desired change is to be effective, not only must leaders influence individuals to do things they do not want to do, but they must also focus on intangibles that create commitment and values. They must exude confidence in others and give them authority to make decisions in a participatory manner. In today's schools, fair process and sound implementation plans are keys to success. When leaders value diversity, are committed to fostering programs that address the needs of all students, and include all stakeholders in the process, change is being made in accordance with standards for effective leaders (ISLLC, 1996).

## MOVING INTO PRACTICE

Review the scenarios in Chapter 6, using the pros and cons of the various situations, and identify several approaches that you would use to address the following school-related issues in an actual school situation. Project yourself in the role of the principal or superintendent and take care to formulate a rationale for your selected behavior.

▶ You have just been appointed superintendent of a large urban school district that is faced with declining achievement scores. The community is very diverse, and the scores are identifiable by ethnic group and by socio-economic status. The community is very upset, as the school district has always had a fine reputation, and for that reason, the city has been able to attract a large number of corporate headquarters. You have been asked to change the climate in the district and to design programs that will increase student achievement. Describe the action steps you would take to fulfill your charge. Take care to reflect various change strategies in your plan and highlight procedures you would use to sell your ideas and at the same time minimize conflict.

▶ Outline the strategies you would use to create and implement a school improvement plan. Support your selected strategies with change theory.

## ACQUIRING AN UNDERSTANDING OF SELF

▶ What is equity?
▶ What meaning do you give to "lifelong learning for self and others"?
▶ How would you determine the services to provide for students who have lower test scores than their counterparts?

## SUGGESTED READINGS

Barth, R. S. (1991). *Improving schools from within*. San Francisco: Jossey-Bass Publishers.

Carrow-Moffett, P. (1993). Change agent skills: Creating leadership for renewal. *NASSP Bulletin, 77*, 57–62.

Conley, D. (1997). *Roadmap to restructuring: Charting the course in American education*. Eugene, OR: University of Oregon (ERIC Clearinghouse on Educational Management).

Fullan, M. (1999). *Change forces: Probing the depth of educational reform: The sequel*. New York: The Falmer Press.

Greenfield, T. A. (1995). Improving changes for successful educational reform. *Education, 115* (3), 464.

Sarason, S. (1996). *Revisiting the culture of the school and the problem of change*. New York: Teachers College Press.

# REFERENCES

Arnold, H. J., & Feldman, D. C. (1989). *Organizational behavior.* New York: McGraw-Hill Book Company.

Ashbaugh, C. R., & Kasten, K. L. (1995). *Educational leadership: Case studies for reflective practice* (2nd ed.). New York: Longman.

Barge, J. K. (1994). *Leadership: Communication skills for organizations and groups.* New York: St. Martin's Press.

Barth, R. S. (1990). *Improving school from within: Teachers, parents, and principals can make the difference.* San Francisco: Jossey-Bass Publishers.

Bennis, W. (1995). *The 4 competencies of leadership.* In D. A. Kolb, J. S. Osland, & I. M. Rubin (Eds.), *The organizational behavior reader* (pp. 395–401). Upper Saddle River, NJ: Prentice Hall.

Bennis, W., & Biederman, P. (1997). *Organizing genius.* Reading, MA: Addison Wesley Longman.

Bennis, W., & Nanus, B. (1985). *Leaders: The strategies for taking charge.* New York: Harper & Row.

Berger, J., Zelditch, M., Anderson, B., & Cohen, B. P. (1972). Structural aspects of distributive justice: A status-value formulation. In J. Berger, M. Zelditch, & B. Anderson (Eds.), *Sociological theories in progress* (Vol. 2, pp. 21–45). Boston: Houghton Mifflin.

Blake, R. R., & Mouton, J. S. (1985). *The managerial grid III.* Houston, TX: Gulf.

Blanchard, K., Oncken, W., & Burrows, H. (1989). *The one minute manager meets the monkey.* New York: William Morrow and Company.

Bolman, L. G., & Deal, T. E. (1997). *Reframing organizations: Artistry, choice, and leadership* (2nd ed.). San Francisco: Jossey-Bass Publishers.

Bormann, E. G., & Bormann, N. C. (1972). *Effective small group communication.* New York: Burgess Publishing.

Bowers, D. G. (1977). *Systems of organization: Management of human resources.* Ann Arbor, MI: University of Michigan Press.

Boyatzis, R. E., & Skelly, F. R. (1995). The impact of changing values on organizational life: The latest update. In D. A. Kolb, J. S. Osland, & I. M. Rubin (Eds.), *The organizational behavior reader* (pp. 1–17). Upper Saddle River, NJ: Prentice Hall.

Bradley, L. H. (1993). *Total quality management for schools*. Lanham, MD: Rowman & Littlefield Publishing Group.

Brewer, J. H., Ainsworth, J. M., & Wynne, G. E. (1984). *Power management: A three-step program for successful leadership*. Upper Saddle River, NJ: Prentice Hall.

Bridges, E. A. (1967). A model for shared decision-making in the school principalship. *Educational Administrative Quarterly, 3,* 49–61.

Campbell, R. F. (1968). Situational factors in educational administration. In R. Campbell & R. Gregg (Eds.), *Administrative behavior in education* (p. 264). New York: Harper & Row.

Chin, R., & Benne, K. D. (1969). General strategies for effective changes in human systems. In W. G. Bennis, K. D. Benne, & R. Chin (Eds.), *The planning of change* (2nd ed.). New York: Holt, Rinehart & Winston.

Christensen, C., & Hansen, A. (1987). *Teaching and the case study method*. Boston: Harvard University School Publishing Division.

Cohen, D. K., March, J. G., & Olsen, J. P. (1972). A garbage can model of organizational choice. *Administrative Science Quarterly, 17,* 1–25.

Conger, J. A. (1991). Inspiring others: The language of leadership. *Academy of Management Executive, 5*(1), 31–45.

Conley, D. T. (1997). *Roadmap to restructuring: Charting the course of change in American education*. Eugene, OR: University of Oregon (ERIC Clearinghouse on Educational Management).

Council of Chief State School Officers. (1996). *Interstate school leaders consortium standards for school leaders*. Washington, D. C.: Author.

Covey, S. R. (1989). *The 7 habits of highly effective people*. New York: Simon and Schuster.

Crosby, F. (1984). Relative deprivation in organizational settings. In B. M. Staw & L. L. Cummings (Eds.), *Research in organizational behavior* (Vol. 6, pp. 51–93). Greenwich, CT: JAI.

Cunningham, W. C., & Cresco, D. W. (1993). *Cultural leadership: The culture of excellence in education*. Boston: Allyn and Bacon.

Cusella, L. P. (1987). Feedback, motivation, and performance. In F. M. Jablin, L. L. Putnam, K. Roberts, & L. W. Porter (Eds.), *Handbook of original communication: An interdisciplinary perspective* (pp. 130–164). Newbury Park, CA: Sage, 1987.

Cusick, P. A. (1973). *Inside high school*. New York: Holt, Rinehart.

Dalkey, N. (1969). *The Delphi method: An experimental study of group decisions*. Santa Monica, CA: Rand Corporation.

Delbecq, A. L., Van de Ven, A., & Gustafsen, D. H. (1986). *Group techniques for program planning: A guide to normal group and Delphi processes*. Middleton, WI: Green Briar Press.

Deming, W. E. (1986). *Out of the crisis*. Cambridge, MA: MIT Center for Advanced Study.

Depree, M. (1992). *Leadership jazz*. New York: Dell Publishing.

Drucker, P. E. (1995). *Managing in a time of great change*. New York: Truman Talley Books.

DuBrin, A. J. (1996). *Human relations for career and personal success* (4th ed.). Upper Saddle River, NJ: Prentice Hall.

Etheridge, C. P., & Green, R. (1998). *Union district collaboration and other processes related to school district restructuring for establishing standards and accountability measures.* (A technical report for the 21st Century Project). Washington, D. C.: National Educational Association.

Etzioni, A. (1967). Mixed scanning: A third approach to decision making. *Public Administration Review, 27,* 385–392.

Fielder, F. E. (1967). *A theory of leadership effectiveness.* New York: McGraw-Hill.

Freedman, S. M., & Montanari, J. R. (1980). An integrative model of managerial rewards allocation. *Academy of Management Review, 5,* 381–390.

French, J. R. (1993). *A formal theory of social power.* New York: Irvington.

Fullan, M. G. (1992). Overcoming barriers to educational change. In Office of Policy and Planning (Eds.), *Changing Schools Insights* (pp. 11–19). Washington: D.C: Office of Policy and Planning.

Fullan, M. G. (1993). *Change forces.* New York: Falmer Press.

Fullan, M. G. (1999). *Change forces: The sequel.* New York: Falmer Press.

Gardner, J. W. (1990). *On leadership.* New York: The Free Press.

Garvin, D. A. (1995). Building a learning organization. In D. A. Kolb, J. S. Osland, & I. M. Rubin (Eds.), *The organizational behavior reader* (pp. 96–109). Upper Saddle River, NJ: Prentice Hall.

Getzels, J. W. (1958). Administration as a social process. In A. Halpin (Ed.), *Administrative theory in education* (p. 153). Chicago: University of Chicago Midwest Administration Center.

Getzels, J. W., & Guba, E. (1957). Social behavior and the administrative process. *School Review, 65,* 423–441.

Gibbs, J. R. (1995). Defensive communication. In D. A. Kolb, J. S. Osland, & I. M. Rubin (Eds.), *The organizational behavior reader* (pp. 225–229). Upper Saddle River, NJ: Prentice Hall.

Gibson, J. L., Ivancevich, J. M., & Donnelly, J. H., Jr. (1976). *Organizations: Behavior, structure, and progress* (Rev. ed.). Dallas TX: Business Publication.

Goodlad, J. I. (1984). *A place called school: Prospects for the future.* New York: McGraw-Hill Book Company.

Goodlad, J. I. (1994). *Educational renewal: Better teachers, better schools.* San Francisco: Jossey-Bass Publishers.

Goodlad, J. I., & McMannon, T. J. (1997). *The public purpose of education and schooling.* San Francisco: Jossey-Bass Publishers.

Gorton, R. A. (1987). *School leadership and administration: Important concepts, case studies, and simulations* (3rd ed.). Dubuque, IA: McGraw-Hill.

Gorton, R. A., & Schneider, G. T. (1991). *School-based challenges and opportunities* (3rd ed.). Dubuque, IA: McGraw-Hill.

Gorton, R. A., & Schneider, G. T. (1994). *School-based leadership: Challenges and opportunities.* Upper Saddle River, NJ: Prentice Hall.

Green, R. L. (1997). In search of nurturing schools: Creating effective learning conditions. *NASSP Bulletin, 81*(589), 17–26.

Green, R. L. (1998). Nurturing characteristics in schools related to discipline, attendance, and eighth grade proficiency test scores. *American Secondary Education. 26*(4), 7–14.

Greenberg, J. (1996a). *Managing behavior in organizations.* Upper Saddle River, NJ: Prentice Hall.

Greenberg, J. (1996b). *The quest for justice on the job.* Thousand Oaks, CA: Sage.

Greenberg, J., & Baron, R. A. (1997). *Behavior in organizations.* Upper Saddle River, NJ: Prentice Hall.

Greenfield, T. A. (1995). Improving changes for successful educational reform. *Education, 115*(3), 464–478.

Greenhalgh, L. (1986). SMR forum: Managing conflict. *Sloan Management Review, 27,* 45–51.

Greenleaf, R. K. (1977). *Servant leadership: A journey into the nature of legitimate power and greatness.* New York: Paulist Press.

Gross, N. (1958). *Explorations in role analysis: Studies of the school superintendency.* New York: John Wiley.

Guarino, S. (1974). *Communication for supervisors.* Columbus, OH: The Ohio State University.

Gulick, L., & Urwick, L. (Eds.). (1937). *Papers on the science of administration.* New York: Columbia University Press.

Halpin, A. (1956). *The leader behavior of schools.* Columbus, OH: The Ohio State University.

Halpin, A. W., & Croft, D. B. (1963). *The organizational climate of schools.* Chicago: University of Chicago Press.

Hammond, J. S., Keeney, R. L., & Raiffa, H. (1998a, September/October). The hidden traps in decision-making. *Harvard Business Review,* 47–58.

Hammond, J. S., Keeney, R. L., & Raiffa, H. (1998b). *Smart choices: A practical guide to decision-making.* Boston: Harvard Business School Publication.

Hanson, M. E. (1991). *Educational administration and organization behavior* (3rd ed.). Needham Heights, MA: Allyn and Bacon.

Hanson, M. E. (1996). *Educational administration and organization behavior* (4th ed.). Needham Heights, MA: Allyn and Bacon.

Hersey, P., & Blanchard, K. H. (1977). *Management of organizational behavior: Utilizing human resources* (3rd ed.). Upper Saddle River, NJ: Prentice Hall.

Hersey, P., & Blanchard, K. H. (1982). *Management of organizational behavior: Utilizing human resources* (4th ed.). Upper Saddle River, NJ: Prentice Hall.

Hersey, P., & Blanchard, K. H. (1993). *Management of organizational behavior: Utilizing human resources* (6th ed.). Upper Saddle River, NJ: Prentice Hall.

Hersey, P., Blanchard, K. H., & Johnson, D. E. (1996). *Management of organizational behavior: Utilizing human resources* (7th ed.). Upper Saddle River, NJ: Prentice Hall.

Herzberg, F. (1993). *The motivation to work.* New Brunswick, NJ: Transaction.

House, R. J. (1971). A path-goal theory of leader effectiveness. *Administrative Science Quarterly, 16,* 331–333.

House, R. J., & Dessler, G. (1974). *The path-goal theory of leadership: Some post hoc and a priori tests.* In J. G. Hunt & L. L. Larson (Eds.), *Contingency approaches to leadership* (pp. 29–55). Carbondale, IL: Southern Illinois University Press.

Hoy, W. K., & Miskel, C. G. (1991). *Educational administration: Theory, research and practice* (4th ed.). New York: McGraw-Hill.

Hoy, W. K., & Tarter, J. C. (1995). *Administrators solving the problem of practice: Decision-making concepts, cases, and consequences.* Boston: Allyn and Bacon.

Interstate School Leaders Licensure Consortium (1996). *Standards for school leaders.* Washington, D.C.: Council of Chief State School Officers.

Interstate School Leaders Licensure Consortium of the Council of Chief State School Officers. (1997). *Candidate information bulletin for school leaders assessment.* Princeton, NJ: Educational Testing Service.

Johnson, D. W., & Johnson, F. P. (1982). *Joining together: Group theory and group skills.* Upper Saddle River, NJ: Prentice Hall.

Kamlesh, M., & Solow, D. (1994). *Management science: The art of decision-making.* Upper Saddle River, NJ: Prentice Hall.

Kanter, R. M. (1982, July/August). The middle manager as innovator. *Harvard Business Review, 60*(4), 95–105.

Katz, D., & Kahn, R. L. (1978). *The social psychology of organizations* (2nd ed.). New York: Wiley.

Katz, N., & Lawler, J. W. (1993). *Conflict resolution: Building bridges.* Thousand Oaks, CA: Corwin Press.

Kim, C., & Mauborgne, R. (1997, July/August). Fair process: Managing in the knowledge economy. *Harvard Review, 75*(4), 65–75.

Kmetz, J. T., & Willower, D. J. (1982). Elementary school principal work behavior. *Educational Administrative Quarterly, 18,* 62–78.

Kotter, J. P. (1985). *Power and influence: Beyond formal authority.* New York: Free Press.

Kouzes, J., & Posner, B. Z. (1987). *The leadership challenge: How to get extraordinary things done in organizations.* San Francisco: Jossey-Bass Publishers.

Leventhal, G. S. (1976). The distribution of rewards and resources in groups and organizations. In L. Berkowitz & E. Walster (Eds.), *Advances in experimental social psychology* (Vol. 9, pp. 91–131). New York: Academic Press.

Lewin, K. (1951). *Field theory in social sciences.* New York: Harper and Row.

Lewin, K., Lippitt, R., & White, R. K. (1939). Patterns of aggressive behavior in experimentally created "social climates." *Journal of Science Psychology, 10,* 271–299.

Lewis, P. V. (1987). *Organizational communication: The essence of effective management.* New York: Wiley.

Likert, R. (1961). *New patterns of management.* New York: McGraw-Hill.

Likert, R. (1967). *The human organization: Its management and value.* New York: McGraw-Hill.

Lindblom, C. E. (1959). The science of muddling through. *Public Administrative Review, 19,* 79–99.

Lipham, J. M., Rankin, R. E., & Hoeh, J. A., Jr. (1985). *The principalship: Concepts, competencies, and cases.* New York: Addison Wesley Longman.

Lundy, J. L. (1986). *Lead, follow, or get out of the way.* New York: Berkley Books.

Lunenburg, F. C., & Ornstein, A. C. (1996). *Educational administration: Concepts and practices* (2nd ed.). Belmont, CA: Wadsworth Publishing Company.

Maier, N. R. (1963). *Problem solving discussions and conferences: Leadership methods and skills.* New York: McGraw-Hill.

Manz, C. C., & Sims, H. P., Jr. (1989). *Superleadership.* New York: Berkley Publishing Group.

March, J. G. (1982). Emerging developments in the study of higher education. *The Review of Higher Education, 6,* 1–18.

March, J. G., & Simon, H. A. (1958). *Organizations.* New York: Wiley.

Martin, J. (1981). Relative deprivation: A theory of distributive injustice for an era of shrinking resources. In B. M. Staw & L. L. Cummings (Eds.). *Research in organizational behavior* (Vol. 3, pp. 53–107). Greenwich, CT: JAI.

Maslow, A. (1970). *Motivation and personality* (Rev. ed.). New York: Harper & Row.

Mayo, E. (1933). *The human problems of an industrial civilization.* New York: Macmillan.

McCaskey, M. B. (1979). The hidden messages managers send. *Harvard Review 57,* 135–148.

McGregor, D. (1960). *The human side of the enterprise.* New York: McGraw-Hill.

McPhee, R. D., & Thimpkins, P. (1985). *Organizational communication: Traditional themes and new directions.* Thousand Oaks, CA: Sage.

Merseth, K. (1997). *Case studies in educational administration.* New York: Longman Publishers.

Meyer, A., Brooks, G., & Goes, J. (1990). Environmental jolts and industry revolution: Organizational responses to discontinuous change. *Strategic Management Journal, 11,* 93–110.

Mintzberg, H. (1983). *The structuring of organizations.* Englewood Cliffs, NJ: Prentice Hall.

Murphy, J. & Hallinger, P. (1993). *Restructuring schooling: Learning from ongoing efforts.* Newbury Park, CA: Crown Press, Inc.

Myers, M. T., & Myers, G. E. (1982). *Managing by communication: An organizational approach.* New York: McGraw-Hill.

Newstrom, J. W., & Davis, K. (1993). *Organizational behavior: Human behavior at work* (9th ed.). New York: McGraw-Hill.

Osborn, A. F. (1957). *Applied imagination.* New York: Scribner's.

O'Toole, J. (1995). *Leading change: Overcoming the ideology of comfort and the tyranny of custom.* San Francisco: Jossey-Bass Publishers.

Owens, R. G. (1991). *Organizational behavior in education.* Boston: Allyn and Bacon.

Owens, R. G. (1995). *Organizational behavior in education* (5th ed.). Boston: Allyn and Bacon.

Pondy, L. R. (1967). Organizational conflict: Concepts and models. *Administrative Science Quarterly 14,* 499–505.

Putnam, L. L., & Poole, M. S. (1987). Conflict and negotiation. In F. M. Jablin, L. L. Putnam, K. Roberts, & L. W. Porter (Eds.), *Handbook of organizational communication* (pp. 549–599). Beverly Hills, CA: Sage.

Rahim, A. (1986). *Managing conflict in organizations.* New York: Praeger.

Rogers, C. R., and Farson, R. E. (1995). Active listening. In D. A. Kolb, J. S. Osland, & I. M. Rubin (Eds.), *The organizational behavior reader* (pp. 203–214). Upper Saddle River, NJ: Prentice Hall.

Ryan, K. D., & Oestreich, D. K. (1991). *Driving fear out of the workplace: How to overcome the invisible barriers to quality, productivity, and innovation.* San Francisco: Jossey-Bass Publishers.

Sarason, S. (1996). *Revisiting the culture of the school and the problem of change.* New York: Teachers College Press.

Sashkin, M., & Morris, W. C. (1984). *Organizational behavior: Concepts and experiences.* Reston, VA: Reston Publishing Company.

Schein, E. H. (1970). *Organizational psychology* (2nd ed.). Upper Saddle River, NJ: Prentice Hall.

Schmidt, W., & Finnigan, J. (1992). *The race for the finish line: America's quest for total quality.* San Francisco: Jossey-Bass Publishers.

Senge, P. M. (1990). *The fifth discipline: The art and practice of the learning organization.* New York: Doubleday.

Senge, P. M. (1995). *The leader's new work: Building learning organizations.* In D. A Kolb, J. S. Osland, & I. M. Rubin (Eds.), *The organizational behavior reader* (pp. 76–96). Upper Saddle River, NJ: Prentice Hall.

Sergiovanni, T. J. (1984). Leadership and excellence in schooling. *Educational Leadership, 41* (5), 4–14.

Sergiovanni, T. J. (1991). *The principalship.* Needham Heights, MA: Allyn and Bacon.

Sergiovanni, T. J. (1992). *Moral leadership: Getting to the heart of school improvement.* San Francisco: Jossey-Bass Publishers.

Sergiovanni, T. J. (1994). *Building community in schools.* San Francisco: Jossey-Bass Publishers.

Sergiovanni, T. J., & Starratt, R. J. (1998). *Supervision: A redefinition* (6th ed.). New York: McGraw-Hill.

Short, P., & Greer, J. T. (1997). *Leadership in empowered schools: Themes from innovative efforts.* Upper Saddle River, NJ: Merrill/Prentice Hall.

Simon, H. A. (1982). *Models of bounded rationality.* Cambridge, MA: MIT Press.

Smith, D. M. (1997). *Motivating people* (2nd ed.). Hauppauge, NY: Barron's Series.

Snyder, C. R. (1988, January). So many selves. *Contemporary Psychology, 77.*

Sobel, D. S., & Ornstein, R. (1996). *The healthy mind healthy body.* New York: Time Life Medical.

Stech, E. L. (1983). *Leadership communication.* Chicago: Nelson-Hill.

Stogdill, R. M. (1948). Personal factors associated with leadership: A survey of the literature. *Journal of Psychology, 25,* 35–71.

Stogdill, R. M., & Coons, A. E. (1957). *Leader behavior: Its description and measurement.* Columbus, OH: Bureau of Business Research, The Ohio State University.

Strike, K. A., Haller, J., & Soltis, J. F. (1988). *The ethics of school administration.* New York: Teachers College Press, Columbia University.

Taylor, F. W. (1911). *Principles of scientific management.* New York: Harper.

Thomas, K. (1976). Conflict and conflict management. In M. D. Dunnette (Ed.). *Handbook of industrial and organizational psychology* (p. 890). Chicago: Rand McNally & Company.

Tichy, N. M., & Ulrich, D. O. (1984). The leadership challenge: A call for the transformational leader. In D. A. Kolb, J. S. Osland, & I. M. Rubin (Eds.), *The organizational behavior reader* (6th ed.) (pp. 476–486). Upper Saddle River, NJ: Prentice Hall.

Vroom, V. H. & Jago, A. G. (1988). *The new leadership: Managing participation in organizations.* Upper Saddle River, NJ: Prentice Hall.

Vroom, V. H., & Yetton, P. W. (1973). *Leadership and decision making.* Pittsburgh, PA: University of Pittsburgh Press.

Walton, S., & Huey, J. (1992). *Sam Walton: Made in America.* New York: Doubleday.

Weber, M. (1947). *The theory of social and economic organization* (T. Parsons & A. M. Henderson, Trans.). New York: Oxford University Press.

Wexley, K. N., & Yukl, G. A. (1984). *Organizational behavior and personnel psychology.* Burr Ridge, IL: McGraw-Hill.

Yukl, G. A. (1989). *Leadership in organizations* (2nd ed.). Upper Saddle River, NJ: Prentice Hall.

Yukl, G. A. (1994). *Leadership in organizations* (3rd ed.). Upper Saddle River, NJ: Prentice Hall.

Zuker, E. (1991). *The seven secrets of influence.* New York: McGraw-Hill.

# INDEX